Talking with the Angels

The Angelus Transcripts

Emrayel A'a Ra iry A'a

Copyright © 2019 by Emrayel A'a Ra iry A'a.

ISBN-9781645506263

All rights reserved. No part of this book may be reproduced or transmitted in any form or by any means, electronic or mechanical, including photocopying, recording, or by any information storage and retrieval system, without permission in writing from the copyright owner.

The views expressed in this work are solely those of the author and do not necessarily reflect the views of the publisher, and the publisher hereby disclaims any responsibility for them.

Matchstick Literary
1-888-306-8885
orders@matchliterary.com

PREFACE

This book is the continuation of the first book: The Angelus Transcripts 2013-2014.

In this book, I will continue what I have started by relaying the messages I had received in the year 2015.

As you read on, you will notice that the messages get more precise, complicated, and downright confusing.

When the Angels decide to relate only part of the message and leave me guessing about the rest, I nearly tear my hair out. They enjoy making me think.

In the book, I have included some of my meditations, lessons, and travels. Maybe someone will learn from them, perhaps not. But whatever happens, it will be unique, amusing, and at times puzzling.

Yes, there are worlds beyond ours, and we need to understand that the end, is not necessarily that. It is infinite! There is more going on in the background than is presented to us in this world, and it is up to us to explore them. Not with spaceships or such, but with our minds. We can travel to these worlds with meditation. Time and Space are nothing to us all when the human mind becomes expanded. 3D physics mean nothing in the 5D world.

So, enjoy the messages and stories in this book. If they make you laugh, that is good. If they make you think, then that is good too. And if they make you learn, even better.

This life is all about learning, and if I can help in some little way, then it's a big step for you.

Again, I have to let you know that I don't control what the Angels say. They tell me what to write, and I scribble it down for them. Now and then I edit some of the narratives due to my dodgy spelling.

I hope this helps with some matters in the book.

Now, in the words of the Angels when signing off: Be well!

INTRODUCTION

Let me introduce myself!

I am an Angel Channel! There you have it in a nutshell!

I am one of the many tools used by the Angels in getting their messages across to the world.

Usually, I receive these messages via Telepathy, but when they wish to be more direct with other people, they merge with my body and use my voice. During these moments I get an energy recharge, boost to my healing abilities, and extra insight.
When the Angel finishes and leaves, I am left feeling as if I'm about to bounce off the walls, More inner peace and a plethora of cheeky comments directed at me.

Who needs coffee!

During a routine Telepathic channeling, I type out the messages that I receive. During which I will often receive the comment; 'That doesn't sound right! Let me rephrase that.' Or I get a 'Stop! Your train of thought has derailed again!'. It depends whether I get distracted or the Angels do.

But I love them all, and they are a crazy extended family to me. Like siblings, they enjoy teasing me to the point of distraction. So fling it back at them.

Who would have thought that the child from the rough side of town would grow such a wonderful, loving gift as Angel Channeling! I find it rather humbling, and yet I feel honored.

I was born in the 60s in historic Corbridge, England. But the family didn't stay there long, returning home to the dingy, smokey town of Gateshead. There I grew up with my big brother, going through various rights of passage as schools, bullies, and poverty.

My mother bringing up two children on her own meant that times were very hard. But I survived – don't ask me how, but I did.

As my mother's family had a few members with psychic abilities, my gifts were encouraged by them. So I did have some support there.

In the 70s, my mother remarried and decided we all should move to New Zealand. By this time, my brother got married and had his own life. So I, my mother, and my stepfather moved to Auckland, New Zealand. And here I am still.

Ah, enough of my rambling on in this introduction. You want to read this book, don't you? I'll shut up now and let you read it.

Be well!

JANUARY

1 JANUARY 2015

Daily Message from the Angels and Ascended Masters:

"As much as you doubt yourself, take note of this: We don't feel the same about you. We know you and believe in you. Do yourself a favor and believe in yourself.

Never doubt yourself, for this weakens you. Instead, trust your instincts, don't hold yourself back because you are afraid of a new path coming up in your life. Never run away from new adventures. Instead, take one step forward and at your own pace, enjoy the new beginnings coming your way. When you are satisfied with what that one step has given you, take another stride forward and learn from what is new there.

Do this throughout your life, and you will regain that childlike wonder of new sensations. A new world will open for you, and you can explore it as much as you want. We encourage it. It helps you grow, and that inner child of yours will be exploring with you.

It's a fascinating universe. You have a beautiful world you have yet to understand fully.

You are an explorer, and there's so much out in your world to see. What you read in books and on your television is just a tiny portion.

Things are much bigger than what is in those books and such. And it is all waiting for you.

Be well, sweet ones. I shall be watching your adventures with joy.

Gabriel"

**

2 JANUARY 2015

Daily Message from the Angels and Ascended Masters:

"Darling ones, think of all the fantastic things that are going to happen to you in the future. Your new year has so many possibilities and so many promises. And you can make them come true.

You have so much power in your body and your mind, and you all don't realize it. Well, know it now. For you can make your future, your destiny, and your path in life. You can even change the world with just your thoughts alone.

You are the gift of the Divine to the Universe, and you share the same creative abilities. You can be a creator in your own right.
Never forget that you are your own master, teacher, and student. You are that powerful, and you need to know it.

Do you want to change the world for the better? What's stopping you? There are many, many more with the same ideal as you, so when you meet with some of them, you are creating a more powerful creative force. The more people there are with this desire, the stronger it will be.
Things are starting now because there are already enough people with the same dream and they have got the ball rolling — the more people that join them; the more significant the change.

Never underestimate yourselves. You ARE much more powerful than you realize. But it is up to you to make things happen.

In the name of our ultimate mutual father, I thank you.

Be well

Gabriel"

***

3 JANUARY 2015

Daily Message from the Angels and Ascended Masters:

"Whatever you want in your world, whatever it takes, and whatever you require, it can all come to one thing: Belief!

Believe that dreams can come true.
Believe that things will happen the way you want it.
Believe that you are lucky.
And above all! Believe in the Divine and us.

The more you have belief in yourself, the more things happen. When you allow that little bit of Ego sneaks in, you know which little bit, that one called "Self-Doubt," then you are not at your full potential. It is a hindrance, not a help.

Believe in yourself to make things happen in your world. There are no lessons, just self-discipline. As soon as one Ego thought sneaks in, block it, and replace it with an affirmation for yourself.
In truth, there is purity; in purity, there is a belief. In this belief, there is action, and in this action, there is a wonder. In your awe and wonder, there is the Divine.

The Divine hears all and sees all.

So be aware, your beliefs are noticed and monitored.

Be well; sweet ones, be well.

Haniel"

***

3 JANUARY 2015

A fascinating moment just now:

I had just closed my eyes and found myself surging forward into a tunnel that had high sidewalls, and the floor appeared to be on fire.

As I traveled forward, I heard Uriel say: "It's alright; keep going." I did.

The tunnel kept changing, and yet I still went forward.

I found myself in an old room with no doors. Inside the wallpaper was peeling off the walls, and filthy. I quickly looked around and then looked up and decided my next action: I smashed through the roof!

I heard Uriel go: "That's it!" with triumph.

I then leaped upwards and found myself following a somewhat dark red light into the sky. I kept following this red light and was in a grey stone room.
There in that room, I saw another angel stand before me and take off, with wings made of rainbow-colored energy. I felt I needed to follow the angel, and I followed.

I soon ground to a halt and could see myself reflected in a large eye which was staring at me. The eye drew back and became a giant head. I soon found myself looking at a male with dark long curly hair that was greying, and he nodded. He moved to one side and let me into a room.

The room was red and gold. There were thrones in a circle facing a small golden stool that was in the center.

I approached the center of this room and looked around. It was then I saw the Egyptian Gods sitting on the thrones. I was indicated to sit on the stool in the middle, and they began talking.

Anubis stood up and came towards me, held my arm, and gently made me stand. He looped an arm through mine and began to talk. I can't remember much what was said, but I got the impression that they satisfied with my progress.

As we strolled back to the center, Anubis quickly looked over my shoulder at Uriel and said: "Angel, what is it you want us to do with this one?"

Uriel's reply was: "Open her up more and let her have what is coming to her, as it is now time."

Anubis put his hand inside my head and began to alter something there, and said: "So be it, you will get what is coming to you."

After a few more manipulations in my head, Anubis said: "Now it's time for you to go back" and I found Uriel pulling me back into my body at high speed.

And here I am. My headache is gone too.

***

4 JANUARY 2015

Daily Message from the Angels and Ascended Masters:

"Do you remember what you did last week that was so important to you then, but now you realize that it was not all that important? That's when you know that you have wasted precious time and energy over something that just wasn't worth it.

What is worth it is you. Yes, YOU!

You are worth all the time and energy you have. You can spoil yourself. After all, to grow spiritually, you must feel happiness and joy. All these make you stronger, more confident, and relaxed. That is good. That's what we want. We want you to be happy.
Stop worrying about things that may not happen. Besides, what did worrying ever give you? Nothing but high blood pressure.
If you can't do anything about the situation, why worry about it. It is out of your hands anyway.

Also, let others worry about their burdens. It's not your job to take on other people's problems. Anyone that tries to offload theirs onto you tell them where they can get off. They are responsible for their problems, and they should act responsibly.
You have your moments, don't stress needlessly over them. As for your offspring that get out of control? Why worry! It's part of their learning process to grow. Experience teaches. Your role is to advise them. If they are adults? Then they are no longer your problem. Move on.

You see, you have fewer problems than you think, and a lot of them aren't worth the waste of energy worrying over. Your main job is to be happy, have fun and above all live your own life as you wish it. Never forget that.

I recommend reading the Desiderata. It has much to learn from and to say.

Be well, my beloved ones.

Be well

Gabriel"

***

5 JANUARY 2015

Daily Message from the Angels and Ascended Masters:

"Let's do an exercise.

Go to your mirror. An ordinary hand mirror will do as you are only going to be looking at your face.
Now, as you look at your face, take note of your eyes. What color are they, are they bright, can you see yourself? If so all these, then your eyes work, and that means they are perfect for their job. It doesn't matter if you are short-sighted or long-sighted, you can still see enough to notice your face.

Now look at your nose, can you breathe a bit through it, is it there, does it work? Again, if so, then that too is perfect for the job it has for you. It doesn't matter if it is large or crooked, it's doing what it is supposed to do. Even if you have a sinus problem, it will pass as it only hampers you now and then.

Look at your mouth, can it speak, can it eat, can it taste? If so, perfect again. No matter if you have lips that you think are ugly, as that is only a cosmetic problem. It is only imperfect to you alone. To us, you are perfect. It doesn't matter if you have a few teeth missing. If you can hold a straw in place through a gap, it's working.

Now, look at your skin. Ignore the battle-scars, birthmarks, and eruptions. It is holding you together, it breathes, it feels, and it is also perfect for you as it is.

Yes, I'm telling you all to look at the real you, and not to compare yourself with the latest pop star. You are perfect as you are. You are probably more so, a lot less plastic involved.

Look at your entire face in the mirror and say this:
'I am perfect as I am. In many ways, I have achieved perfection naturally just by being myself and not a shadow of someone else. I am perfect in the eyes of my Soul, of the Angels and the Divine. They see me as I am, and they see me as perfect, just as they intended me to be long before I was born. And so be it.'

There, you are perfect. And now I must leave my laughing channel.

Be well,

Michael"

***

6 JANUARY 2015

Daily Message from the Angels and Ascended Masters:

"Smile and the world smiles with you. How true is that?

Well, it is very accurate. When you smile at a person, make it a genuine smile. Be pleased to see them, greet them in friendship. Even if the person is someone you find antagonistic, smother that negative feeling, and show them your positive side.
Keep on doing that, and you will soon find that the person will not try to annoy you so much. In time, they will return that

pleasant feeling. They will start to look forward to meeting you with some pleasure and will enjoy your company.

Friendship is such an attractive target to reach. For it has no boundaries. Friends are as close or even closer than family at times. For friends will know you more and judge less than what family can.
You can't help your family, but you can choose your friends.

Your choice!

Do you have an enemy who continually harasses you and tries to make your life terrible? Why do they do this? It's because they don't know you, and you make them a bit frightened.
To get rid of an enemy, try to gain a friend who will be an ally in times of stress.

I repeat, your choice and your choice matters.

Be well, dear ones, be well. For life can be hard at times, but never more than you can handle. You are stronger than you all think, and in that strength, there is confidence. In confidence, there is more strength to help you along.

Be aware of what is around you, for the world has many aspects that change with the tides of time. And time is infinite. No matter where you are in your life, it was personally planned by you and your Guardian Angels. Every happening in your life is by your own choice.

Never worry about those people who try to play you like a toy, for they are of no importance to you. Let them walk their path, and you walk your own. Be free with compliments and thanks, and in turn, you will find others will be open with theirs about you.

No matter where you are or what you do, all is happening as it should. No matter how bad it can get, you will persevere and strive. It's meant to be, and you know it deep within you. You are strong, you are our beloved children, and you are the light of your world.

Let this light show and let others follow you to the divinelight: The spark of enlightenment. For is it not the ultimate destiny? As you become enlightened, your inner light shines so much brighter. Let this be so. Those who do not understand this are the ones you need to teach the most.

Understanding is the best lesson anyone can give and take.

Be free with your love also, for it is this that will bring others to your presence. Give them hope too because it will brighten their light even more.

Be strong, and you will find that those who lean on you with Love, are doing so because they are supporting you.

So be it,

I shall return later.

Abraham (El Morya)"

***

7 JANUARY 2015

Daily Message from the Angels and Ascended Masters:

"When you feel lost and alone in this big world of yours, stop and look around you. Though you see others walking by, some you don't seem to notice. It's these that appear to be invisible.

You see, it's us.

We are the ones that walk with you, holding you by the shoulder, whispering words of love and encouragement to you.

We are the ones that are with you every hour of your life and beyond.

We are the one who laughs with you at your jokes and antics.

We are the ones who try to make things easier for you if only you would ask.

We are also the ones who will never abandon you, no matter how bad the situation is. It is because we love you so much, it saddens us if harm comes to you.

Please, never do anything that could bring harm to you, for we want you to be safe and happy.

We love you, and that is love beyond words, for there is no end to it.

Be well, dear ones, be well.

Chamuel"

***

8 JANUARY 2015

Daily Message from the Angels and Ascended Masters:

"Sing like the joy of love and life are alive within you.
Dance your feelings of happiness and live it.
Be full of such emotions, let them rule you and bring you high on life.
Such feelings are that of peace, happiness, and light.

Never shy away from being happy by hiding and thinking that you don't deserve such feelings. To that, I say RUBBISH! Yes. I said Rubbish. Those emotional guilt trips and self-pity are that: pure rubbish.

You deserve to be happy. You have earned that right the very moment you were born into this world. To be happy is your Divine Right!!! Because the Divine gave you that right with all the love, the Divine has for you.

So yes, be happy like you earned that right. Because you have, and no one can stop you.

Those who will try to stop you? Don't let these people do that. Just walk away and carry on, feeling your joy. In time, if they see enough people smiling and laughing, a seed germinates within them. If some of these happy people talk with the unhappy ones, that seedling will grow more and more, until it takes over and destroys that unhappy emotion.

Yes, the first sign - they smile.

Well my children, what's stopping you? Hmm?

Be well

Jophiel"

***

9 JANUARY 2015

Daily Message from the Angels and Ascended Masters:

"Take a moment to yourself. Step back from anything you are doing and let yourself stay still in the moment right now. Feel the air around you move, feel the weather caress your cheek. Let the day's troubles wash away with the moment. For this moment it is all about you. Nothing else - Just you.

Why do I ask this of you?

It is so that you can feel the peace and tranquillity that lies within you and is waiting for you to reach it. Take this moment of peace to feel the love we have for you, and which is fed by us always. This love is your heart, your soul, and your center of Oneness. Let the peace of this moment take over.

Forget about all your troubles and problems, for at this moment, they don't matter. You do!

Problems seem minor, and they are. Stresses can be removed and do. A moment in time, which is all about you, and the peace you can gain just by tapping the inner core of divine love that is within you all.

Never forget about it as it is ever available to you and is never empty. We will make sure it remains full for you at all hours of the day and night.

It is a moment for you to learn how beautiful you are inside. Never mind what other people think or say about you; they aren't significant enough to warrant your attention. This moment is about you, and let it always remain about you.

Dearest ones, you alone are the most crucial thing in the world to yourself. For every path you make, every decision; it all starts with you. Choose wisely and with the right choice; you will find that your inner core of divine love will burn ever brighter. For that to happen, call upon us to direct you to the right path.

Enjoy your moment of inner peace. It shows off your perfection within.

Be well, and with love, I bid you be yourself.

I am Sananda Jesus"

***

10 JANUARY 2015

Message from AA Raziel:

"The stars in the sky are beautiful, aren't they? So high, so far, and thus beyond your understanding.

Think about this! The stars are all part of the body of the Divine. Yes, the body. Your planets and sun are also part of this body. You too are a part of the body as well. You all are.

Never think yourself as so unimportant that you are nothing. Since you are part of the body of the Divine, you are something special.

The Divine has made many concessions to all and many, and it is all due to one thing: The Divine's love of their children. You are the children of the Divine, just like we are. The Divine is our ultimate father; we are kin.

We are all made of the same divine energy. You are the physical embodiment of the holywill, but the Divine made us befriend, teach, and help you on your path. Yes, you could say we are your older siblings, looking after our younger ones. It has its perks. Your antics make us laugh with you.

When you fall in love, we encourage that love and give you our blessing.

When you are angry, it saddens us because it is harmful and often enough there is no need for it. Save your anger for a more worthy cause, than just because something didn't turn out the way you wanted it.

When you are sad, we come forward and hold you in our arms, stroking your head and comforting. We want you to be happy, and we are delighted when you are.

All this is for one thing only; the Divine and we do it because we love you. Nothing more, nothing less. Just pure love and there's nothing better in this universe.

If you have a problem with someone that is making it hard for you to maintain your equilibrium, walk away. There are no real reasons why you should have to put up with it. Just walk away and let the other person reap what they have sowed.

Never let others try to take away your freedom either, for it is yours and was given to you by the Divine itself. Treasure it and never give it away either. Walk the path of light and leave behind your negativity. Yes, the 'negativity' that is part of your past and therefore no longer relevant to you.

You could keep it if you so wish, but what good will it do for you to dwell and fester in such adverse situations that no longer exist. Leave it behind, let go, and live for yourself.

After all, you deserve to be happy. You earned it since the day you were born, so you may as well stand up, step forward, and grab that happiness with all hands and your soul.

There is no happiness in material objects. They are just that: Objects. There is no real happiness in it. Real joy is listening to a bird singing, a cat purring, children playing in the grass, the wind in the trees. Oh, I can go on and on, because there are so many beautiful things in your universe.

Above all else, remember this - you can be happy if you want. You were made to feel joy, laughter, and love. It is all part of you right to the very atomic level. Emotions are a part of you. Therefore you are quite capable of giving the same opinions out.

Be with love and joy, for they are always with you.

The time will come when all you need is such feelings to help you understand the Universe of which you are part. It is what holds you and the world together. The Divine has created the Universe from such feelings, and so the Universe will remain.

You will soon explore such new worlds and meet many wonders. Such wonders that we won't tell you about because it would spoil the surprise and delight of discovery.

But one world we will tell you about is the world of Atele'ai'a. It is a world that you won't discover for a long time, but when you do, Humanity will have evolved so much and become more energy than physical.

You know the world as Eden.

I shall now leave you with my words, my siblings, and let you think upon them.

Be well!

Be free and above all, be love

Raziel"

***

10 JANUARY 2015

Daily Message from the Angels and Ascended Masters:

"Go in peace in your world, for your paths are many. Let the road be smooth, and the crossroads give you clarity in their direction. Let the knowledge of the world rest lightly on your shoulders and be the solution to problems and not the cause.

Be with good terms with your inner soul so that you may walk forward in confidence and gentle humility. For love is your path towards all blessed things in this world of yours.

Believe in what gifts you have been given by the Divine, for they were made especially for you. Accept with love all that you have received.

And above all, accept without judgment, all persons into your sphere of love, for it is there that the blessing of divine love will start upon them.

Judge not those who have hurt others, instead accept that only the Divine knows the full extent as to what happened, and will deal with them in its way.

Instead, concentrate on giving yourself love so pure, that it will transcend all barriers.
Such people who do this will Ascend.

For your path is a long and winding one, it will teach you more about yourself than you realize. But it has only one ultimate destination: Ascension.

Go in peace.

Jesus"

***

11 JANUARY 2015

Daily Message from the Angels and Ascended Masters:

"A meditation lesson for you all!

In meditation, let your mind run like the river, let it trickle over the stone bed and ripple into the deeper rivers.

Let your mind run down that river of blessed light and dip into its depths of gold.
The mighty river of light runs fast and deep.

Let it run through your mind, down your spine, and into your Chakras.

Let the golden light run through those areas, and let it set you on a higher vibration.
The higher vibrations give you: Peace, tranquillity, and pure love.
The higher the vibration, the nearer you are to the divine gift: Ascendancy.

Let this river of light pour through your entire body, soaking each cell and atom in its golden glow.

Bathe in it and absorb its healing powers.

Take your time in bathing in this light, for there is no shortage. You can go to it whenever you want. It is there for you.

Let that golden river of light run through to your feet and back up, stirring dormant energies and bringing you to the surface.

Now you may awaken, and feel enervated, at peace and above all, healed by love.

Our meditation is a lesson that we are very willing to teach you, for it is something we all do, and we love it. It is to bathe in the light of the Divine itself.

Bless you all

Gabriel"

***

12 JANUARY 2015

Daily Message from the Angels and Ascended Masters:

"Beloved ones, do you not know how miraculous you all are? You were created from the divine light, infused with divine love and then placed on your world to grow, learn, and become enlightened.

We were created to nurture, teach, and open you up to the beauties of your very own divine born self. Never be indifferent to your blessed origins, for it is all within you. You have a name for it: The Soul. You must treasure that divine light within you, for it is what makes you so strong, powerful, wise, and loving. Never lose sight of that gift placed within you. For without it, you will be like the very rocks on the ground. Never moving, never speaking, never knowing.

Treasure your self and treat yourself kindly. For you cannot perform your miracles if you don't look after your mind and body.

But remember, there are those whose bodies are not perfect at all but deformed. Respect them and love them, for their Souls are at their highest in your world. They are in their last incarnation and will not return when they have passed. Rejoice in this, for they have reached spiritual perfection. They will Ascend soon. They are learning their final lesson by having such a body. Please respect these beautiful Souls, for they have reached the goal on your world: Ascendancy.

Take note though; not all souls need an imperfect body to Ascend. Some do very well without having to go to that path.

It is all up to you. You decide on what incarnation you want, not us. You do! It is your choice, your free will. All you and will ever be.

Be strong and be well our beloved ones.

Haniel"

***

13 JANUARY 2015

Daily Message from the Angels and Ascended Masters:

"Wherever you are, whatever you do, don't forget to stop and look around you. See your world through the eyes of a child, and you will see how magical everything is.

The single pigeon! A common bird, but perfect in its design.

The baby! As noisy as they can be, and yet so full of new life.

A single daisy on a lawn. So small, delicate, and beautiful in its simplicity.

Look at your world with the eyes of a child, look around and enjoy the new adventures and wonders that will come.

That is the secret, never to grow old. Be young in mind and heart and enjoy yourself.

Don't let anyone else try to make you feel old; tell them to go away. And if these people don't? Walk away yourself.

To be young in heart and mind, and you will find your Spirit will be young too.

Carpe Diem!

Be well

Gabriel"

***

14 JANUARY 2015

Daily Message from the Angels and Ascended Masters:

"Believe in yourself my dear ones, simply because we do believe in you.

Never underestimate yourselves and think you are not worthy of us or to the Divine. YOU ARE!!! You are all worthy in our eyes. Even those who fell by the wayside, they are loved by us too. We take an interest in those so that we can teach them, make sure they learn what lesson they received. And then they come back in the next life and practice what they have learned.

You have a will, use it. You have a mind, use it. You have a heart, use it. Use all these together, and what do you get? The will to recognize and open your heart to those who need it the most. And that is to us perfect!

We all need love: you, me, us, the Divine. And we, in return, give you the same back. It is all free and precious.

Start loving each other instead of fighting.
Embrace each other in friendship, instead of arguing.
Laugh with each other instead of crying.
Talk to each other instead of hiding your feelings.

You all need love, so yes you are worthy of that and much more.

Be well, sweethearts.

Michael"

***

15 JANUARY 2015

Daily Message from the Angels and Ascended Masters:

"Cherish the life on your world, for it is precious and unique to it. No other planet has a creature called a Panda, or a Whale. Your animal life is unique to your world.

Something else, look after your world. It is more than just the ground on which you stand. It is your only home right now. And you will have nowhere to go if you ruin it.

Cherish your mother Gaia and all her children. Each creature was born from Gaia, and this includes you. You were given this higher intelligence so that you can look after your world in the best way, nurturing and helping her children. Please, look after your world the same way as you would like to be in turn.

There is one world, one home, and one chance. Never spoil it for yourselves.

Be well,

Ezekiel"

***

16 JANUARY 2015

Daily Message from the Angels and Ascended Masters:

"Take time to be yourself. For there is no better person than to be. Do not follow the pop star or the football player, for they are not you. Instead, support yourself.
You are the right one for yourself, for you are no less than the weakest and no more than the strongest.
You are both healthy, and you should let your strength carry you to new heights in your life. Your weakness is your Ego, for it will forever try to hold you back. Let your strength rule, not your Ego. Your strength is that of your own will, your mind, and your own Spirit.

Exactly, you are as strong as the most influential person in your world when you use that will. Don't hold back, my dears.

Your weakness? Don't even give it the time of day. Get active, get going, and you shall fly!!

Spread those wings of strength you have and fly to new words, paths, and hopes.

Be well, dear ones.

Raphael"

***

16 JANUARY 2015

I was feeling over-emotional and weepy for nothing at all. I heard a voice tell me to go into a meditation state. So, being a well-behaved (coughs) medium; I obeyed.

As I slipped into a meditation state, I found myself going through a tunnel at high speed. This tunnel was dark, and I asked was I okay in this? I got reassured that I was on course.

An angel soon appeared in front of me, but at a distance. This one seemed wispy and changed shape and form. I got the impression that I was to follow this one. The voice told me that this was Fleur, my Guardian Angel. She is to be my guide for this.

Soon I saw a red flower made of stars opening and glowing upwards. I followed that glow towards a distant doorway which shone with an inner light. Fleur always ahead of me and leading the way.

I headed towards that doorway again at speed and went through it.

I soon found myself in a courtyard with a white marble building ahead of me and smaller buildings around me. There was marble decorations, balconies, and balustrades. All covered with patches of Ivy. As if neglected, but in reality, it wasn't. It just appeared that way.

At my right, sat a huge dragon who told me to wait for a moment. I recognized my Guardian Dragon friend. He said to me that someone was coming to see me.

At that moment, I heard a voice behind me say, "I'm already here."

I looked around and saw Michael approaching me and had a big broad smile. He reached forward and gave me a big hug.

He then turned to Fleur and acknowledged her, stating that she was doing an excellent job in looking after me. He even made sure I saw her. Fleur is beautiful.

He told me the reason why I was all over the place emotionally was that I had been downloading big time during my sleep periods, and that makes my sleep broken and at times shift into a deep trance.

Michael then walked me to the entrance of the big building and led me into a hallway.

The hallway was ornate, red carpeting, and red decorations — the same hall where I first met with the Egyptian Gods.

There on a podium in the middle was a white/blue broad light that seemed to be coming from the ceiling and hitting the floor - I had been linked to Zelrith there – my Dragon friend (but it had a throne at that time).

Michael told me to stand under it, and I did.

Michael then grabbed my wrists and told me not to worry. The light changed into a silver color and surrounded me.

Michael reminded me to keep breathing as my physical body seemed to stop. He then told me to breathe in the light so that it went through my entire body.

Soon the silver light stopped.

Michael joined me on the podium, still holding onto my wrists. This time he related that the next light was one we will both share as we both loved it. And soon we were covered in the golden light of the Divine.

Michael was smiling with joy at the light, and occasionally reminding me to breathe it in.

Soon the light stopped and still holding onto my wrists, Michael gently brought me off the podium. He related to me that the silver light was enervating, cleansing, and protective. The golden light was the Divine giving love to all.

Still holding onto one wrist, Michael brought me outside. He led Fleur and me to a door made of a grey stone that had symbols and decorations etched on it.

The door opened into a corridor which again had a red floor, but with appeared to be wood-paneled walls. Very comforting look.

As I walked down this corridor, there was a pair of large imposing doors at the end, but Michael led me down a hallway to the left, walked past a couple of doors, and made a hard turn right. He opened the door that was there, and we walked into a room which had books, books and more books. They lined the shelves.

Michael stated that these books were mine to read and to use. They are readily accessible to me. The rooms and garden that had belonged to Emrayel (my Higher Self) no longer existed. This room was to be mine.

There was a large table in the middle. The books were on a wooden Mezzanine floor, with a rail separating it from the main floor. There was a Globe in the corner and some statues. Sunlight beamed from a window.

Michael then told me that after my time on Earth is over; I'm to help in the Halls of Healing. So as a Healer, I must remember my job there. As a messenger, I was to learn my duties. My duties are to work with the other Ascended Masters and Angels, and that there was to be another meeting soon. They will call me to it.

Michael then brought Fleur and me back outside and met up with my Dragon friend.

Curious, I asked what he meant in an earlier conversation that I had the mark of the dragon? Michael then took both my wrists and brought them up to my eye level. He showed me the golden Dragon bracelets on them.

He told me these were the Marks. While I had them, I always had a friend in the Dragon who gave them to me. At the same time, I also noticed that my energy was no longer all shades of blue but seemed to have a silver sheen to it.

Michael then leaned forward, kissed me on the forehead, and said that it was now time for me to go back to my world.

Soon I found myself heading forward at high speed with Fleur beside me. Fleur slowed down over the Harbour and let me enjoy the view. She then brought me over my house. I rushed down to the house and found myself rousing out of meditation.

I was told to type the whole thing down, so that others may know that such things are not scary, but fantastic. And for all to learn.

***

17 JANUARY 2015

Daily Message from the Angels and Ascended Masters:

"Why don't you all sit down and write down what you want in your life on a sheet of paper. Okay? You can even add photos or drawings to personalize it or as a helpful guide to make you think of it more.

It all helps. Just write down your heart's desire on that paper. Be realistic though; no angel is going to drop George Clooney or any other person on your doorstep.
Keep your wishes on that paper to the point and no dithering around. Be precise, and spelling is not necessary, the meaning is.
When you have finished, read what you have written and promise yourself this will happen.

Tell us out loud what you have written. Tell us, and we will hear.

As you are doing this, you are telling us what you want, and we feel how much you need it. In writing your desires down, you are communicating with us.

We hear and see all you have written, and that tells us what you want, and angels will be sent off to arrange such happenings, and we Archangels will supervise this and make sure there are no stuff-ups.

Be warned though; we do take things very literally, so be careful of how you write things. For example, don't ask for a 'break' or you will find you'll end up with a break in your leg bone or arm. That is how literal we can be. It can be a bit of a problem at times.

A holiday? No problem. Write it down; we see it. We will make things happen so that you will get that holiday. It's not instantaneous, but you will find that things will start clicking into place at the right time.

Be well, dear ones, I shall now leave you with my message, and I'll try to calm my giggling channel.

Gabriel"

***

18 JANUARY 2015

Daily Message from the Angels and Ascended Masters:

"Open your soul to whoever is closest to you in life and love. Just let these people join you there - heart to heart. Whether it be a lover, a sibling, or your closest friend, it does not matter.

Just let them in, and when they open their hearts to you, be flattered. For they too consider you the closest to them.

It is the same with everyone. You all have someone so unique that the bonds are unbreakable. That is what happens when two hearts that open to each other join in a link of love. No power can break that link, and no one can take it away from you.

Even death is no barrier. The bond will forever remain steadfast and true. It is what is meant to be and will forever be.

Let the bonds remain strong; let them stay unbreakable. For it is part of your spiritual strength and your emotional strength. All have each other.

Single you are tough, together you are indestructible. The bond of the heart is also a bond of souls.

Each gives each other strength and hope.

Let it be so, as I wish it to be.

That is all.

Jesus"

***

20 JANUARY 2015

Daily Message from the Angels and Ascended Masters:

"Let those who shine a light in your life, know that they are loved. They have shared with you their joy and happiness. They have shared their soul.

Let those who have stood by you in thick or thin know that they are appreciated, for they have shown you how much they loved you by being there for you.

Let those who have shared tears of joy and sadness with you that they are unique, for they have bared their very innermost feelings with you. They will be close as family to you.

Let those who have made you laugh and play that you consider them close to your heart, and they will keep on making you laugh and play, all because of the love they share with you.

Let those who have given you a helping hand unasked but needed that you thank them for their help, and they will help you again.

Let those who are strangers who came out of nowhere and gave you strength and assistance, and then left with no trace. Thank them and show your appreciation, because we loved you and helped you. We will always be there for you.

So be it.

Kuan Yin and Ariel"

***

21 JANUARY 2015

Daily Message from the Angels and Ascended Masters:

"I am aware of all those who need my help. I am aware. Be assured that I have listened to you all, but remember, all will take time to make things happen as they are supposed to happen.
Nothing sooner, nothing later. Always at the right time.
If too soon, it will make things worse for you. Too late, then it won't help you at all. Always at the right time, and ever for the right reason - for you to learn from the incident so that you may grow.

Never underestimate your powers to help yourself. For those who ask my help and carry on working to make things happen as they wish, will get my help better. I work best with those who work with me on the same goal.

To those who ask for my help, and then sit back doing nothing to help themselves. I cannot work with anything, for you have a part to play in helping yourself. I cannot do it for you.

Always be aware that if you need my help, ask me and I will work WITH you and make your job easier.

It is how it is meant to be, and always will be. For the idle will never make an effort to help themselves.

Be well, dear ones, be well.

Masniel"

***

22 JANUARY 2015

Daily Message from the Angels and Ascended Masters:

"Do you remember what it is like to have fun, laugh, and feel full of the joy of life? Did you know that some cannot sense those emotions because life has hit them hard? A death happened or because they have no one left to share their experience.

Such people are lonely and feel the weight of their sadness lying heavily on them. That is all it is: Loneliness. They need someone to care for just as much as you do.

Do you have such a person in mind?

Sometimes such lonely people get crabby because they're unable to express their emotions appropriately, as they don't know how to interact with others.

Again, do you have such a person in mind?

Are you willing to give them a small bit of your time to provide them with your company? Even just 15 minutes of chatting, joking, or just being caring can change their world. That person in your mind, give them some of your cheer and joy.

Be well

Amitiel (likes to be called Amit)"

***

23 JANUARY 2015

Daily Message from the Angels and Ascended Masters:

"Believe in your inner self, for what better way to thank the Divine for your existence.
If you believe in yourself, then you believe in the Divine's will and gifts.
You believe in miracles.

Once you start believing in yourself, my dear ones, you will find yourself growing in confidence, strong willpower, and above all: Love.
So much comes from believing in yourself, so much! You find that you can do things you never knew before. You can even perform your miracles.

Never give the time of day to those who are jealous and try to knock your confidence away from you. Just walk out of their influence; you don't need that negativity at all.

Hold your head high, shoulders back, chest out, and say: "I believe in myself to be strong and confident." And SHOW that confidence. The more you do it, the easier it gets, and that is because you are becoming that new you. Your mind and body are starting to believe in you.

That is all part of the Grand Design. Empower yourself, and in doing so, you will find things will improve for you significantly.

Be well

Raphael"

***

24 JANUARY 2015

Daily Message from the Angels and Ascended Masters:

"When you thought that life was terrible and hurting you, and you think you can't take any more. Stop and rethink where you are in your life. It is better than you thought. If things you hoped for don't come your way, it is because your life path doesn't belong there, and of course, it is something that would have done you more harm than good.
If you lose out on a specific job or a competition, think that. Something much better that is coming your way. Why settle for average, when you can get better?

It is your happiness that we want. Losing that job or competition, means you are now free to pursue a much better future, which of course is heading towards you at the speed of thought.
You can, of course, take more of what life can give you. Much more.
Always realize that as one door shuts in front of you, another much better door shall open. There are no dead ends if you strive

to further your path. The dead-end will only happen if you stand still and do nothing to help yourself.

Also, remember this, we are always around you and listening to you. We will not ignore you in any way. Of course, things don't happen in an instant or at a snap of the fingers. If we did that, your mind would not be able to cope with it. Changes are gradual so that you have something to look forward to in hope.

All the universe is in flux, and changes must happen at the right time, or chaos will ensue.
Changes within you must happen at the right time, or the balance of the universe will topple into chaos.

We are very, very careful about how we work with you, so please take care of yourself first. And remember, you are all destined for better things, but they will happen when they should - no sooner and no later.

Be patient, be happy, and above all, be confident in your internal link to the Divine. It makes you special.

Be well, my dear ones, we will speak again soon.

Gabriel"

***

25 JANUARY 2015

Daily Message from the Angels and Ascended Masters:

"Whatever you do, wherever you are, please take the time to stop and thank the Divine for the love the Divine has given you. This love can take the form of a good life, a good job, or even just the feeling that someone out there is sending you their love.

Your existence is proof that the Divine loves you.

Also, remember this. No matter who you are or what you have done. The Divine loves you, whether you are black, white, yellow, or red. Straight, Gay or Bi. The Divine LOVES YOU AS YOU ARE! Never let those who spout hatred and prejudice turn you away from being yourself. For those who do that, are ignorant and wallow in their ignorance. In time they will reap what they have sown.

Such is the way of learning of the Divine will. The Divine notices, and it is never wrong.
You are loved by the Divine and by us. Rest your heart in that and be sure that you will always be welcome. We accept you as you are, a perfect human being.

Praised be to the Divine One!

Be well

Uriel"

***

25 JANUARY 2015

This happened to me today during meditation, some things of interest here:

I was told by Uriel to go into the meditation state. As I knew he would be asking me of this soon, I did so. I slipped into a meditation state. Uriel was talking me into this state and holding onto my shoulders. He said he was going to keep me in that state until I finished my business.

Soon I found myself in a large round hallway that had glass windows that showed that we were under the sea. There was a broad set of stairs that led to a doorway that was glowing. Uriel told me to go up the stairs and through the door. And so I did.

On the other side, I found myself in the upper levels, way above the planet. I got the impression that the doorway was a portal.

On this level, I was in front of a large grey stone building that had rounded bay window like extensions, that showed that there were rooms there.

I went into the building and found myself in a very familiar hallway. I turned left into the first corridor, and I went straight to my assigned rooms there. I noticed I had a small water fountain in the room. Uriel responded: "The sound of water is soothing and helps to relax." Then I was told that I needed to pick something up there.

I searched the desk, and I couldn't find what I wanted. I moved to a cupboard and opened that up, pulled open a drawer there. In it were some documents and a silver pendant – I was looking for these.

Uriel told me to put on the Pendant as it was a symbol of where I am assigned, and to take the documents.

I donned the pendant and gathered my documents, and headed out of my room, turning left towards and into the main hallway. Red carpet and wood-paneled walls lined the main hall. This time I turned left again, went towards the large ornate doors, and went through them.

Beyond the doors, there was a large arena with a podium in the middle. I went to the nearest empty seat and sat there, documents opened in front of me.

The meeting began.

Holographic-like images began to appear above the podium and appeared to be showing the Planet Earth. small models started to form in front of all of us on the same planet. The topic was Global Warming and what was required to fix it, and what are the effects. All this via telepathy.

As I sat and studied my image, Uriel began to chat with me through the link. Explaining what was happening, what the background was, and generally bringing me up to date on what I needed to learn. In time the meeting was ending, and Uriel brought my attention as to what was happening. Via telepathy, I heard: "Does anyone agree to this, and if so, raise your hand." I heard Uriel say: "Raise your hand." I raised my hand.
I quickly asked Uriel what I had agreed to do, and he replied: "Combat global warming in your way."

Then the meeting was over, and Uriel asked me to: "Go outside." I headed out, but as I was just about to step out the door, another entity came up to me and asked for the documents and pendant. Uriel advised me to give them to the being as they will put them away for me. I thanked them.

I walked outside and felt the nudge to go into the garden.

As I approached a large fountain, I saw a Cobalt blue light form and take shape. The light then appeared to be an Angel with a silver circlet on the head that had many twists and turns on it. He wore Cobalt blue clothing that seemed to have stars in them. He introduced himself to me as the galactic Archangel Orion. He wanted to chat with me.
He asked me to walk into the forest and talk.

As we walked deeper into the forest, we began to chat about what problems humanity may face, and how I can work with other Angel Guides.
We soon reached what appeared to be a cottage. I saw it was my old cottage that I used to use as a stopping point whenever I visited the Higher Realms, and no longer needed anymore.

Orion then turned to me and said, "Now it is time for you to meet someone else, and they will take you home too."

I looked up to my left and saw AA Cassiel standing there, grinning away. He came forward and hugged me. I teased him with the words "What? No showing off today?" And Cassiel laughed, saying it wasn't necessary with me.

Orion then went away in a flash of blue light.

Cassiel told me that though normally Uriel or Michael would bring me home, he asked if he could, and they agreed.

We chatted, and one part of the conversation I do remember was that I mentioned that he was the Angel of Tears. He laughed and said that there were tears of joy, laughter, memories, and loss. All were to be treasured.

Then came the time I had to go home. Cassiel held onto one wrist and brought me to Earth, at such a speed that the land and water nearly blurred into one another.

Soon Cassiel brought me to my room and watched me settle into my body.

As I roused out, I heard: "Now write this down as much as you can remember. You won't remember much of the conversations and meeting as your world isn't to know yet."

***

26 JANUARY 2015

Daily Message from the Angels and Ascended Masters:

"Whoever you are, when you feel the need to rest, then you must. Resting is part of the healing process that is necessary for your body. Regular hours of sleep at night is also part of this healing. Do not burn the candle at both ends, it will not help you rest or heal, but instead, make the problem worse for you.

Let your rest happen at times when you won't be disturbed. The night is the best, but during the day, try those times where you are alone.

Sleep is not necessary during the daytime periods of rest. Just sitting with a book or listening to music is restful. Even the daydreams are equally as good, for they also tell us what you want in your life. Resting is again necessary. You need it, or you cannot function properly.

Don't drag yourself through the burner so that you can meet a deadline. Start working on that issue long before it becomes a problem. That way, you will find that you have less stress, and you will rest better.

Be well and rest well

Ghamion"

(I have never heard of Ghamion and can find no reference in the 'Net)

***

27 JANUARY 2015

Daily Message from the Angels and Ascended Masters:

"Why do you worry about how you look to others, and what do others think about you? Why do you?
You are here to learn and live for yourself, not for them.
You are the only one you need to please, not them.
You are the one walks in your shoes, not in theirs.

Stop letting others tell you how you should look, live your life and giving them control of you. You are not them; you are, in fact, a beautiful bright individual in your own right.

If what these others suggest you do make you feel wrong inside, then it is not for you. Tell them that you are quite capable of making your own decisions. You should make your own decisions, and if they don't like it, not your problem. They shouldn't have interfered in the first place.

It's your life, and you can do whatever you want. You are a free spirit, and you can only learn in your life when you make the decisions.

Be free, be wise, and be yourself. For there is nothing more perfect than the individual who is comfortable being who they are: their very own self!

Just be being you and ignoring others telling you how to live your life, you are cutting down your stress levels. That is much healthier for you.

I shall leave you now.

Be well, my children.

Ambriel"

***

28 JANUARY 2015

Daily Message from the Angels and Ascended Masters:

"What is it about money? It has limited use, and it's not worth the stress over. Well, that will change soon. As this world changes to a new age, money is going to be useless. It will be obsolete as it is not a reliable way of trading.

Instead, you will find that the trade in skills will rise. There will be another way of what you call "commerce."

No, money has no further place in the future, significant changes are coming, and they will create upheaval in some parts, and new fresh beginnings in others.

Those who have relied on money and are somewhat obsessed with it— Ah! That's where the upheaval starts. Your funds will be useless.

Such is the New Age that is coming, an age of enlightenment, greater freedom, and above all, instead of paying with pieces of paper and metal, you trade in love and skills.
For food, you trade in a skill. And besides, there will be enough for all.

It will be a time of peace, knowledge, and revelation — an age of exploration, understanding, and light.

Is that not worth it? I think it is, for we will have a direct hand in this.

Be well

Michael"

***

29 JANUARY 2015

Daily Message from the Angels and Ascended Masters:

"Love! Yes, that's what I said: LOVE!
They say it makes the world go around. Is that all? It makes the Universe grow, it makes the stars, and it is the pure embodiment of the divine will. Love is all around you in each ray of light and every tiny flower. Each living thing in your world is love. The stones and the stars? Same again - all made from the divine LOVE.

And what about you?

Yes, you too, are made from love, and the Divine knows it. After all, the Divine made Humanity and taught it to love also.

As a parent of a child, the Divine will always nurture you, care, and love you.

As a child of a parent, humanity will give love back, embracing, and adoring.

As an older sibling, we love you and will look after you, giving you strength and courage when asked.

That's what Love is — unconditional acceptance and care for each other.

What more do you want?

Be well.

Chamuel"

***

30 JANUARY 2015

Daily Message from the Angels and Ascended Masters:

"What a sweet world you live in, and yet have anyone of you noticed? Isn't it beautiful and colorful? Yes, it is.

Look around you and see what your world has to offer you. It has plants, flowers, birds, animals, trees, insects, sunshine, rain, clouds, the sky and so much, much more. But the most important thing of all? It has YOU!

You are the Guardians of your world, so please, don't ignore that duty. Don't slack at it. Be aware that the fate of your entire world is in your hands.

So please, look after it. It is at this moment, the only one you have. All living things in this world need you to nurture and love it. Nature is powerful, and you are all children of Nature. You were all sent to this world to look after it.

Take care of your world and mend its hurts, and you will find that Nature will, in turn, look after you.

You are all one, and all are one with you. You are all one with each other, and the same goes for every living thing in your world.

Appreciate your world, its beauty, and variety. For it is the richest and purest thing you have within reach.

Be well, Guardians of Earth.

We await your response.

Muriel"

***

31 JANUARY 2015

Daily Message from the Angels and Ascended Masters:

"When the sun goes down in your world, the birds and beasts all lay to rest, and the creatures of the night then rule. Relax! There is nothing to fear in these creatures for you know them as the Owl, the spider, and the cricket. There are many more, but these will do.

Remember please that these also deserve the light just as much as the creatures of the day. Think of the night creatures too when you ask for the warm glow of the Divine to shine on your world.

The divine light is invisible to the human eyes, but it is evident to us.

The love you have for your world, send some to the night. For the night time is also beautiful in its unique way. The soft silver glow of the moon brings out the ethereal quality of whatever abilities you have. The moon is a nurturer as well as being the Night Sun.

When you pray to the Divine for the healing golden light, think of the night creatures too. After all, they also are made with the divine will.

They belong to your world too.

Be well, dear ones, be well.

Ariel"

***

FEBRUARY

1 FEBRUARY 2015

Daily Message from the Angels and Ascended Masters:

"Do you believe in Magic?
Do you believe in the miracles of love?
Do you believe in yourself?

Magic exists, and it is within you. For it is magic that created you, and through manifesting your wishes into reality, you create magic.
Magic has another name: Miracles. They are the same, but a different name. After all, when a miracle happens, doesn't it feel like there's magic in the air? It is so!
Then again, that too has another name: YOU!
You have the magic; you are magic. That means you can create your miracles, and also you are miracles. This miraculous magic is you. It created you, it is part of you, and you to us are magic.
Be your magic self, be filled with the warm puregolden light that is fuelling your magic and spread that magic of yours.

All this can be narrowed down to one word: LOVE!
Love is magic. Love is miraculous. Love is you. And you are all that in turn.

Spread the love dearest ones, spread the love.

Emmanuel"

***

2 FEBRUARY 2015

Daily Message from the Angels and Ascended Masters:

Listen to the sweet sound of the music of the light. It is a song that ripples through the very core of you. This song energizes your soul and making it shine brighter. The music of the light is the music of the soul. It is also the music of the divine will.
Such purity has the music, so gentle and fluid.
Our voices carry the music to you so that it caresses the aura that surrounds you.

It is healing; it is pure; it is true. It is wonderful.

The golden light of the Divine has the purest sound. It is perfect. Nothing can surpass it, and it is infinite. Bathe in the golden light and feel the music.
It is given freely for you all to enjoy, to absorb, and to relax in. We too love this light, as we are part of it also. We will share this light with you. Join us in bringing this light into our core. You are very welcome.

Be well dearest ones,

Gabriel"

***

3 FEBRUARY 2015

Daily Message from the Angels and Ascended Masters:

"Do you realize that every decision of yours has consequences? The consequences could change your path of destiny from just a slightest to a significant shift.

A decision made without thought but with impulse is a decision with the most significant consequences. These could drag you down. Instead, when a decision is in front of you, think about it. Feel what your intuition is telling you. Does it feel wrong? Then don't follow that choice but head for the other.

Does your choice seem perfect for you? Then you have made the right decision.
The right decisions can make your path more accessible and your life more rewarding. Such it is meant to be.

So please, speak with your inner voice, and feel with your intuition before any significant decisions, and you will be amazed at what will happen. Nothing short of miraculous.

Why deny one of your great gifts: Intuition. It is for you for this very purpose.

So be it.

I AM!"

(Note: Straight after this, I had a conversation with this one, who said to me..."You serve my will; you serve my light, you serve my love. You give your love to me freely. I am pleased." Then I broke down crying, but not with sadness. But because the love energy was so powerful and pure, that it overwhelmed me.)

***

4 FEBRUARY 2015

Daily Message from the Angels and Ascended Masters:

"Beautiful ones, such harmony in your eyes. Let your voices sing the praise of the Divine.

Let your heart shine with love and let your mind open to the Universe in rapture.

For it is the time to release those that have troubled you, whether they are problems or people. Now is the time to let go and embrace what is to come.

Yes, the new era is coming. The master is coming, and his very touch shall enlighten you.

Be with the truth and be with the golden one: His voice will be like the fire that runs along a grassy plain. His eyes will scan far distances and yet see things close. His mind will know the universe.

It is time for the chosen one: The golden one.

It is time for new beginnings and new horizons. And it is time for you to let go of your burdens and sorrows. Let them go and walk away from them and instead, take on the light.

So be it, so be it. In the light of the Divine, you are ALL worthy.

And it is so.

Matriel"

... Illuminus Dei... ist ra del, marat de dumis veit mar... Istus mur iris dem curit...

(Note: To be honest, I don't know what the words mean, I was told to write them down as they said it. So, I'm none the wiser)

***

5 FEBRUARY 2015

Daily Message from the Angels and Ascended Masters:

"Be free in your mind and your hearts. For the gift of Freedom was given to you by our very own hands.
Be free to walk the world.
Be free to feel the wind.
Be free to hear the trees.
Above all, be free to worship the Divine in your own very own way, for the Divine will listen to the prayer that comes from the heart.

It is those prayers that are the most precious and truthful. They are prayers that have originated in honesty and love. They are valuable to the Divine.

Open your heart to the Divine and be honest with your intent. In doing so, the Divine will grace you with divine blessing and love.

You cannot hide from the Divine, and you cannot hide the truth. We know what lies are, so never lie.

Be free with your love for the Divine, and we will return that love to you. Love from us is unconditional, and we love you for the pure spirit.

The Divine sees all and hears all, so be honest with yourself, and be true to your inner light.
You are loved and will always be loved. So why do you run away from it!

Be well

Ariel"

***

6 FEBRUARY 2015

Daily Message from the Angels and Ascended Masters:

"You are not in this world to serve the demands of people who don't care for you.
You are not in this world to be browbeaten into submission by abusive people.
You are not in this world to be enslaved by prejudice and fundamentalism.
You are here to be free.
You are here to be alive.
You are here to be happy.
You are here to be yourself.
You are loved.
You are treasured.
You are beautiful.

Believe in yourself! And the more you do so; others will start to believe in you.
We believe in you and have done so since your creation.
The Divine believes in you and never will stop doing so.
Trust in yourself and bring good thoughts and laughter into your life. The happier you are, the stronger you will become.

Be well

Cassiel"

***

7 FEBRUARY 2015

Daily Message from the Angels and Ascended Masters:

"When you feel like there is nowhere to turn, nowhere to run to, nowhere to live for; think again.

You have the Divine to turn to, who is always waiting, watching, and ever-loving. There is no rejection.

You can run to us and the Divine, we will give you comfort and shelter. Again, there is no rejection.

You have us to live for, for we want you to live the way you find best. The path that gives you comfort and security in yourself and the path that helps you start new steps in a new direction in life.

That is one path you will stay on, and you are always welcome.

Never turn away from your destiny, dear ones. For it is always the better and most accessible path of all. When life gets hard, it's because you choose the more extended and rockier path. But the destination is the same.

Think about this, my dear ones, think about this.

Ambriel"

***

8 FEBRUARY 2015

Daily Message from the Angels and Ascended Masters:

"Let us into your life and let us take over all aspects of it. In doing so, you will experience miracles, love, and joy. You will feel our presence and even interact with us.

Feel your world open and new fantastic possibilities will come through.

We are the agents of the Divine, and we were made to serve humanity. We are your friends, family and more.

Let us both work together and create this world anew, into a much better world filled with harmony and peace. This future world is the world we all want you to have — a world of laughter, joy, freedom, and light.

Let us both join in friendship and help this world to become a better place for you all. For, after all, your world is beautiful, and it would be much better for its health if we work together in helping it get better and grow.

Let us help you put aside differences. Agree to disagree we say but remember this - If you were all the same, wouldn't your life be tedious? So, variations are to be treasured, not abhorred.

Be with the Divine and let the Divine work through you via us. That's the way we will work.

Be well, dear ones, be well.

Gabriel"

***

9 FEBRUARY 2015

Daily Message from the Angels and Ascended Masters:

"Do you feel the force of the light, the sensation of love it gives you? Such is the will of the Divine, and the Divine turns it into love. The sensations of this touching you are that of love, a caress on a cheek, a tingling warmth that seems to surround you and grow inside you as well, a euphoric state of bliss when that Love focuses on you.

That is the force of the light; you can feel it.

When you feel these sensations, relax. Just open yourself up to this light and let it flow around and through you. You will find it healing and ecstatic. It is such a wonderful feeling, and there is nothing like it in the entire universe. The divine light is one of the many aspects of the Divine.

There is no need to hide from it; thelight will never harm you or your family. Instead, it will protect and nurture you. You can put your trust in it.
Nothing can harm you while you are under the protection of the Divine. Nothing! The golden light is the personal light of the Divine, andthe Divine wants to share it with you all – their children.

Accept that light into your life, and you accept the Divine into your life. That is meant to happen. Accept it and be filled with love.
Even if you reject it, you will still feel the light as the Divine still loves you. But the sensations will not be as intense. But if you suddenly change your mind and accept it willingly, you will receive that light as you are meant to be.

There are no closed doors in the eyes of the Divine, and in what you call Heaven. All are open; all is ready, all is available to you all. The divine light is also a doorway that is permanently open to you all.

So be it.

Be well

Matriel"

***

10 FEBRUARY 2015

Daily Message from the Angels and Ascended Masters:

"When you think things are getting on top of you and causing you stress. Relax! That's right! Relax! Don't let anything destroy that inner peace and serenity that is within you.

For the times that your stress levels start to peak, walk away and go to a place that you can call your area of calmness. Some have a favorite tree, a space in a park or near a stream. Or even a drive out into the country will do. It must be your area of peace and let it make you part of it.

Always have this space within your heart and go to it whenever you feel a need.

Don't get into arguments; walk away.
Don't let the small stuff get to you, leave them.
Don't let an abusive partner, family member, or a stranger near you, walk away and don't stop.

Let this space of peace be your haven — a place of rescue, solitude, and sanctuary. Even a church can help there.

All moments of peace are to be treasured, for in those moments; you start to heal, and in healing, you become stronger.

You are meant to be at peace. You all deserve moments as such. Take these moments and treasure them. They are your moments to interact with your very own soul.

Be well,

Michael"

***

11 FEBRUARY 2015

Daily Message from the Angels and Ascended Masters:

"Let the light shine on you and your loving soul.
Let the stars glow in pleasure at your smile.
Let the sun glow with love at your laughter

And above all!

Let the Divine see the pure loving energy glow from you. Be like children in the Divine's eyes, for as children, you will find joy in life, in play, and your adventures.

When you are asked to "Be like children," it's not about innocence, but it's about your inner child. The inner child that wants to jump into puddles, but doesn't because of the adult mind that rules it.

Forget that 'adult mind' as it is not so much adult as pure ego. And a human-made ego has no place in the grand scheme of the universe.

Let go of that ego, let go of its hang-ups, grumbles, misery, and ignorance, and instead allow that curious, open-minded and laughing child rule.

We want you to laugh, have fun, and learn at the same time. Besides, you go ahead and jump in that puddle, you want to, and you know it. Do it! If anyone looks down their nose at you for doing it, remember this; they are envious and would like to do the same thing themselves, but are frightened.

Be as a child and let the light energy shine on you. While you are like this, the Divine finds great pleasure in you.

Well, what is stopping you, dear ones?

Be well

Michael"

***

12 FEBRUARY 2015

Daily Message from the Angels and Ascended Masters:

"Let the truth of what is about to come to be known. It is all around you and the messages around the skies.
Are you ready for the next step in your evolution?
Are you willing to take the risk and join in a new adventure? Perhaps a new beginning even!

Never falter in your steps and walk forward with your decision firmly in mind. For those who have chosen to take the next steps, we will help each one of you. You will grow to new heights.
Those who back away in fear or blind ignorance? Your turn will come. And it will be a time when you and your future come together as one, and you will find yourself embracing it. It is because you were born to it.

No matter how much you back away and hide, you will embrace the new beginnings: The new era of light. It may not be in your current lifetime but will be in the next. That's why you will never be left behind. You back away because you are not quite ready for it.
That is quite normal, and nothing to be ashamed. Accept it for what it is, a sign that your spirit has not quite finished its lesson.
As for those who do step into the new era of light? You have learned your lessons well, now is the time to learn new and more wondrous lessons. They aren't lessons that you can learn about in your 3D world.
We await you all, every single individual. No matter who you are, in the eyes of the Divine, you are all one. Accept that, and you will find you have a very extended family because that is what you all are.

I shall leave you now with these words to ponder and say this: Are you ready, my dear ones?

Be well

Gabriel"

***

14 FEBRUARY 2015

Daily Message from the Angels and Ascended Masters:

"Reach out with your heart and hands and take the new beginnings that you deserve.

Every day a doorway is opened for each of you, every day you choose whether to step through it or past it. Every decision you make is a doorway.

Each doorway is the start of a new path, a new beginning, and even an end of an old problem. Doors are made for you all every time.
If you ignore that doorway? No worries, that is your choice. And that doorway will close but will never lock. So later on, if you choose to take that doorway, turn the handle and step through.

Your doorways never go away, and they will be presented to you each time you desire it. The only condition is that you choose whether to step through or not. And if you step through, be prepared to work at your choice. For it will be a learning decision and you are here in this world to learn, aren't you?

Let your choices be the correct ones and be the ones to take you higher in life. If you want something badly, you ask us, and we will work WITH you to gain it. After all, the Divine does help those who help themselves, and this means you work with us to your destination, doing your part in reaching it. In doing so, you learn more.

No good letting us do all the work, for that means you don't learn anything, and we can't help you then either. You do your part, and we'll do ours. A working partnership as it is.

Just ask, choose, and just be yourself. And that is all good in the Universe.

Be well, dear ones.

Gabriel"

***

15 FEBRUARY 2015

Daily Message from the Angels and Ascended Masters:

"Now you have made your day with what you have done, now is the time for you to make someone else's day with something you can do.

Look around you, see those who aren't as fortunate as you. These people need someone like you to give a smile, a greeting, and perhaps a hug. These people are lonely, and they need you to show them that there are others out in the world who do care.

They are lonely because they have been disillusioned by what other less worthy people have done to them.

It's your turn to show them that not everyone is as wrong as the person they experienced.

Humanity has many excellent gifts and many faults. It is the faults that make you human. It is the faults that teach you how to grow beyond. And part of that learning is showing these people, that you accept their faults, and that you see them as perfect.

Assure them that you also have your faults and that you accept them as well. In mutual acceptance of each other's faults, you are all growing and learning. It is the first step.

Let those lonesome people become friends. In mutual respect, you will both become strong.

You get my understanding.

Be well

Ambriel"

***

16 FEBRUARY 2015

Daily Message from the Angels and Ascended Masters:

"Children, do you realize how much we love you? Do you know what we will do for you? I suspect you only have a little inkling.

I shall tell you!

You are made with love, and the Divine made this love in you also. You are the physical proof that this same love formed you. We also are created from that very same divine love, even though yours is a human form, and we weren't. We love you because we are kin and made with the same energies from our ultimate father.

You are placed in this world to learn what it is like to be human and to learn every aspect of it. We were kept on our dimension to help you learn and direct you to your direction. We are more than just kin; we are your teachers and protectors.

The divine love within us all are all part of the Divine within each of us. The Divine can see and feel what we can through that link. In other words, you are the Divine, and you share the Divine's will.

We are all part of the Divine, and the Divine is part and within us all.

We share a kinship, little siblings. We are kin.

In loving your fellow man, you also love us at the same time. You even love the Divine at the same time too. For what you sow, you reap. And the Divine knows what you have done and what you feel. The Divine knows the results and hopes you will learn from that result.

I could go on forever, but my messenger is tiring. I shall leave you with my thoughts on the matter.

Be well and be with our love.

Metatron"

***

16 FEBRUARY 2015

I went into meditation by the Angels, and this is what happened:

AA Metatron came and told me to go into a meditation state. On hearing this, I did as he asked. Metatron then stood behind me and sped the process up.

When I reached the right level, I found myself rushing forward through a track in a forest. Metatron was with me.

As soon as I came to a stop, Metatron picked me up and placed me on his shoulder. He stood about 15-20ft tall. He carried me down a side path.

We came through to a courtyard that appeared neglected. Rubble everywhere and overgrown with vines. Metatron picked up some broken branches and cleared some broken stones, all the while he was explaining this is what it was like within me.

He then told me that Zelrith (my Dragon Guide) wouldn't be visiting me at this time and said to me that I was safe with Zelrith, as I was his latest charge and he tended to be picky over who he watches over.

Soon he took me to what appeared to be a balcony. We were looking out towards mists that were glowing and seemed to be silvery.

On a balcony lower and further forward than mine, was another angel with another person with them sitting on their shoulder.

Metatron brought me down to the lower level and met up with this other Angel and their human.

They let us both down on the ground and stepped back.

This other human and I began looking closely at each other, peering closely yet nothing hostile, just curiosity. This other human appeared to be female, with long brownish wavy hair, aged around 20 something, delicate skin, brown eyes, had an orange-like glow about her.

Metatron started telling me that my current life and soul has a link to this other human. I asked in what way. Metatron just laughed, and with a mischievous look in his eyes and a big grin, said: "Partners in crime" and chuckled to himself.

In time we were both picked up by our respective Angels (mother hens?), and I then was taken to a room that had walls made with white stone. There was a slightly sunken circle in the middle of this room, and I stood there. Metatron told me to remain in this place.

At his words, a door opened, and another Angel walked in. This Angel was wearing black and silver clothing; they had white hair and silver eyes. He took his place on the side of the circle. Behind him came other Angels. They all stood towering over me.

I appeared to be encircled by all these Angels. There seemed to be around 10 of them.

Metatron approached me and told me not to worry. He pointed to one of the Angels to the left side of me, and I recognized Michael, who was smiling. He indicated to my right, and there were Gabriel and Chamuel. I saw Raphael to the right of Michael. Cassiel at the left of Michael.

Familiar faces indeed!

Metatron explained that I was right in one way: That the only time he ever came to me was when he was going to do work on me. He mentioned he was contemplating opening me up 100%. I told him that I didn't think I was ready enough. He smiled and nodded, seemingly at ease with my answer.

His hands began to glow and the light began to form the shape of the Merkaba. He placed this Merkaba light on my chest, saying: "Let the Merkaba be part of you. Let it be with you and let it flow through you. As it does, so be it. Let the symbol release you."

The Merkaba seemed to surround me.

The other symbols of the Sacred Geometry began to place themselves in a spherical formation around me.

Metatron placed his forefinger on my third eye and went behind me, holding my head still.

The other Angels came forward and began to do the same thing, one by one, placing their forefinger to my third eye.

They came closer and surrounded me, and they all put their hands on my head where the Crown Chakra was and poured energy into me. I felt myself get warmer and feel like I was about to explode into energy.

Eventually, they all backed off, and Metatron took my hands and raised them to my eye level. Instead of blue energy with bands of gold, they were now silver energy with bands of gold. My Soul had changed color!

Metatron held my face then said: "Time to go home now. You need to rouse out".

I soon found myself settling back into my own body and feeling as if I was off my face.

The Angel in black and silver was my gentle friend, Ambriel.

***

17 FEBRUARY 2015

Daily Message from the Angels and Ascended Masters:

"Go forward sailing your ships of light, for they follow the blades of the day. The seas of harmony and peace will let you travel with ease into the growing day.
No storm shall sink you and set you off course, for we will be your beacon to guide you on your path of truth.
Stand up and raise your soul to the winds of change and promise, for you are part of the new future. Change with the breezes, and envelope them within you.

You are the new future.

As the day lengthens, your strengths and power will be like the stars above, directing like others to your path. If they are meant to be with you, they will steer towards you and help you on your way.

In time the day will shorten to let the night through. Then it is time to slow down and rest. Let the moon shine on you with its light of tranquillity, calming you to more profound peace and meditation. Use this time to commune with us, with like-minded companions and to sleep. The night is beautiful and protective. We take this turn to stand guard over you and clearing your path of obstacles.

All this in preparation for the journey ahead on the ocean of opportunity and growth.

Such is the way, and always will be. Let your hearts unfurl like sails in the breeze, catching the divine light that beams on you.

Such is the way, so be it.

Be well,

Sandalphon"

***

18 FEBRUARY 2015

Daily Message from the Angels and Ascended Masters:

"Let those who wish to walk away, do so. For it means their path and yours are starting to diverge.
They are on their journey of discovery and learning now, and it is not your path to follow them. If you decide to follow the path of someone else, the only result will be unhappiness.

Follow your path, no matter where it may end up. It will always have the lesson you need to learn. Your way is for you only, just like your now distant companion's path is for them alone.

Follow your path, and you will find new lessons and adventures. The road was specially made for you and will be the smoothest.

If you come to something that needs a decision, feel the answer inside of you. You will know then. Note I said 'feel.' That's right. The answer isn't in words but feelings.

Let your inner spirit direct you. It cannot lie or deceive you for it doesn't know what it means. Nor does it want to know, for your inner spirit is at its happiest when you are joyful.

Do not let others try to hold you back or hang on to you. They fear their path and don't want to take it, and they are afraid of the fact that you have found your own and taking it. They will hold you back, and that is negativity you don't need.

Cut cords and wash away their attachments.

Step forward into your path in life, complete with its destination.

Be well

Habbiel"

***

19 FEBRUARY 2015

Daily Message from the Angels and Ascended Masters:

"Believe in the essential thing in the Universe: The Divine. For the Divine is the Universe, and both are part of you.
In believing in the Universe, you believe in the Divine. And in turn, you believe in yourself. As such, you are near invincible. Once you realize how the Divine and you are linked, you will appreciate how much you can create.

You can create your path; you can create your answers to problems. You can make people.

Yes, you are so close to the Divine.

Believe in yourself completely, and you will find out how strong you are, and how perfect you are.

A long time ago, a promise made to you all and now lost in the depths of time. The vow was that if you respect yourselves and each other, you will be rich spiritually.

There are people whose opinions differ from yours. Let these opinions be with their owner alone. Do not destroy them or put them down, for even the weak and the helpless have the right to have a voice, but it is not your right to condemn it.

The Divine knows your opinion but respects it by not condemning it. And such is the way you should all be.

Did we give you a little food for thought, maybe? I shall leave you with it.

Be well

Ambriel"

***

21 FEBRUARY 2015

Daily Message from the Angels and Ascended Masters:

"Are you feeling alone in your world of solitude? Alone in the spirit and life?

Well, stop right there! Stop feeling that!

You are not alone. You will never be alone. Not while we Angels exist, you will always have us as companions.

We listen to every word you say. We watch everything you do, and we are always within an arm's reach of you.

When thoughts of depression hit you, remember this: You are not alone.

We surround you with our love for you; we will protect you. And above all, we are your closest friends. We will never let you down, and that is a promise we will keep.

Whatever happens in your life, we are around you, listening, and helping.

Do you want to get something off your chest? Tell us! Vent! Let us take the burden of what is holding you down. Let us have the problem, and you can relax, knowing that your issues are in our capable hands.

We can do things with your problems that you can't, so relax.

Be well sweethearts,

Ariel"

***

22 FEBRUARY 2015

Daily Message from the Angels and Ascended Masters:

"Do you like to laugh, to joke and to relax with your friends? Well, so do we. We love to laugh and have fun, and we do relax with our best friends: YOU!

When you laugh at a joke, we laugh with you and all because we enjoyed it too.

We feel joy when you enjoy an enjoyable experience.

When you relax under the sun with your favorite book, we read with you.
You are our best friends, and we endeavor to be yours.

When you look at a beautiful painting, we too enjoy its beauty.
When you show love to your pet, we will make sure your pet is in our circle of protection, just because you love your pet.

If you are a person who loves all animals and nature? You will fight for the cause. Then we will fight with you, making sure that you win your battle, one piece at a time. We don't want you overwhelmed.
If you are a home-body? No matter! We will shield your home with protection so that you can relax more.
If you are enjoying a moment in solitude, we too can step back up to a higher vibration to leave you with your thoughts, but you will always be within our sight and protection.

We do this because we wish to be your most fabulous friends and part of your spiritual family.

No matter where you are, Guardian Angels will always be at your side. That is because they are part of your spiritual family. Your Guardian Angels will be as close to you as your nearest sibling. They are ever protecting and watching, always encouraging you to new adventures.

That's what we all do and want.

Never think you are inconveniencing us, you never will. We are always ready and willing to listen to you. We will hear you no matter where you are.

Be well my friends

Gabriel"

***

23 FEBRUARY 2015

Daily Message from the Angels and Ascended Masters:

"When you feel such an all-encompassing sensation of joy, it is because you are sensing our emotions. You are feeling our happiness.

A lesson:

Relax and breathe deeply.

Go deeper and deeper into your mind, feel the stillness of the soul settle within you.

Let the stillness reach into your mind and keep breathing deeply.

You will feel yourself sinking deeper into the stillness. When that happens, ask us to come and join you. We will.

You will feel our hands touch your face, stroke your arm, or a cheek. Some may feel us embracing them.

This stage is an early step in communicating with us on a deeper level. It is where we can touch you, and it will give us joy, and you can even feel our emotions during this stage if you tune in deep enough. But if not, something within you will sense our feelings and will relax.

Just take your time at this stage.

And when you feel ready to wake up, envision yourself sitting back within your own body and expanding your awareness of what is around you.

It is a gentle way of rousing, and it won't trigger a headache. If anything, you may feel more relaxed. That is because we have removed some of the tension around you.

Now that is a lesson well worth learning.

Be well sweet ones.

Rachiel"

***

24 FEBRUARY 2015

Daily Message from the Angels and Ascended Masters:

"Do what you want and when you want but note that what you do will incur consequences.

You help someone who needs your help; you will incur gratitude and love. Harm someone, and the consequences will occur. Always there are consequences and results. No short measure there, for the outcomes and effects will be thrice-fold back.

Do not destroy what beauty lies within others, with malicious words or actions. Instead, bring them forward and show that beauty to the world and encourage it.

Do not put anyone down for their opinion. After all, the view of these people has as much right to air as yours.

Let those who seek the best in you, come into your life. You will never regret their blessings.

Do not ever forget who created you, for you are in turn, not forgotten.

As love resides in your heart, it lies in everyone else's heart. Don't tear at the other person's love for you. Instead, cherish it and coax it out more. You will, in turn, receive love.

There are many possibilities in your lives, many open doors. No matter how much you run from them, these doors will remain open for you.

You cannot hide from me, and you cannot ignore me. I can see deep within you all and know the truth and power within you.

Let that come forward and raise its arms to the light. You will fly to me on the wings of love. And when that happens, something beautiful will happen inside you.

Never forget how beautiful you are to me and others. We can see the real you, and I made you so that you shall glow with your beauty. It is not about looks and other opinions. It is about your Soul and your personality.

What is within you is perfect to my eyes, because I made it so. So never turn away that part of you. Let it show, for I can see your inner truth.

Let it be so, and I will make sure it is.

I AM."

***

25 FEBRUARY 2015

Daily Message from the Angels and Ascended Masters:

"There are many things in this Universe of yours. So much that no matter how many times you incarnate, you will never learn it all. So that's why we teach you only what you need to know.

It's no good us teaching you about what is the culture on planet Meled if you are never going to be even a light-year near it. We will inform you what you need to know to learn and survive your corner of the Universe.

If the time comes when you need to know more than the usual, that's taken care of too, and we will teach you precisely that knowledge.

The reason is we don't want to overload you. We want you to be happy with yourself and what you know. We don't want to stress you out.

If you should come home to us, where the knowledge is readily available to you all, every single bit of it, the restrictions are gone, and you can learn as much as you like and take your time about it too.

These sources of knowledge in our universe have many names for many races and creatures. But on your world, it is known as the Akashic Records. We have ready access to it on our side, and the people on your planet have limited access, and only through intense meditation, spirit work, and light energy manipulating. It involves a lot of concentration.

But still, a few of you have reached them. And these people are the "prophets" of your world. It is a nurtured skill.

That is my little bit of information to you all. It is not a message of Love or harmony, but a message of knowledge.

Are you prepared to reach the Ultimate Library of Universal Knowledge?

We are waiting with open arms.

Be well, my beloved kin. Be well.

Uriel"

***

26 FEBRUARY 2015

Daily Message from the Angels and Ascended Masters:

"Just when you thought you had learned it all and seen it all. Well, you haven't learned much at all.

Have you learned of the infinite love within your own heart?
The powers of the belief that lies within you?
Or even the strength of your mind and will?

I think you have all scratched only the surface there.

The infinite love can encompass the world and every living thing that dwell upon it, including the plants.
This skill is within reach of your abilities, so what better way to start, by spreading your love further and further out into your world. When it meets up at the other end, your Earth Mother will surround you with her love too.

The powers of belief I mentioned earlier? That too, is within reach. Believe in truth, honesty, love, joy, laughter, innocence, yourself, your own will, and the Divine. So what better way there is to open your self to better things. Believe in the Divine and us, of course. We believe in you, after all.

The strength of your mind and will? Again, that is possible. In an abusive relationship? Believe in your self and soul and get out. All the best things in this world are for the taking, better than that sort of life. You are much stronger than you realize, and that's why the weakest try to dominate the stronger, it's jealousy and fear.

With your mind and will, you can move mountains. You can change the world to a much better place. All you must do is merge your strength with the other two qualities: Infinite Love and Belief.

When all three are combined, then you will realize how powerful and significant you all are. For you will then also realize how much the Divine is within you all. You will be on the first steps beyond enlightenment.

You will start to become receptacles for the divine light and grace.

You will become superhuman.

I will leave you now with my lesson. Learn from it and realize all is much, much more than you have found, and that there is a lot more to learn than you thought.

Be well

Raziel.

***

27 FEBRUARY 2015

Daily Message from the Angels and Ascended Masters:

"Be what you are and believe in it. You are perfect in your Soul and light. You are physically perfect for your task in this world. We do not put you into the wrong bodies. The one you have is the one that is perfect for your role in this current life of yours.

You don't like having something wrong with it? But it is there to teach you something. Maybe to show you compassion for those who are similarly afflicted.

Nothing is accidental, and all is more than it seems. Don't forget that and learn from what your lot is in life. The quicker you learn it and take the lesson to heart, the quicker things can move on.

Instead of complaining about your situation, thank the Divine for giving you the chance to learn this lesson in preparation for your next stage in spiritual growth.

As I said, there are more than it seems — wheels within wheels, and fortunes within fortunes.

You need to learn all you can about your current life. Once you have mastered it, you move to the next lesson. Those who don't learn from it and keep on ignoring the experience, well, they must come back to re-sit the training again. And will continue to do so until it sinks in that they need to wake up and learn.

I'll let this end for now. Be well among your selves.

Raphael"

***

28 FEBRUARY 2015

Daily Message from the Angels and Ascended Masters:

"Where do you think you are going within your life, work, and home?
You go to work, you come back from work, watch television and then sleep. This life is not for you. There is more to your life than that.

There is much in this world that is waiting for you, and we have prepared it all for you.

See the clouds in the sky; they are never the same. The clouds change with every second of your day: the birds that sing, the flowers, and their pristine beauty. Even the lowliest of beasts have their singular glory. They are fascinating aspects of your life that you have hidden from you.

Why?

Trees, plants, birds, insects, and beasts all have their unique part in your life. And you have a role in theirs.

You are the Guardians of your world, and this means you need to protect all living creatures, no matter how small or inconsequential they are. They are yours to look after.

You too need looking after, so that is why we were created in the first place, to prepare the way for you, and then watch over.

That is the way it is meant to be.

You have only one world, so don't destroy it, please.

Our Father has watched you all through the ages and seen how you all have grown. He tells us that it is soon time for you all to step up a level in the vastness of the Universe. Even the creatures and plants are going through this. It is a time of strange changes within you, but you are aware of it. But the plants and animals aren't so much, know the cause. So hence you are needed to be their protectors during this time.

But don't forget to look after yourselves at the same time. Put yourself first and foremost, for you cannot help others if they weaken you by illness.

That is my words to you, my beloved ones.

Be well within your hearts and spirit.

Melchizedek"

***

MARCH 2015

1 MARCH 2015

Daily Message from the Angels and Ascended Masters:

"Do not ever fail yourself. You are your own best friend and your own worst enemy.
 If you give up when you're only at the beginning, then you have failed yourself. Your EGO has now taken over you. You have become your own worst enemy.
 Fight back and push that ego away. You know it has taken over you because you weakened.

The ego has its place in life in helping you to cope with stressful situations and in decisions, but when it comes to communicating with us, it is a hindrance. It doesn't like it and will try to stop you.

Push back that ego and bring forward your Light-Self. Let that Light-Self take over instead, and you will find your rewards in love, compassion, joy, and laughter.

We don't work with the ego as it tries to block us off from you. It is selfish and narrow-minded. Instead, be your true inner self; without ego. Such a beautiful person you become.

Though my message is brief, it is relevant. For it is the ego that is stopping a lot of you from contacting us and nature.

Some will argue the point about this, but that is because they have let ego rule them, not the other way around which is what it should be.

Think about that, be well dear ones.

Gabriel"

***

2 MARCH 2015

Daily Message from the Angels and Ascended Masters:

"When you bring a dream into reality, you are manifesting it into reality. It also has another name: Creation.
Yes, you are also Creators in this beautiful Universe, and this is because you are all essences of the Creator. Each one of you that was born was given that spark of light by the Creator them self.

You are, after all, like us! We are all children of the Divine, and the Divine made us all. We are one. We are a family. You are our little siblings, so it is a duty and a pleasure to look after you, teach you, and guide you. And like family, we love you.
We are one in this. We are one family. We are united, and what is more beautiful than this gift from the Divine, our Creator, and Father. We are all blessed with this gift.

We will bring out this spark of Creation within you so that you can bring your dreams to life. We will guide you on your path to it.

In return for this, all we want is your love and trust.

Nothing more, nothing less! We, in return, send you that love and trust.

We are the divine Children.

Be well.

Gabriel"

***

3 MARCH 2015

Daily Message from the Angels and Ascended Masters:

"Have you ever wondered why you seem to have problems in your life? Well, sit back and see it from my side of things.

Your problems are mainly of your own making. Every decision you make comes with a cause and effect with it. Each choice changes your path, creating new adventures and new problems. The best way to deal with them is one at a time and never make it more than what it is a temporary setback.

What has caused this problem? Why is it there? What can you benefit from it?

You can learn from the situation so that you can recognize it before it happens. That way, you can stop it.

Each situation has a solution and a lesson. Learn from it, and you will find yourself able to avoid the instance in the future. But if it is a big problem, so big that it's getting out of your control. Well, that's where we come in. You call for us and let us take care of it. We can reduce it into a simple small issue. Not instantaneous as that can create a problem in the vortex of time.
We can see the solution far beyond what you can see. We will set events in your life to help you fix the situation.

You see, that is how it is. That's how we see it and work it. And that's how we work it.

We are here to help, but we need you to call upon us to help you. We cannot interfere, but we can direct you to the right path.

Let it be so.

Be well, dear ones.

Michael"

***

4 MARCH 2015

Daily Message from the Angels and Ascended Masters:

"Well, what have you decided? To go with the flow of what others tell you to do, or do you want to dance to your rhythm?

If you go with the flow, you will a face among many similar faces, denying your true potential and your inner light. You will be as the sheep, flocking all together and easily led from one drudgery to another disaster.

But if you go your way in life, you will shine out above others. You will find life exciting and fun. That is the way it is meant to be. Nothing is static, so you go out and enjoy yourself. Be your own master and your pupil.

Many things in this world of yours are magnificent. Your Grand Canyon has a breath-taking beauty of its own.

You are all meant to dance to your drum, not to others. For it is by doing so, you will find your life fulfilling and exciting. The people who are like sheep will never know the thrill of nature's wild beauty. They will never experience anything of such wonders while they remain as sheep.

But these people too can get out of that rut if they so wish, all have got to realize is this: they have no obligation to anyone else but to themselves. Your Destiny and path are in your own hands, not anyone else's.

The only one who is master of you all is the Divine, and the Divine is a kindly loving master.

I shall leave you this to ponder on.

Be well, dear ones.

Chamuel"

***

5 MARCH 2015

Daily Message from the Angels and Ascended Masters:

"Let your soul sing to the Divine of its love for everything that the Divine has created.
Let your voice join in the song of praise.
There is no sweeter sound than a voice raised in a song of happiness, joy, and love.
For it is the song that comes from the heart and gives happiness at your joy. It pleases the Divine.

Sing your words of passion and glory, let the tones ring in the higher vibrations.
Let the song be from your heart, not from someone else's command.
Be the song and be the source of all that joy and love.
You are so beautiful when you do that, it gladdens ourselves, and the Divine finds the meaning and tone fascinating.

Sing your words of love and sweetness, be true to its words and let the words rule your soul, for there are wonder and beauty in your voices raised in song.

Sing like the whole world is waiting for your voice, for it is.

It doesn't matter if you are off-key or have a voice that sounds grating, for the real song is the one that rests within you, and only the truest of hearts and hear it. For that is the song of your soul, and as your soul, it is perfect.

You can hear your song; we can listen to it too. The Divine finds the song as exquisite as do we.

Sing my dear ones and let us hear your voices raised in joy.

Sing!

Be well, dear ones.

Emmanuel"

***

6 MARCH 2015

Daily Message from the Angels and Ascended Masters:

"Never forget your origins, for you originated from this world, made with divine will and stardust. Your roots are miraculous, but you are all heading towards a bigger miracle: the miracle of transition.

Your world and all its beautiful life are heading towards a New Era in understanding, energy, and spirituality. As your world travels from its current energy level to a much higher one, its powers will become temporarily disrupted. A change that will cause sleeplessness, tiredness, headaches, and a feeling of being 'out of sorts.' It is only temporary.

Once the energies have settled down into their new level and rhythm, then you will find your health improving, your understanding of spirituality growing and above all, you will be in touch with Gaia and all her Protectors; the Fae.

It is the start of a new level of awareness. And quite a few of you will Ascend due to this.

Some will not adapt to the journey and will feel left behind and frightened. It is up to us all to help those left behind along a lonely path bit by bit and ease the stress. But it isn't forever. As time passes, all will age and then move onto the next incarnation. These lonely ones will be fully adapted to this new world of yours and will love it.

Sit back, relax, and enjoy the ride. Be considerate of those who will find it challenging to adapt. And above all, be patient with these people, their path will be much, much harder than yours.

So be it, dear ones.

Michael."

***

7 MARCH 2015

Daily Message from the Angels and Ascended Masters:

"Gentle ones, will you all ever learn that what you have yearned, lusted, and bought in your material world, is not all that important. That much hunted item that you searched for and finally obtained. What is it really in the grand scheme of things. Nothing more than a pretty object.

Jewelry is a work of art, but the diamond is nothing more than a pretty crystal. Gold made into shapes pleasing to the eye is art, but basically, it's just metal.

Art is what you have made of essential everyday items. But you can't take it with you when you leave your world. The most valuable thing you have is the one you don't recognize; it's YOURSELF!

Your soul is part of you, and that is the most beautiful thing you will ever have, for it is a part of the divine will.
You are more critical than any jewelry, excellent works of art, and other branded items.
You are unique, beautiful, and perfect in our eyes. You are the most precious and rarest object of all: YOU!

The rest of all your world's greatest treasures are nothing but mere objects. You are the only treasure in your world that is priceless beyond measure.
You are our most precious ones.

Be well.

Ambriel"

***

8 MARCH 2015

Daily Message from the Angels and Ascended Masters:

"When times are hard, and your energies are low, you must remember the three most important words in your life.
When things go wrong, and your patience is worn through. Remember the three words again.
When you are sad and near to grief, again, those three important words.

If you feel lost and alone, Yes, those three words again.

If you are riled up and frustrated, again, those three words come to mind.

Yes, whenever your life has taken a downward turn, or you have fallen temporarily off your path, those three very, very important words will come to mind.

The reason why those words are so important? It is because we say them to you all the time. The Divine says them to you all also. And you even mention them to each other a lot too.

That's why these words are so important, for they have the most significant depth and power of all. The words can even change Galaxies.

What are these three critical essential words? Simple! They are: I LOVE YOU!

What can better words there be?

Be well, dear ones.

Gabriel"

***

9 MARCH 2015

Daily Message from the Angels and Ascended Masters:

"Blessed ones, when you were small, do you remember your most memorable Christmas? The excitement, the anticipation, and the joy?

Why did you lose such feelings? Is not every day just as exciting? After all, are you sure that every day is going to be the same hum-drum existence? It shouldn't be! Every minute is different. Every day brings new wonders. Retain that excitement as you travel through your day.

Look forward to the next one with anticipation, for you never know you may be surprised.

Manifest that excitement. The more you look forward with excitement to the day, the gleeful feeling of hope of a future reward, the more likely it is going to happen. The more you want it, the more likely it will happen.

Your inner child knows this. Let that child run free.

Each day is a promise of new beginnings and gifts. Each moment has a guarantee of a happening.

Never hide your head and think your life is boring. In believing that, you have made it so. Again manifestation.

You are what you make yourself be. Your immediate world is what you wanted, so you can easily change that for the better. Nothing can stop you, that's for sure. We'd help you.

Dream your dreams, take the next steps into making them a reality, and watch your world begin to unfold like a sunflower, a petal at a time.

Be well, dear ones, be well.

Metatron"

***

10 MARCH 2015

Daily Message from the Angels and Ascended Masters:

"Where are you all going in your lives? You, who have so much to aim for, are missing the point. You are not in this world to chase after money and kowtow to other people's demands. You are here to pursue your happiness.

Money is not the real source of happiness; you are.

Where money rules, then things will collapse. Money is just nothing in the grand scheme of the universe.

I wish to see services returned for services rendered. You do something for another person, and in turn, they pay you with something you need. This trade of skills works very well and can gain greater friendship and peace within you. It brings the joy of giving and taking back into its perspective.
No longer will money serve its purpose, namely bringing down this world. For the give and take, I wish, brings more harmony in your world. The time will come when money will no longer make you serve it. You will, instead, help yourself.

A world at peace is a world without outrageous greed. It's also a world that is in harmony with nature.

Things are already beginning to change, and the time will come when such financial needs will pass. You all can bring forth what you want without such an unnecessary thing as money. You have everything that you need.

Let it be in peace, when you follow this path, for the ending is in harmony. No longer will you serve greed with its pieces of metal. Instead, you will tender to me. You will be for me, and I will give you joy and freedom in turn. I am not a demanding master but a loving one. It is my will, and it too serves me.

In peace, I shall give you my love, my children. For all is working out as it is meant to be.
You who are beautiful in my eyes are also beautiful in my other children's eyes. Let my children of light help their siblings, the children of Earth. And you will find treasures beyond any riches, and that they all are within reach and you.

With love, I shall now release my channel.

Be well, my children and let your love flow like the spring from a flowered meadow. Let my light flow on you and show you how much I love all my children, no matter what color they are and what faith they follow. For all are equal in my eyes.

I am your Creator, my children, and that is most important of all. The fact that I see and know all, and still love you.

The Divine."

***

11 MARCH 2015

Daily Message from the Angels and Ascended Masters:

"Now is the time to contemplate on the greater scheme of things in the Universe. Times are changing, and so are you.

Your world is entering a new phase in its path, a step which will involve you and every living creature. You must be ready for this, as you will find your abilities grow.

Those who don't think you have any unique gifts or talents? Think again! They will soon become noticeable once this shift happens. All will be revealed later when the change is near completion.

You will find that headaches and lethargy are regular during this shift. It is your body and soul compensating for the energy changes and making sure you don't overwork yourself. Once this phase is over, then you will find your energy levels increased.

Never mind what those who have closed their eyes to this; they too will wake up and realize what is happening. Some will not be affected by the changes, and that is because it is part of their life path and must learn from it.

When all is over, then you will find your world will also have changed. Different ideas and thoughts will start to show. Your voice will be able to make things happen. You will find yourself altered and more powerful.

All is change; nothing is static. All is truth in the universe; nothing is ignored or missed.

That will be so.

I regard you with my love

Cambiel"

***

12 MARCH 2015

Daily Message from the Angels and Ascended Masters:

"When you sit back and relax, you are taking a mild type of meditation. Just by sitting still and resting, you trigger that session off.
But when you further theresting phase into a deeper state, which can be triggered just by daydreaming, you are in communication with us. We see your daydreams, and these give us clues as to what you want in your life.

There are times where some people have even gone further and have spoken to us. We reply while you like that. And you hear us as well.

Your daydreams are not a waste of time. And don't let anyone tell you otherwise.

Your dreams are your way to communicate with us.

When you sleep, we are interacting with each other. There is no waste of time there. It is your way to reach our level. And it works perfectly well.

Even in sleep, we can teach you and upgrade your knowledge. It is all teaching and learning. It is all part of your growth.

So never be ashamed of being caught daydreaming by others, ignore what they say about it. You are talking to us. And that is a lot better than derogatory comments by others.

Dream your dreams, and when you decide to start living those dreams, let us know, and you can then take the first steps towards it. Yes, you must make an effort to live the dreams, for then the opportunities will lie in your path. They won't come to you; you must go to them.

That's what dreams are. For communication between dimensions can be tricky for you living ones, unless you can dream.

That is a bit of knowledge to help you understand what you need to do. Dreaming is a part of sleep also and is also better in that you can come into our part of the world.

And it is so, be well dear ones, be well.

Gabriel"

***

13 MARCH 2015

Daily Message from the Angels and Ascended Masters:

"Let's start with a lesson.

Take a bit of alone time with yourself, far away from the noise and confusion of daily life. Make sure it is in an area which is quiet and filled with the vibrations of nature. A park or a spot in a forest that is a bit off the track. Preferably near water.

Sit on the ground and let nature caress you with her music: the birdsong, the rustling of leaves, and the laughing sound of water. Let the sounds envelop you, and then you slip into a meditation state.

Remain in this state and start to envision yourself slowly walking through a forest.

You go further in deeper; you see a small meadow. Once in the center, sit down in this forest glade, on a pedestal of your choice. Surround yourself with the white light. Inhale the white light deep into you. As you do this, add another color of your choosing. Inhale that light too.

Feel both the lights coursing through your body and every cell. Feel it changing and cleansing you from within, as it makes beneficial changes within you.

You will likely feel a tingling in you, or what appears to be a cold breeze rushing around you. Don't worry that is just us, helping you focus the energy.

Deep in your vision of the forest glade, look around you.

Invite nature spirits to show themselves. They too are watching you from within the branches so that they will hear you.

Each experience on this is individual and varied, so take note of what you see.

After approximately 15 minutes, you would have had an exciting experience, and it will be time to rouse out. Do this slowly and gently.

A step at a time, see yourself slowly walk back to your current spot where you are physically sitting, and then merge back with your body.

That is the time when you should write down what you have learned and experienced. For this too will teach you.

What have you seen, dear ones?

Raziel"

***

14 MARCH 2015

Daily Message from the Angels and Ascended Masters:

"It's a beautiful day. The beauty is in that fact that the sun is in the sky, the rain falls onto the soil and giving life to those who are thirsty
.
All is meant to be for a reason.

The sun feeds and brightens the day. Gives you light and warmth enough to survive.
The rain gives you water to drink, and plants will take in that water to provide you with food.
Snow, with its pristine beauty,too, is helpful. Does it not help to warm the soil underneath its layers?
Ice breaks up hard soil so that the tilling in Spring is more leisurely.
Wind spreads the seeds of life to around the globe and helps the birds to travel.

The seasons are such made that way, so that all can work to keep your world clean, fresh, and alive.

So why do you pollute the world with chemicals?

All you are doing is creating your extinction, and that is something we don't want, even your Divine parent doesn't want it. But we cannot interfere because it is your path, not ours.

I ask of you all, choose wisely, be responsible for your actions, and help your Mother Earth. She needs your help. When you do this, you will be surprised at how she can fix things.

Help her dear ones. Ask us, and we will help you with this task.

It is not too late to change.

Be well, dear one.

Ariel"

***

15 MARCH 2015

Daily Message from the Angels and Ascended Masters:

"Welcome to the world of beautiful light. The gift that the Divine has for you is within this light. And what a gift it is!
It is the gift that goes beyond all understanding, for it is a gift that we hold for you.

When you cross over to our side, we hand your gift to you; a gift made of light and contains all your memories from previous lives and of course, interwoven with love from us. It is the gift that belongs to you.

Where is this gift we hold for you? It is deep within your very soul, hidden and waiting to be released. Some of you have managed to open your presents early, and that is because you have earned it well.

The releasing is triggered when you reach a certain level in your spiritual growth, and you will have rightfully earned it. For you have worked hard to reach that level, haven't you? Well, take your reward, dear one.

The light protects those memories from interfering with your lives until you reach the right level. By that time, you have done your primary task, and you are deemed worthy of receiving those memories.
Such is the way, to receive this gift, is to be blessed by the Divine and us.

You are all wonderful, and your souls are such beautiful lights. Your Soul knows when to release those memories. It won't open them up until you are ready. Those who have undergone hypnosis for the memories should note, not all the details will be correct. Certain things will remain hidden by your soul because you aren't yet ready.
If releasing those memories at the wrong time, your conscious mind would not be able to take the additional stress and unbalance; then it would become unhinged.

Let the knowledge come at the right time and when you are fully enlightened.

There is no better time than that, dear ones.

I shall leave you with this thought; all rewards will be given at the right time, no sooner, no later.

Be well,

Gabriel"

***

17 MARCH 2015

Daily Message from the Angels and Ascended Masters:

"When you think that nothing new can come to your world, and there is no more to discover... Hmm wrong!
There is a lot more to explore and learn in your world than you have realized. You are only just touching the edges of discovery.

The wonders of Divinity are infinite, so it is on your world. Still, there are some creaturesnot discovered, unexplored land, and waters to reach.

Your world is more special than you thought. And it is all yours.

Even in your backyard, you can observe the wonders being seen in the eyes of a small child as it follows a humble beetle for the first time. See the curiosity and awe in that child's eyes, for there is proof that the world still holds wonders yet to be seen. And it is all new and beautiful to the child. A child is not born to fear the simple snake or spider. The child sees them with wonder and no fear. It is the adult that teaches the child to fear.

To learn from your world, you must not fear it. Instead, be cautious with the more dangerous forms and treat them with the respect they deserve, and you will get along. Teach your children such respect towards your world and to others. In turn, they will find their life will be that much more comfortable, and there will be more peace.

There is another wonder on your world that is so readily available, but few use it. It has many names: Love, Respect, Joy, Laughter, Compassion, and Honour. They too are worthy of being learned and applied. Explore those too, and you will also find that mountains are moving.

I shall leave you to think about this, dear ones.

Matriel"

***

18 MARCH 2015

Daily Message from the Angels and Ascended Masters:

"Believe in yourself, for in doing so, you are the most potent force in the world. Nothing can stop you, and nothing can put you down. You are indestructible while you believe in yourself.
You can also believe in others, to be what they want to be.

You are all different in many ways. Some can do things that others can't, and so be it. It is the way it is meant to be.

You get frustrated in that others don't think the same way you do. So what! That is the way it is meant to be, accept it as that. If you all felt the same, acted the same, and so forth, you wouldn't be human anymore; you would be sheep — nothing original, not even your thoughts.

You are NOT sheep; you are your own perfect individual selves. And each of you has your paths to follow. No one has the right to try and change you to their ideal. If these people can't accept you for what you are now, then they have the problem, not you. You can walk away from them, as they will try to suck the energy out of you.
Such is the way of those tainted by the darkness.
In time they may realize what is wrong and step into the light, some may not. It is a choice, remember!

So, they have their beliefs, and so do you.

Belief in yourself is trust.

Trust in yourself is acceptance.
Acceptance of yourself is growth.
The growth of yourself is enlightenment.
Enlightenment is the path to ascension.
Ascension is the path to the Divine.
The Divine is a spark within yourself.

Believe in yourself, and you will believe in the Divine at the same time.

All are The One, and The One is within you all.

So be it, and let it be so.

Farewell for the moment.

Uriel"

***

19 MARCH 2015

Daily Message from the Angels and Ascended Masters:

"All those who come into the light of the Divine are welcomed. For in their hearts, they feel the call to be at the Divine's feet and to worship him. We welcome you into the presence of the Divine and will aid you on your path to do the Divine's will.

And what is the Divine's will for you?

It is the Divine's will that you live your life to the fullest. To sing with happiness, to feel the Earth's living pulse under your feet as you dance in the grass. You exist with joy and love in mind, and you are then placed on this world to pursue it. Once found, you can be the most brilliant star in the Universe.

Seek your happiness, and you will find you won't have to look far for it. It is within you all the time.

Choose to be happy. And keep that in mind that happiness will find you.

Choose to be loved, and love will find you.

What you give out to the world will be returned to you thrice-fold. Give the world your love; expect more back. Same goes with compassion and laughter.

As you help others not to stumble on their paths, those who are loyal to the light, in turn, will help you remain safely on yours.

Walk away from the negativity that threatens to sneak up on you and take you. Just stare at it and say: 'You don't own me, I am free to be happy and loved.' then walk away. If the others follow, lead them to the light instead. Lead them to us, and we shall take care of their learning and opening.

That's all the Divine's will is. Be happy!

That's all.

What more does one want?

I leave you now, dear ones.

Gabriel"

***

20 MARCH 2015

Daily Message from the Angels and Ascended Masters:

"Be within your own space and time, for there is no better place

Be at peace within your soul, for you have the right to be happy.

Be at the feet of the Divine, for the Divine is the parent of all.

Be part of the greater scheme of destiny, for you can move mountains.

Be at one with your heart, for Love can change the Fates of others.

Be at the side of Angels, for they are your most faithful friends and kin.

All will come to pass as it should be. Follow my simple rules above, and you will discover more light and love in your life.

We are not the ones who will walk out on you or argue to the point of meltdown.

We are not the ones who will cast you aside like a used piece of paper.

We are not the ones who will make derogatory comments and insult you.

We are the ones who will stand by you in all weathers.

We are the ones who will encourage you to reach the stars.

We are the ones who will protect you from all things dark.

We are the ones who genuinely love you for yourself.

We aren't interested in what you have done in the past. We are only interested in the real you, the one that resides in your body. You and you alone, and no other negative force can harm you if you ask for our help.

You only need to listen with your feelings and heart, for only a few can hear us with other senses. Your senses are your best friend, allow them to tell you of any dangers around you. We will work on communicating with you via those feelings.

Need I say more than what I have already stated? I think not. I shall now leave you with my words and thoughts.

Be well

Melchizedek"

***

21 MARCH 2015

Daily Message from the Angels and Ascended Masters:

A Message from The Divine.

"When I see you all looking around you, judging others. Putting each other down, I sometimes wonder why?

Why do you do this?
What do you have to gain in this behavior?
What sense is it?

I ponder hard and wonder what my children are becoming to be. It is something that is negative and should not reside in your hearts.

Then I look around further, and I see others helping those who have fallen, feeling compassion, and even being each other's strength — showing love for all.
Then I think this, 'That is what it is all about. That is what it is meant to be.'

Let those who have let the light into your hearts be the Beacons to bring forth those who have fallen. Be aware of those who have judged others without any reason and show them that their judgments were wrong. Show them that they would have more power if they showed encouragement to others, instead of discouragement.
The more you help others, the stronger your inner light becomes. Even the inner light that belongs to Gaia grows more.

That is what I want. No more of the weavings of the threads of negativity going through your lives, they are to be removed and destroyed.

I did not intend for you to follow a path leading downwards; my intention was for you to learn, grow, and become one of the members of the light.

No more do I want you to follow the wrong path. I want you to come to me in your full glory, light shining brightly within you and the universe in your eyes. That is what I want. You to be one with this light.

Some have already reached there and are readily available to help you.

I call upon the children of my world, the children of Earth and start to take your gifts and use them to take the first steps towards the light.

My children of the light and I will help you every step of the way. Even those who hide and deny me will feel this call. They may not understand, but they will feel it and unknowingly follow the call.

All is not lost, dear children. All is ready for the next stage of your growth. And never has your world seen the likes of it before. Are you ready my children, if not, then get prepared? Nothing can stop it, and I want you all to be one with the light.

Are you ready?

I am your Divine hope."

***

22 MARCH 2015

Daily Message from the Angels and Ascended Masters:

"As much as the stars in your sky, you too glow as brightly as them. It is because life is from the same elements that the Divine made the stars. All linked to those stars and every solar system in the Universe. Star children you are. And in the future of your world, you will return to the stars.

You feel them calling to you, don't you? Not for long. The stars await your return patiently.

In time, when the future comes, you will return. The universe and we shall be with you, bringing you to the wonders found in the will of the Divine.

Star children you are, and always will be. Never forget that. Your destiny lies beyond your world.

Some of you don't feel the call, don't worry. It means you have been chosen to look after your world. Someone must do that, and it is an outstanding job, indeed. For without you, there would be no world.

Each of you all has an essential job in the grand scheme of the divine will and the universe. Today, tomorrow, and beyond, you all have a necessary task. Each little thing you do will help in your growth. And a criminal act will delay that growth. An evil deed is unrewarded.

There is more to come, but one step at a time. I will say more when you are all ready to reach the next stage. At this moment, concentrate on what you can do now.

Be well

Ashtar"

***

23 MARCH 2015

Daily Message from the Angels and Ascended Masters:

"Beloved ones, I speak to you today to let you know that your sufferance of the shift in your energies and of your world, is almost over.

You all need to rest until the shift ends. Once it is so, then you may start anew on your lessons and work. It is a time of rest until then.

When it is over, you will find things have changed within you. Your abilities may have increased. Or you see the old life no longer serves you. It could go many directions, but the results will be the same: You have changed within.

Do not fear the change; it is due to happen at the Divine's bidding. And it happened. These changes will bring about a new awareness, new powers, new skills, and new friendships.

All will go through with them, and all will find something different.

All we require you to do is wait until the shift is over, and then try them out. Yes, try these gifts out, for what is the point of giving the gifts to you if you don't? Or in your words: If you got it, flaunt it.

If you have difficulties, call upon your Guardian Angels. They are aware as to what has happened and are willing to show you.

Some of you will be very surprised at what has happened to you. Dear ones, you are only scratching the surface. More surprises are coming.

The Age of Aquarius is upon you, and this is the shift to it.

Go with peace and understanding within your soul and be prepared to give help when asked. You will need to give to others what you want to receive back for yourself. Karma works miracles to those who perform them for others.

Be well, dear ones, be well. And you will find your world advancing into a new age.

Raguel"

***

24 MARCH 2015

Daily Message from the Angels and Ascended Masters:

"Peace upon you all. Let peace reach within you and grace you with its love.

Sit back on a lawn of grass and place your back against a tree. Let the tree shelter you and let the grass feed you with its grounding energies.

Let this moment of peace surround you, and know that Mother Earth is watching over you, cradling you in her energy. The tree will support you, and grass will comfort you. The buzzing of insects will soothe your mind. Birdsong will lighten your spirit, and the wind will caress your cheek with Gaia's love.

If you wish to meditate during this time, go ahead. It will be rewarding and enlightening for you. If you want to rest and be at one with your thoughts, that too is welcome. For such moments can be inspirational.

There is nothing wasted on such moments, for these are the moments that you must treasure — a time for rest, peace, and harmony with Mother Gaia.

All within your sphere of peace will be rested, even the tree will remove any negative energy from you. The grass will take most of it away and give it to Mother Gaia to cleanse, then return it to you. The tree will help. Flowers are pleasant to the eye, and in doing so, your soul feels joyous at the sight of nature's true beauty.

All is well in your Garden of Peace. Take this garden and place it into your soul and feel the Peace within you start to grow.

It is how it is meant to be, dear one. No more, no less, and all areintended to be.

Just like you are meant to be.

Be well

Nathaniel"

***

25 MARCH 2015

Daily Message from the Angels and Ascended Masters:

"Believe with all your heart that you are lovely, you are perfect, and you can do anything you wish in your world. Believe in that, and you will find your dreams coming true. Nothing can stop you once you ultimately believe in yourself.

So what if you have been brought up to think you are worthless, or others have browbeaten it into you. You need to stop and think: "I am perfect, and I can do what I want." You see, you must keep on thinking that. You must come out of the dense covers of imposed negativity and show yourself fully. No longer restrained or hidden away. Instead, you show yourself for what you are, a confident, intelligent, and beautiful person.

You are not beholden to anyone but the Divine. No other can tell you what you are, for the Divine truly sees the real you and loves you for what you are.

Don't hide away my friends, but instead be like the Lotus Blossom with its many layers slowly opening to reveal the golden heart at the center. So beautiful you are, and you will become more impressive when you open yourself up to that way.

Why not give it a try at least, you have nothing to lose, but much to gain.

Believe in yourself, just like we believe in you.

Be well, dear ones, be well.

Michael"

***

26 MARCH 2015

Daily Message from the Angels and Ascended Masters:

"When you wish for something, you are starting to manifest a dream. A wish is only part of the manifesting process. The rest of the process involves you showing us what you want, how you want it, and where you want it. In other words, show us more details about obtaining your wish. Every aspect! Every single detail. It is so that the more feature there is, the less chance of a mistake or misinterpretation; we are a very literal type. Think about what you want, as much detail as possible, and in their correct sequence in time, and let us bring it about. Let us guide you to that dream.

That's the way how to make anything work for you, step by step, idea by idea, thought by thought. All will come to pass, if thought out clearly, with detail, love and of course, you must tell us with your voice. Words that come from your heart are more important than words that you are forced to say by others.

Dreams are what worlds you make. Ideas make the most celebrated novels, and thoughts bring the greatest of all changes.

Dreams are great in making things happen. After all, without ideas, would not a lot of your inventions and creations will cease to exist?

Dreams make your world go around and make your heart sing for u — daydream on, little flower.

Be well, my friends and keep dreaming.

Emmanuel"

***

27 MARCH 2015

Daily Message from the Angels and Ascended Masters:

"Be your selves in honesty and love. For you are what is all that is needed.

Truth is the most honest way to say I am with the Divine. For you are with the Divine and the Divine is with you.

Love is another way of saying "I love the Divine," and after all, the Divine loves you unconditionally.

And of course, laughter is a way of saying: "I am part of the Divine" and of course, the Divine is part of you.

In all actions and deeds that you do in this world, the Divine witnesses every single one. Sees it through your eyes and knows how you feel. The Divine sees all, so the truth is the best way to go. You can lie to yourself, pretend you are something else and even try to cheat others, but the Divine sees through all this and knows. So why be something you are not.

It's not the lies we are interested about; it's the truth, the real you. That is what we want to show forth. The real you can be so beautiful, and why is it hidden from the world? Only you and we know the reason. We want you to become the real you, show the world that what you are is the most beautiful thing they have. Your personality, laughter, and joy are one of the greatest treasures you have, so don't throw them away.

Your love is strong, so don't waste it on lost causes that will never understand. Instead, show yourself some love by looking after yourself, a little bit of pampering to your body is good, and so is having fun. Don't be afraid to spoil yourself now and then; you deserve it. Instead, enjoy it. A happy person is a person who can make others happy in turn. So be happy.

We all see your happiness when it shows, and it is beautiful. The divine light within you shines through your skin when you are happy, this is what we want, and it is perfect.
Please, glow like the stars in the sky and show the world that you are a beacon of light that can bring illumination to others in the darkness of their minds.

Be happy and above all, love all livings. Even the dull and ugly have their beauty, and it is not on the surface but within their souls.

That is where the most magnificent beauty shows. It's in you too.

I shall leave you with those thoughts, dear one. I hope that you will heed them and show your love and light to others.

Be well,

Uriel"

***

28 MARCH 2015

Daily Message from the Angels and Ascended Masters:

"Just when you thought things were going down into the pits of depression, and that you had nothing more to give to your world? Think again, dear ones. You have a lot more to give to your world, and you are all stronger than you thought.

Remember that the world does not revolve around you, but you are part of this world, and you are working around it. Your world needs you to look after it in your gentle way and at your own pace. No pressure.

If others are draining your energy, leave them. You don't need that sort of thing in your life. Energy vampires are negative people and gain pleasure in removing you of your vitality and joy. Please leave them; they are not worth your time.

Go out and enjoy the company of other people who share your love and happiness, who believe in the same as you; that you all belong to the light. As you work together in your world, you will find that beautiful things will happen to all of you and often. And in joy, you are helping your world, by spreading your light to others.

And if you wish to help your world physically, no harm in keeping a small plot of land full of flowers for the bees. Or even just gently loving a tree that is nearby. Every little thing is, in fact, far more significant than you realize. Much more prominent, and it is beautiful.

When enough of you put your heart into your world? You spread enough light to surround it, then wait for great miracles far beyond your imagination. And there is proof that the fire that you have all been spreading is starting to show itself. It is continually growing and will soon envelop the entire world. We await that with anticipation, for then, we begin helping the Divine with the next stage. And that is the greatest miracle of all to come.

We wait, and we are patient.

Be well, sweet ones, I will be around.

Cassiel"

***

29 MARCH 2015

Daily Message from the Angels and Ascended Masters:

"Those who try to take away your will and force theirs on you, let them go, and never look back. No one has that right to have that much power over you. No one can make you say something you don't want to say; no one can make you think their way. No one can make you do things you don't want to do. No one!
The only person who can do that is yourself. Only you can do things for your self first. And when you can help others with no thought of reward, then you are ready to help the world.
Some thanks and a smile is rewarding enough; no other required.

As you do someone else a favor, let that other person pass the support on. Spread the deed of love around the world, for it will change people, countries, and laws in its passing. Let it happen and feel the reward of love back. You never know, you may be the recipient of such an award at a time when you needed it the most.

All connected to one and another and Karma has many names. And one of those names is Love.

Never neglect yourself for others, dear ones. Look after yourself first and foremost, so that you may be active in mind and body to help others. It is what is meant to happen. Do it and feel our blessings upon you as you help others in their time of need.

Let it be so, dear ones.

Emmanuel"

***

30 MARCH 2015

Daily Message from the Angels and Ascended Masters:

"When the world gets too much for you, go to your 'special' place where no one can interrupt you, and all is peaceful there. Just half an hour at least per day will give you that needed space to collect yourself and relax.

You all have moments like that, don't you! Well, make sure you have that special place for yourself. No other site is best, just your spot.

You need to have that area, for if you don't de-stress and relax, then you will suffer as this negative energy will harm you. In some case, make you physically sick. You don't need that, not at all. Hence the need for your area.

It is all in the name of good health and spirit. For all need that moment away to collect and calm themselves, before joining in the rest of your busy day.

Find your spot to relax in, make sure it is off-limits for that time. If you think you can meditate during that time? Good! Do it! Meditation is even better for you.

As I said, all in the name of good health and spirit.

Are you willing to do that, my dear ones? I await you when you do decide.

Be well,

Raphael."

***

31 MARCH 2015

Daily Message from the Angels and Ascended Masters:

"Sweet ones, lift your joyous spirits to the sky. Sing your happiness to the stars above. Laugh with us and show you are pleased with what life has given you. Be at one with your self. For in doing so, there is harmony within. As you and your soul are in complete agreement over what your happiness is, your world will expand.

All is love, and love is Divine. And in spreading your passion and joy, you are praising the divine presence. All is complete when you and the Divine are united in happiness. For that is what the Divine wants you to be. You are his beloved children, and no one can ever deny that. Some will try, but their argument will remain forever weak. You know deep within you that you are blessed and loved. The Divine will never neglect their children.

Sing, dance, be happy, and the Divine will be pleased with you. We will help in making you happy; after all, your happiness makes us happy too. We will sing with you too. Dancing? Yes, that also.

So welcome happiness into your life by going out into your world, get out of your comfort zone, and see the smiles on the children faces. Listen to the birds and look at the wonders of nature. They too are a joy to behold.

Sing a song for me, my friends.

Be well.

Gabriel"

APRIL 2015

1 APRIL 2015

Daily Message from the Angels and Ascended Masters:

"Go with peace in your ever-changing world. For as your world evolves, so do you. Nothing is static, for your world to stop at a favorite time, means you will stagnate and will forever remain left behind.
Your world changes to accommodate and teach you to step further into your future. As you take those steps forward, so does your world. Time is relevant to how much you learn. As you learn to evolve spiritually, your world opens new possibilities for you. It has moved with you, opening doors long closed to you.

Evolution of the spirit is growth, learning, and above all, enlightenment.

For the enlightened ones: They are the ones who have stepped beyond your usual boundaries and will keep on stepping forward. Do not be afraid to test your limits; they are there for you to check — those who do not are those who will go no further into their path. You must always move forward, not backward.

It is your process of spiritual enlightenment we are talking about here, and it is to wake some of you up. Those who do not need this wakening up, because they have already reached enlightenment will encourage those who have not yet.

My dear enlightened ones help those who have yet to be enlightened so that they too can reach the next stage of their journey.

It is all that is needed.

Be well,

Michael"

***

2 APRIL 2015

Daily Message from the Angels and Ascended Masters:

"Do not run away from your world, for no matter how much you hide and back off, we will always find you. You can't shy away from those who can see everything. You can't run away from what is inevitable. No matter how much you bury yourself either in your world or your past, you remain seen by us. To us, you were never lost or hidden. We are around you always.

You may as well stop hiding and, instead, come out to your world with lights flashing, and trumpets blaring. You're in this world, so make the most of it. Live your life to the fullest, and don't worry about what happened a long time ago. That part of your life is gone and finished; it won't come back.

If you want to go to new places? Ask us to prepare the way for you. We shall arrange doors to open for you and even guide you to them. All you must do is make an effort to take those first steps. Beyond those doors is your new life, new adventures, and above all, a new future.

That is why it's a waste of time hiding or running away. You will end up going in the right direction no matter what. Destiny has its plans for you, and Destiny goes by the title of the Divine.

Well, you go along for the ride, because no matter what, it's all yours. We will take care of the details; you will take care of the physical work part of it.

Think about it, dear ones, think about it.

Be well.

Gabriel"

***

3 APRIL 2015

Daily Message from the Angels and Ascended Masters:

"Whatever you believe in or whatever you do, be aware of one thing, that all paths lead to the One. No matter what religion you are, there is no one path. There are many, but they all lead to the one destination: The One. The Divine One.

Those who preach hate and segregation, you are saddening the One. The Divine wants unity in peace and harmony. The Divine wants you all to know that though you are apart, you belong to each other and the Divine.

Stop the hate, stop the bigotry, stop the fighting. It serves no purpose but to encourage the negative energies to grow in your lives. You don't need that. Let the light in your lives instead.

To do that, let in love, acceptance, tolerance, and friendship grow. Your human-made religions are not natural. But to accept the Divine as your spiritual leader is. The Divine is also your helper, nurturer, and believes in you, so never doubt that.

No human-made cult can meet up with that love and trust, and so it must be left behind. Accept the Divine in your hearts, and you don't need a church, temple, or mosque to do that. Just standing in an empty field and opening your heart is much closer to the Divine than any human-made promise.

The reason why?

The most precious center of worship to the Divine is you. You are your temple, your church, and your link to the Divine. Your relationship is the strongest, so there is no need to feed on other people's connections to feed greed.

No, be yourself, and follow your love and link to the Divine, and you will find yourself doubly blessed with the Divine's love for you.

You are the perfect Temple in the divine universe, and we know it. The Divine can read your heart, and if your love for the Divine is true, then you will find your path in life to be golden.

If your heart isn't pure, then you will find yourself learning lessons in your life to make it right. The Divine knows when your heart is like that, you're not quite ready and understands. We will show you the way to the Divine and teach you.

You will not be forgotten or forsaken. We will all teach you.

Are you ready?

Sananda Jesus"

***

4 APRIL 2015

Daily Message from the Angels and Ascended Masters:

"Make a wish, any wish, and hold it in your heart. Believe in that wish coming true and tell yourself that it will. A request from your heart is an honest wish. Just like a promise from the heart.

Any feelings or oaths taken by heart, have the highest importance in knowledge, for they have grown from deep within you.

Not all wishes get granted, because if they were, would you learn anything? You would gain absolutely nothing. Most of your desires, you must strive towards, for the gaining of that wish, is your path towards knowledge. It is a very efficient way of teaching as all learn the details very well.

Rest that wish within your heart, give it love and hope. And when that dream shows signs of blossoming, your energy levels are higher. And of course, as you know, the higher the energies, the easier it is to talk with us. And in doing so, we have a more unobstructed view of your wish and greater detail of it.

Yes! That's when WE go into action.

Oh, it is a shame that the written word here cannot convey the laughter within me, but then again, when you manage to get to the level to speak with us, you will feel us too and laugh with us.

Wish your love into your heart and treasure that little bit within you, for love is a gift to humanity from the Divine. As you treasure that small piece within, you will begin to love yourself more. That's a good thing, you know. I'm not talking about vanity, but more happiness and inner peace.

Makes a good wish, doesn't it!

I shall leave you now with my love, my heart, and my blessings.

Gabriel"

***

5 APRIL 2015

Daily Message from the Angels and Ascended Masters:

"Wherever you are in this world, you are meeting new people and learning new lessons. They are all meant to be happening. After all, remember that there are no such things as "chance" meetings. They are all orchestrated with one thing in mind: Your education towards enlightenment.

Enlightenment is a state of awareness that provides much new knowledge and heightened skills. It is the first of the lower targets on your path towards us. When you reach the level of enlightenment, then you will walk the path towards Ascension.

There are many levels towards Ascension, and all have their lessons. And some of these lessons are provided by strangers unaware. They will be part of your teaching, and they don't even know it. But it's for you to work over. You may not know it's a lesson either, but how you deal with the stranger or maybe work with the stranger, could be your lesson.

No matter how dull the person is or how slow they are, they all have their story to tell, and in that story is your lesson. The one you thought dull might be passionate about a hobby they have got. They may even feel the same about you, not knowing what your favorite past time is.

As you look in the stranger's eyes, you are looking at yourself. You are the stranger to this other person. And your paths will match at that time. Before you judge other people, look deep within yourself, and see the real you. Another lesson? Could be!

Hence the path towards enlightenment can be a confusing one and must be taken one step at a time. And work at your own pace, you can't rush this path. It is rewarding in the end. It is a path that is smooth, but if you find a few potholes in it, they are of your own making. These potholes are often called Procrastination, Self-Doubt, and Ego. The potholes are easy to avoid if one is more diligent.

Enough, I have said enough. I shall let you contemplate my words and learn from them. All become clearer as time passes.

Be well and be safe

Ambriel"

***

6 APRIL 2015

Daily Message from the Angels and Ascended Masters:

"Sweet beings, all is not lost. Your world is undergoing a transition from one energy to another. And this new energy will bring much changes and awakenings. It will cause some disturbance in others, but all you can do right now is rest.

Yes, I have seen the messages around the world from people saying that they are unsure of their paths, and of their direction. I heard your voices complain of feeling down, tired, headaches, and body aches. I thought it was time for me to intervene and say my piece.
You will have the usual headaches and stress that you just can't put your finger on the cause of it. It's new energy.

Be patient, all of you. You have a saying: 'Rome wasn't built in a day.' Well, this counts for you too. Try to do too much right now, expect your abilities and mind not to work very well. Hence the quiet time. Let things settle, then start exploring.

It won't be for much longer though. It is nearing the end of this current phase. Yes, I said, 'Current Phase.'

You see, there is a set of energy shifts, and each one is higher and stronger than the other. You are all just going through them one phase at a time. When you are going through a stage, the best option is to sit back and rest a lot, or you will exhaust yourself much quicker than usual.

Right! You are nearing the end of this phase. And the next step is due within a few months. Settle down for now. When this phase is over, then you can go back to doing what you usually do with a few changes to everyone. I shall let you find out what they are, for they are different for everyone.

I hear you and understand.

I shall now let this message rest with you all.

Be well, dear ones. Be well, indeed.

Melchizedek"

***

7 APRIL 2015

Daily Message from the Angels and Ascended Masters:

"Walk in the light with peace in your heart. Let the love shine through your eyes. Be one with the Divine in your will. And never let the beauty of your soul dim in the darkness.

You are a beacon in the darkness of despair. You shine brightly and call upon others to follow you. You bring the light to those whose own light has dimmed. You are their leading light.

When you come across these who are lost, shine brightly, and light up their paths to you. Lead them from out of the darkness and into the vision of the Divine. Lead them to the eternal One.

You are that beacon. You are the guide. You are an instrument of the Divine.

That is the path of every Light-Worker in your world. To light up the ways of those who are lost and bring them into the divine light. All Light-Workers do this out of love and dedication. Love for you and respect for the Divine. Such a commitment should not be ignored but honored.

My fellow Light-Bearers, shine on your loving light and help the lost find themselves. You are perfect, and your inner light is excellent too. You are beautiful and breath-taking. You are the stars to lead humanity to the light side. Show your inner light and make it flare. You are beloved and honored by us.

We will help you, my friends.

Be well.

Michael"

***

8 APRIL 2015

Daily Message from the Angels and Ascended Masters:

"Let us see you at peace when all war is gone, and all is calm. Be at peace with your world and with others in it. Let this peaceful state last throughout your life and bring you gentle harmony and rest.

You have all earned this peace, and it was a hard-earned peace. Some have long gone, and have paid the ultimate sacrifice for this peace.

Be at peace and rest. Tomorrow is another day and brings that peaceful knowledge and feeling into that moment. Carry it around within you, and gently smile at all troubles that are around you. As you hold this gentle feeling, you will find that your problems will become smaller, and others will find themselves relaxing in your presence.

Peace feels good, and others can feel it within you. Such will find you an excellent person to be around with and will look forward to seeing you. Enjoy their company, and spread your peace among them, so that they too can spread it further afield.
All people love peace, and so it must come to be.

Do not let others try to ruin it for you. Avoid such people, for they will waste your time and try to rile you. If you see one, walk away and never turn back. These others will find their peace on another path, but not to the expense of yours. These people are antagonistic, but deep within them, they too have their beauty. It just needs to be shown the way to come forward. If they irritate you, then you are not the person to show them.
The correct one will be the one who will be immune to these people's irritable qualities. They are then drawn to each other to meet and help - just like you have been brought to help some other people, and yet not to others. You all have different paths, but only a few will meet up. It is to stop you from feeling overwhelmed.

You can't help everyone, but you can help a couple.

Be well, sweethearts.

Chamuel"

***

9 APRIL 2015

Daily Message from the Angels and Ascended Masters:

"Beloved ones, are you not ready for your next step in your life? The new presence of the next dimension is upon you, and are you willing to move with the change?

Right now, your world is shifting. Yes, it's no longer at the starting point, but right in the shift. The energies surrounding your world have a higher vibration, and it is, of course, playing havoc with your emotions, from what I have seen.
You need to relax and don't stress about it. This shift will be much easier on you all if you relax and don't do any demanding tasks. Start the demanding stuff, and you'll start feeling irritated.

Now is the time to be with family. Make peace with those who have faulted you. Forgive all the wrongs that were done to you by others, and above all, forgive yourself for the mistakes you have done to your self and others.

Let loved ones reunite when they have been driven apart by situations that have exploded to irrational behavior.
Seek those who have nothing but the clothing on their back; they don't have a roof over their head or food. But you can help them by simply giving them a sandwich or even a hot drink. A little will help a long way.
Give the lonely who have no one left for them, a little of your time and listen to their story.

It is time to relax and to help others. All will become clearer at the end of the shift.

Do not fight it as it is inevitable. And those who reject the shift will feel out of the loop and unhappy in life. It is due to the dimensional vibrations are operating at a higher level and bring those people with it into the 5th Dimension. Clinging onto a 3rd-dimensional life will only bring dissatisfaction and unhappiness.

Ah, I've gone too long, I see. I shall now let you go and think.

Be well, sweet ones.

Barachiel"

***

10 APRIL 2015

Daily Message from the Angels and Ascended Masters:

"In the grand scheme of things of the Universe, your politics and struggles are small to non-existent. Your problems are nothing, and your world is minuscule.
Despite all that, we have noticed your troubles and will help you to work your way through them. We have also seen something beautiful that is growing stronger in your world: Light!

As the numbers of the Light-Workers are growing day by day, the light they encourage is growing and starting to encircle your world. That is good. In time the Light-Workers numbers will exceed your million, and they will bring the divine light to surround your planet.

Yes, your world is unique to us as it has you. There are many other worlds out in your Universe, and many teem with the life of many types. Did you know some of these worlds have an experience that is like yours? Well, you do now. We take care of those worlds too, as well as their subjects troubles. The presence on these worlds have the same origins as you: The Divine Parent. This life is also human. In time you will meet this race and interact. You will find that there are differences, but there are similarities.

Long ago, when humanity was in one world, there was a cataclysm which made their world unstable. Humans had to move out to new worlds to ensure survival.

They set off in their starcrafts and spread out in all directions. And humanity was already established on other worlds. Some of the planets have kept their knowledge. Those much further out, fell into a primitive state. These worlds are starting to reawaken to their inheritance - like your world.

You see, no matter how small or distant your world is in the Universe, you still have made your mark on it. You are not lost anymore, because members of these planets that have kept their knowledge have seen and visited your planet. They will visit again, but this time with a direction to bring your world up to scratch.

Exciting times ahead, indeed, but in theright way.

I shall leave you with this little bit of knowledge. I bid you farewell for now. We will speak again soon.

Metatron"

***

11 APRIL 2015

Daily Message from the Angels and Ascended Masters:

"In the days ahead, you will find that much will happen to bring your world to your consciousness.

People who drill oil are hurting your Mother. People who mine for metals and jewels, they too hurt your Mother.

Pesticides and chemicals are not the answer, for they poison the ground and your food.

We have provided you with everything in your world. There is plenty of food, clean water, fruits, and even herbs for healing. All is there in your world. You insist on poisoning yourself and your world. Not good, my friends, not good at all, you deserve better treatment. You deserve fresh spring water, fruit fresh from the tree, herbs from the ground you walk on and above all, vegetables that you find for yourself in the field, all food without poisonous chemicals.

As for the pests that hurt your food? Do we not supply other creatures that prey on those pests? They keep the pest population at a reasonable level.

That is the original plan for your world. It is other people's greed that makes others poison the ground. Not good.

Herbs can make a safe pesticide, without harming your beautiful Mother Earth.

But all is not lost though; there are people right now who are risking their all to try and make your world a cleaner, safer and more beautiful place to be. I thank them for their concern and care and say this: Your quest is not in vain, but welcomed with love because you love your Mother Earth.

I shall leave you with these thoughts, my friends. Be well and be with love for your Mother Earth.

Gabriel"

***

12 APRIL 2015

Daily Message from the Angels and Ascended Masters:

"When all the world seems going by you at a fast pace, and you feel stressed out by the day's frustrations. STOP! Forget the stresses and strains.

Instead, take the time out of your hectic day and look around at what is around you. See the person across the road, they may have more significant problems than you, or they could be missing someone. Spare a thought of compassion to them.

The child running to an adult, it could be lost, or only happy to see its parent.

The beggar at the side of the street? Yes, that one has more significant problems than you, but will still see the humor in a situation. You see, that is my point. There are always two sides to a story, and yet they still have their happy moments. It is these moments within you that you need to encourage.

The more you bring up those happy moments, and create them in your life, the more often they happen. Like attracts like. When you feel the day starting bad, stop, and encourage happy moments.

If a problem is too big for you to cope with, that's when you ask us for help in it. We are not sitting here twiddling our thumbs, watching. We are here to help; we can change things to make it easier, and even cause the problem to transform into an advantage. Nothing is too big or too small – despite if it is just finding a decent parking spot. Yes, we can do that also.

So instead of feeling stressed out, feel something better like a happy memory or your life mate.

All are within your range, and all are waiting. You can't miss us, even if you are a lousy shot. We are waiting for you to call us to help.

Now I must leave my now-laughing channel and let you ponder my words. I bid you a temporary farewell.

Gabriel"

***

13 APRIL 2015

Daily Message from the Angels and Ascended Masters:

"The stars are many, and you are few. But you belong to the stars, and they are the home of the future of Mankind.

There is always hope and promises, and they will come true when the time comes for your kind to move to your new homes.

There will be those who won't leave your world in the future, because they are the Guardians of this world of yours — a great responsibility indeed and worthy of respect.

Yes, your whole race is on the edge of expanding out into the Universe. You are all so close to it. And right now, your consciousness is changing, compensating for what is to come.

You call it the Age of Aquarius. We call it the 'Time of the Dimensional Shift.' Either name will do for the same event. Right now, people are noticing changes within themselves. Accept the change as there's no going back.

Answer this question: What changes have you noticed with yourself? And listen to your answers. Don't worry about it as the changes are meant to be. Humanity is growing and evolving, and you are evolving with it.

We know what will happen in your future, we know all about it. We cannot say what evolution has for you, due to free will and all that. But it is there. I can say that some of you may be able to visit new worlds with your mind and abilities.

Not all daydreams are dreams; some are a glimpse into new worlds. You are all more potent than before.

Though my lesson here is brief, there is a lot said, and a lot more unsaid if you read between the lines. I shall, therefore, leave now.

Be well Dear Ones.

Michael"

***

14 APRIL 2015

Daily Message from the Angels and Ascended Masters:

If you have all the power in the world, all the talents, and skills, what would you do? Will you help others with this gift? Or will you self-indulge?
All the answers lie within you. For you already have that power, and it is in a form that isn't visible in your visual wavelength. It is visible only to us and those who can see your soul.

Your soul has access to all power and often does, but only to help you. All souls in your world can access this power. All souls can speak to the power,and the power is the Divine.
You all have access to talk to the Divine.

If you use the Divine's love and gifts to help others, then you will be blessed by all on your world and in ours. Such is worthwhile and to be treasured. These are the realchildren of the light. A lot of Mediums do help others.

For those who use these gifts for selfish reasons, and harm others, they are the "Vampires" of your world. They are not of the light, but of the darkness. In time, they will approach the Divine. They say they won't, but they always do. Patience and tolerance in coping with these dark children are required.

Never let the darkness tarnish your inner light. Darkness is just an absence of light. Shine your light into the night and chase away the shadows.

And mostly, look after yourselves first. You cannot help others if you can't help yourself to remain in good health and heart.

I shall now leave you with my words and allow yourself to shine forth. Never forbid yourself from showing love. Always permit yourself to be yourself. Yes, your own true loving and gifted self.

Be well, dear ones. Keep showing your love.

Jeremiel"

***

15 APRIL 2015

Daily Message from the Angels and Ascended Masters:

"Sweet as the flower that gives the honey to the bee, you are just as sweet.

You are the Honey, and your world is the flower where you live. The bee? Anyone who has your heart in love will be the bee to sip the honey of your gentle self.

Such beauty in the world is rare and so needed. So never let anyone take away such a rarity from this world of yours. You are all beautiful, and no dictator or violent person has the right to destroy it. They will be the fools if they did, and you will be the one to suffer their foolishness.

Avoid those who wish you harm, as they will take pleasure in your suffering.

Ask us to only let in your life those who will honor you, treat you with great respect and above all, be at your side when things get rough. You all deserve the best and only the best.

Negative people will try to take you down. They will change eventually, but let someone who is not attached to them, do the work on improving them. If you are too emotionally involved, you will end up being dragged down.

Wear a black tourmaline jewel on you. Smokey Quartz, Onyx, and Obsidian will do just as well. Wear one of these, and they will absorb negative energies that try to get to you. And at night, clean the stone of negative energies, by placing it next to a Carnelian. At night you can wear another of the protective rocks until morning.

I would not like to see your beautiful self harmed by others, and you deserve to be well.

Walk away from what does not serve you.
Walk away from what does not honor you.
Walk away from the one who does not treat you well.

You are much, much better than those who are negative. The reason why? I shall name them:

You are beautiful.
You are sweet.
You have the divine light of love in you.
You are precious.
You are loved.

I could go on non-stop about this.

But I shall say this instead. You are perfect!

Be well, sweet ones, be well

Gabriel"

***

16 APRIL 2015

Daily Message from the Angels and Ascended Masters:

"Tears and sorrow from what appears to be of no reason, are a sign that you need to rest, that your body is telling you to have more sleep, to do your own thing and just 'slob' out.
Exhaustion is not a pretty thing, nor is it beneficial to you or anyone else. For your light to remain bright, you need to take time off now and then. You need to do that.

Once you have had your rest time and slept more, you will find your divine light shining even brighter than before. Your health will pick up also. Rest and take in a show or also do a favorite hobby. All help towards healing the cause of the tiredness: Exhaustion.

During this time, we will ask your Guardian Angels to give you healing energy and help you relax more. That is part of their job also, and they too do it out of love for you. They are, after all, closer to you than your current family, as they have been with you throughout every incarnation you have had. You are their prime responsibility, and they love you deeply. Let them into your life and feel their love.

Tiredness can trigger depression; this can also be attractive to negative entities. Rest again is essential to repel them.

I don't tell you all this without reason, for you all need to rest at times, just for the sake of body and soul. Yes, even your soul needs to have a moment to relax.

Even we Angels need our moments where we can relax and rest. We go into the Garden for this. In time you will visit this protected Garden. You know by its other name: Eden. All are welcome there.

Rest and be with your Guardian Angels and let them help you heal.

Let it be so, beloved ones.

Daniel"

***

17 APRIL 2015

Daily Message from the Angels and Ascended Masters:

"When all is at disarray, and you are feeling lost in the big full world. When you are alone, and everyone is a stranger who ignores you while in pursuit of their direction. You must not give up. You must not despair. You are not alone!

We are watching over you and hearing your voice. We see what goes on in your heart and your mind.

If you feel you need help? We are here.
If you want company? We are here.
If you want happiness? We are here.
If you want peace? We are here.

We are here to help you with your problems, whether they are big or small.

When everyone is a stranger, call upon us, and we'll send one of those strangers to your aid, and will become a friend.

Companions are easy to get; we are your companions, your spiritual friends, and family.

No matter what happens in life to you are those around you, we are there, and we have your back. Hence you are never alone, not while we are hanging around you, directing you and loving you. We will make sure you know it too. Ever sensed what feels like a hand stroking your face, and yet there's nothing there? That's us! That feeling of intense love which surrounds you from out of the blue; us again.

Yes, we have our ways of letting you know you're not alone and never will be, no matter what happens.

Be well, dear ones

Michael"

***

19 APRIL 2015

Daily Message from the Angels and Ascended Masters:

"Beloved ones, do not ever despair that others will forget about you when you are left behind or moved on. They won't! They may act as they have, but deep within their minds, you are there. You are also in their hearts.
If they loved you enough when you were with them, then you will forever be loved by them when you have moved away.
Love is more powerful than you realize. So close friends and family will never forget you.

Those who look at you blankly and appear indifferent aren't your friends in the first place. They were using you for their purposes. You may as well forget about them; they are not worth the trouble. And if a person close to your heart has passed on, they haven't gone far, for they will forever rest in your heart, your mind and spirit.

Whenever you think of them, it is like a beacon calling their name, and they will come to visit in their spirit forms. Never forgotten and never left behind. You may or may not see, hear, smell, or even feel them. They are with you in thought and spirit. They visit because they sense your love for them, and in turn, their love for you has drawn them to you. All is a win-win situation.

You see, do not mourn those who have passed on. Instead give these loved ones your love and blessing, for they have now gone to a more beautiful place. See it like that: A promotion. Even those who take their own lives will be looked after by us. They will go to the Halls of Healing, and there they will be gently healed. Their troubles removed, and their emotional instabilities cured. They too will be drawn to your love for them, and they will realize how much they love you in return.

All illnesses will receive treatment at the Halls of Healing. ALL!

I shall leave you now to think about my words.

Be well

Raphael"

***

20 APRIL 2015

Daily Message from the Angels and Ascended Masters:

"Don't let yourself to make wrong assumptions of people you do not know, for you show yourself to be judgmental. Instead, listen to them, see them, get to know a little bit about them. Then you will see the other person in a different light.

Your thoughts, when spoken out, reflect on you.

Instead, remove those negative thoughts and let in fresh, peaceful, and beautiful ideas.
The other person won't change, for it is their nature and they don't know it. But you who are reading this can change yourself.

Give the other person space, for they may be more than you realize. They could be the lesson you need to learn from, and that lesson could be tolerance, awakening, or just patience.
Yes, every person you meet in your life has a lesson for you to learn. No matter how big or small the experience is, it is still there for you to take in.

Never judge others on just hearsay, instead form your own opinions by studying the other person. The other person could be very likable. Don't let others try to cloud your mind with their views on a person. Take time to reflect on this for yourself.

Never listen to poison but listen to gold.

You are all creatures of the divine will. You are all created from the one light. You are all aspects of the Divine. Accept that you are all different, yet all the same and you will find tolerance, acceptance, and friendship. Also, be patient with yourself. Everything in your future takes its own time in coming forward. You can't rush it. Patience is also teaching yourself to take the time to reflect and meditate.

I shall leave you now, dear ones. I bid you well.

Uriel"

***

21 APRIL 2015

Daily Message from the Angels and Ascended Masters:

"I wish you all to be free in the golden light of love.
I wish you all to laugh and sing with joy from above.
I wish you to show the world you are good.
I wish you allow the divine love to run through your blood.
I wish you all a happy ending.
I wish you to in harmony blending.
I wish you to sigh with a thankful heart.
I wish you to be with the One at the start.
I wish you love and all its power.
I wish you to relax under a rose bower.
I wish you to feel the ground below.

And let in the energies of Gaia flow.

You are the ones I wish to bless
With harmony, beauty, and nothing less.
You are the stars, and the universe knows
That you have the divine light within, it glows.
You are energetic and with faith within you,
Your heart will then be healthy and be right.
You are the carriers of the light
Your spirit glow sends the stars to flight.

And let the world hear of your sweet story. Surround yourselves with wings of glory

You are one with love and our presence,

Nurturing you with power, and our essence.
Never alone, and never will be lost at all.
You have the power to stand and be tall.
You are the light, the beacon, and the tower.
You stand tall and proud, like the sunflower.
You are our blessed friends and kin.
We share the divine love, and we will win.

I shall leave you now with the words of love.

It is sent to you from the divine power above.

Gabriel"

***

22 APRIL 2015

Daily Message from the Angels and Ascended Masters:

"Remember the days of laughter, joy, play, and innocence? Your childhood should be composed of all those factors. They belong to the child you were, and they belong to the child that is still within you.

For those whose childhood was of pain and sorrow, it's not too late to remove that inner darkness and replace it with the real wants of a child: To be happy and to be what a child is supposed to be.

It is not too late, you hear?

The things that can help you the most are in front of your face. Grasp the joy and laughter. Play is essential and can help you grow. Release that real innocent inner child within you and let it play, let it have fun and make it laugh with joy. You all need to make the inner child come out often; play is essential for emotional strength.

Sure, there are times for business and times for work. But there is also time for play. If you have small children of your own, it's easier for you. And for those who don't have small children, look among your relatives. Failing that, no worries. You can still have fun and lighten your load.

Alone, you can dance in the sunlight. Laugh at the way nature interacts with each other. Butterflies dancing in the air can create such laughter. Even on rainy days, the way water plays can be exciting.

See life with the eyes of the child, and you will find life fascinating and infinite. You will discover the beauty of your world enhanced. And you will find your connection to us improved also. We encourage this in you all so that you can feel what we feel when we look at nature and you: JOY!

Be well dear ones

Ambriel"

***

23 APRIL 2015

Daily Message from the Angels and Ascended Masters:

"Just when you thought it couldn't get any better? Think again. It can!

You all have doors of opportunities opening to you all the time. Each entry is always open to you, but it's up to you to take the first steps. Don't expect the door to open and bring you in.
All opportunities in your life all begin with you. You must make the first decisions, the first motions, and the first steps. We won't do them for you. It's all about YOU!

If you decide not to take the first steps now, you can still make them several years later. The door never closes but waits for you. Indecisions are a sign you are not quite ready yet to take the path. But once a decision suddenly comes to mind a few days or months later, it's the perfect time for you to open that door.

We will support and guide you every step of the way, and even open a few more doors for you on your new journey. Doors that will let others into your life that can help you further on your path.

All is meant to happen that way; it is both a learning journey as well as an enlightening one. Your Guardian Angels will make sure that all things happen at the best of times and will help you grow and learn on your way.

Never give up on yourself, for you are far greater than you thought. You can make decisions, you can open doors of opportunities at any time, you can learn and grow within them, and above all, you will become stronger than ever. All chances are for your happiness, so take the first steps.

Those who continuously ignore the opportunities and yet complain that other people are holding them back; blame your selves, not others for your issues. Take responsibility for your actions and realize other people are under no obligation to make your decisions for you. They are yours alone, no others.

I shall let you think about this and open your doors to your futures.

Be well.

Sandalphon"

***

24 APRIL 2015

Daily Message from the Angels and Ascended Masters:

"I wish you all to see what I can see within you all. You are so full of the divine light that you put the stars to shame. You glow with the colors of the rainbow and more. Some colors have no name in your world or language.

You are the vessels of divine light and joy. You are worthy of this task, and yes, it is YOUR task to work through. And what is that task?

Your task is to share your light and love with the world, show your divine presence within you to lead others towards the divine light at the source.

Yes! The Light-Workers are the beacons, and they will lead you to the way of the Divine. It is their task, and they share it with you.

Join them dear ones and help to spread the divine word and promise to all. In doing so, you too become Light-Workers, and your divine light will grow stronger and brighter.

It is healing, loving, and above all, divine.

Will any of you join in and help us spread the light of the divine love to the world? Will you help, teach, and nurturing those who need it, giving your time freely and willingly? Any of you willing?

Of course, you will meet some who will try to dim your light and pull you down. That is when you can either walk away or rise above these people. Either way, you don't have to take on their problems or attitude. It's theirs, not yours.

You don't have to be around such people if you don't wish to be, and you will not be condemned or told off if you walk away. You are human that we know. And you must walk away from negativity if you wish to remain shining bright.

If you start feeling others negativity beginning to affect you, despite what steps you have taken to avoid it, then ask for us to help in removing it. Call upon the divine golden light to flow through every cell of your body; to the molecular level. It's cleansing and healing. And we can help you with that too.

We understand more than you think. We see more than you realize. We see within the hearts of every living creature and know their destiny.

I shall leave you now, sweet ones. Are you willing to join in the forces of light, and help others?

Let us know with your real voice from the heart. We will see it.

Be well, dear ones, be well.

Nathaniel"

***

25 APRIL 2015

Daily Message from the Angels and Ascended Masters:

"The blessings of the Divine are showered on you all. You have met with expectations that were given to you, my Light-Workers. You have succeeded where a few have failed. You have reached the next stage of your growth. All is in readiness for your growth and the path that will open up in front of you. There are no obstacles.

Some of you have thought of a few blocks: Family, friends, and responsibilities. Yes, those blocks. Well, you are not leaving your loved ones at all. They will remain at your side. Same with your closest friends. As for the responsibilities? Some of those are not important and never have been. You just made them an excuse. Won't work!

A problem that brings joy is not a problem.
A problem that drains your energy avoid it.
A problem you can't avoid is of your creation. Fix it for once and for all.

There are no excuses. The family members and parts of your life which you have loved so much shall remain with you.

You see! Nothing to worry over. But plenty to look forward to, as this next stage is part of your growth and will bring benefits to you all. New jobs, opportunities, friends, and new adventures. All are there.

Do you wish to have fun? Yes, we all do. Note that I said, "We!" For we welcome fun into our lives and yours. We love to have you join us in humor, laughter, and just everyday chatting.
We will take you on your next steps, dear ones. Don't worry about that. We will guide your actions. An accommodating bunch aren't we and won't let you fall.

Your Guides will help you as well as the people we have sent to you — all part of the grand scheme of things.

Your next step in your new path means new skills, so be aware of lessons coming your way. Learn and teach others, so that they too can learn and teach others also.

There are circles within circles, spheres within spheres. All is oneness and all circle around the One. Let the light of the Divine shine upon you all and cleanse away the darkness of other people's negativities that have latched onto you.
Never take on more than you can manage, for it is not a race but a growth spurt.

The stars are the eyes of other souls watching you; they wait for your growth to reach the state of divine light, so that you may show that you have Ascended. You are all unique to the Divine One, and the Divine One has plans for your world.

Your world is beautiful but is under pressure. Let those who can help, do so. For these people were sent to help and bring forward the new age of songs.

The songs are the voices of the Divine and the divine messengers. Open your hearts to them and let them help you in return.

That is all I need to say.

Be well.

Gabriel"

***

26 APRIL 2015

Daily Message from the Angels and Ascended Masters:

"Welcome to my world of love and learning:
    A world where the most considerable knowledge comes from the divine heart.
    A world is full of beauty and joy.
    A world in which all are equal.

You are all growing up fast, and like children, you will enter our world with love and understanding.

There is no threat within my world but welcomes and invitations.

Humans will be once more welcome to join us in mutual friendship and love.

What is my world? - I hear some of you ask? My world is just outside the range of yours. It is beside yours, around yours and before yours. It is a world that is of another dimension, a world of spirit and energy.

Your world is starting to merge with mine soon. And we all shall see new wonders on it. Oh, I could go on and on, and I will never have the time to put everything down. So much to say, so little of your time.

Never mind, it's happening, and it's beautiful!!

Learn your gifts as they are starting to open. Those who thought they didn't have any psychic abilities? Think again! You are beginning to open, and all you need is the training.

I love to see the beginners come into their gifts, the look of joy on their faces as they contact some of us. It makes us happy too.

You will need those gifts soon enough. No worries about that, and of course, you are not alone and never will be.

Now a final word.

I ask of you to all say a prayer on behalf of those who have suffered the latest cataclysms of your world. They need your love and thoughts to help them cope with the loss of their beloved ones. Help them heal in body and spirit. And help those who have passed on in such circumstances. Your love helps them too.

I thank you for your help and hearing my words.

Be well.

Azrael"

***

27 APRIL 2015

Daily Message from the Angels and Ascended Masters:

"Beloved ones, when you came into this world of yours, you came pure and clean. You had no such thing as sin. No infant contains sin. You were all born of pure mind, heart, and soul.

You learned all the problems from when you started to grow up into adulthood. That's when others began to force their opinions onto you. The 'Peer Pressure' of your teens is that. Annoying isn't it! It is during those moments that your strength will show. If you carry on following others, and hunting for their reasonable opinion of you, you are not living up to your full expectation and will not get far in life.

But if you reject those opinions, which others have of you, it is because only your view of your self that is important. And that you are not in the world to live up to other people's expectations, then you are showing your real inner strength.
Yes, the strength and confidence to be yourself and only yourself. Be answerable and taking responsibility for your self. That is a step forward, my dear ones. Get the hint? Hmmm?
You are encouraged to what you are best at, being yourself. Also, look after yourself first and foremost. In doing so, you are helping others at the same time. You do better work and play when you are healthy and sound, and I bet others appreciate that. Your pets, your family, and friends; I could go on.

Never compromise your moral compass and standards, as some will feed on you like a leech if given a chance. Avoid them, walk away, push them away with a barge pole if you need to.

You ought to look after yourself first, understand? Never neglect yourself for others, as you can't help those others if you can't help yourself. I know I'm confusing. Good! A mind who tries to work out that comment, is an enquiring mind and a quick one.

Enough with my chit-chat. I have noticed with Azrael that you have sent healing thoughts to the countries that have had cataclysms happen in them. We are thankful and ask that you keep the healing coming. Much more is to happen, and help in all areas wanted. No matter how large or small, each bit helps. Your time helps, your love and healing energy help too.

I shall leave you now, my beloved ones. I love you all and wish you well.

Be blessed.

Gabriel"

***

28 APRIL 2015

Daily Message from the Angels and Ascended Masters:

"Be at peace.
All of you!

Stop the fighting as it serves no purpose.
Stop the hurting, as it hurts your soul.
Stop rioting as you only fail yourself.

You need to all stop. Violence has never solved any problem, but it has created more. You all think you have just causes, but I see the truth and notice that not all the reasons are right. They appear more self-serving and ego than just.

Stop the violence and let all rest. You have more important things in this world of yours to fight about, like climate.
You have the environment to care for, and you need to protect it.

Small children and the defenseless ones, they need your care and protection also.

But violence for the sake of violence is not what I want in your world. What I want is all of you to stop, look at each other, and call each other BROTHER. Be like brothers and help each other.

No more of this strife, no more of this trouble and no more of your petty egos trying to destroy what good is within you. It is not what I have wanted for your world.

There better things to do in your world, so leave those egos on the ground, where they belong. Forget them, and instead, let your true inner self show. And let it show in peace and love. I did not create you to hate each other.

LET IT STOP!

No more and enough is enough. Instead, focus on those who are the innocents and have suffered. The place you call Nepal does not need your hate; it needs your help. That is a much worthier cause to choose.

I have said what I need to say, and I shall leave you to learn from it.

I am somewhat disappointed in some of my children, and I am proud of those children who do help. The helpers are the ones that I want you all to follow as the example.

Enough. Let it be so, and heed what I have said.

So be it.

The Divine"

***

29 APRIL 2015

Daily Message from the Angels and Ascended Masters:

"In all the problems you are having, remember one big thing in your life, a crucial big thing.

YOU!

Your own body, soul, and mind are linked, and they make you become the most critical being in the world. Even though others have the same links, they are not YOU!

YOU, as an individual, are essential. Your opinions and thoughts are important, and so is your love.
Take time to pamper yourself. Look in the mirror and tell yourself that you are beautiful, smart, and healthy.
Believe in yourself, for you are the only one who knows you the best. Trust in yourself and your abilities. As you do so, you are in a way helping others to do the same.

Self-love that is in a rightway is healthy for all. Because those who are feeling down, will see you and the example you are setting; of courage, confidence and above all, open-heartedness.
Encourage those who need those same ego boosts. Compliment them, thank them, smile at them and even give them the pep up they need.

Show them self-love, the same way I have asked you to show yourself.

You are important.

Be well.

Gabriel."

***

30 APRIL 2015

Daily Message from the Angels and Ascended Masters:

Just before I wrote this message, I got these words: "Brace yourself."
So here is what the Angel meant by those words:

"Well? What are you waiting for, my friends?

Someone does a good deed, and I hear a lot of voices who noticed the act, saying: 'There should be more like that person' or 'There should be more people like that.' Guess what! You are those people who should be like those who do good deeds.
Don't leave it to others to do it for you. Don't sit around on your backside saying such things and doing nothing, because it doesn't work that way, my dear.

What works is for you to get up, get out and doing the good deeds, no matter what form they take.

Yes, charity does begin at home, and this means that charity begins with YOU, not just others helping their own country. This world is your world, and so it is HOME to you.

No excuses! I've heard them all before in one form or another — time for you to shake a leg and get out.

Best way to go about it is the 'Pass It Along' way. As you do one good deed for a person, tell them to pass the act along. In time, it will take the entire world, but not in a storm, but a wave of love. These good deeds are what makes the world turn. You are doing a kind act for others. You never know, there may be a time when you will need a kind act done for you. As you do for others, may it return to you threefold. A good deed returns to you threefold.

Stop the whining about things. Instead, get out there and do something.

Now I've had my say and now going to perform a retreat before the rotten tomatoes head my way.

Be well, dear ones.

Gabriel"

***

MAY 2015

1 MAY 2015

Daily Message from the Angels and Ascended Masters:

"You wish for this, you wish for that, but you never say the magic words: 'Please, can you arrange this.' to us. Wishes are nothing but empty dreams. You must ask us directly if you want action.
　I know it won't be immediate in happening, as we must arrange things and start events up to make what you want to happen. Just like the wings of a butterfly will stir up the air enough to create a storm at the other end of the world. Little things can create more significant events. So be patient. It will come to fruition at the right time and place.

　We know you better than you realize. We hear all and can read your dreams, fantasies, and thoughts. It's how we can work with you.

　Patience is a virtue. Rush things, and you will find yourself held back more. We will not bring the situation forward to please you as we have the entire universe to consider. All must be balanced and sequenced at the right moment.
　You are not the only one in theuniverse, but you are part of it.Like you are part of the Divine, and so is the Cosmos.

　Be patient, be happy, and be loved.

　I shall wait and see your decisions and dreams.

　Gabriel"

***

2 MAY 2015

Daily Message from the Angels and Ascended Masters:

"Relax! That's all you need to do. When the world appears to you to be going haywire, and others seem to find every nerve in you, and getting on it. Find your peace and solitude by moving away from the drama and relaxing.
No need to start fights or arguments, walk away.

If that doesn't work, and you find yourself still a bit hot under the collar, then nothing like a decent vent will help release the strain. But not in a violent way. Write what you want to say on a piece of paper, and don't hold back on it. Keep writing your feelings until you feel you have calmed down. Then read what you have written down.

Tear that paper into pieces and throw them into a fire or flush them down a toilet. As you destroy those pieces of paper, you are destroying the link that the argument has created between you and the other person. You are then free from that person and can move onto whatever you wish to do. That other person will have no hold on you. And if they persist, time to put them out of your life permanently - walk away or tell them to leave.

Your choice.

It's up to you from here on, dear ones.

Anabiel"

***

3 MAY 2015

Daily Message from the Angels and Ascended Masters:

"Do you ever wonder what it is like in our dimension? How it must be and how it feels? I shall give you a glimmer into my world.

In my world, there are no buildings or artificial constructions. It is a world of light – a light of various colors, and we are the contributors to it. It's a world of colors, lights, stars, and music. Surrounding that planet is a golden light, nurturing and protective. A world that is far more vast than your Universe, for it is the world that lies within and around the Divine.

The Divine is our world, our light, stars, and our music.

You too are part of this world, but on a much, much smaller scale, and separated by dimensional barriers. These barriers will stop you from being overwhelmed by the powers and energies of our world. Your human minds cannot take in the vastness and range of our universe; your brain never was designed for that.

In time, you will visit our world but not in your solid human form. Only your soul can comprehend our universe -for it was made in our dimension and returnsto us regularly.

The world of the Divine is indeed beautiful, massive, and beyond your words and understanding. But you will know it as soon as you see it.

I hope I have explained a little bit about what we have here.

Be well

Matriel"

***

4 MAY 2015

Daily Message from the Angels and Ascended Masters:

"Blessed ones, you are the miracle that the Divine has strived for in creation. You have the spark of divine life within. You have the prize and the treasure of the Stars. You are the wonder that we all have worked hard for and received.

You are beautiful.

Rejoice in the fact that you are one of the miracles of the universe and you are beloved by us all. You are ours to teach and look after. You are the Divine's children, for us all to help grow into enlightenment. You are our kin.

Why all these compliments and beautiful words we say to you? Well, why not! You are all that, and it's about time you knew it. So many of you are always putting yourself down, holding back and putting others down.
No more, we implore you. You are all individually beautiful in your own right, and you need to stand up for yourself and show it.

The blind child is beautiful to us and can see far more than you realize.
The deaf is treasured; they hear more than you know.
The beggar in the street is far more abundant in nature's treasures and life than the millionaire who can only see monetary wealth.
The disabled ones travel far and wide with their imagination: seeing and experiencing far more than the most traveled tourist.

Never underestimate the powers of your self and your soul. You all can become far more than others think of you. You are all divine made gifts of love and beauty.

We all love you and would like you all to know that, for you deserve to know it. I feel we need to make sure you do.

Be well, dear ones, be well in heart and mind.

Gabriel"

***

5 MAY 2015

Daily Message from the Angels and Ascended Masters:

"Life has many pleasures, and I'm sure that you know quite a few of them. Love, laughter, joy, they are all part of your life.

There is one pleasure you have forgotten to think about, yet you experience it so often. It is a pleasure of close friendship. A soul mate or a twin soul, someone who is your shoulder to cry on during times of duress. Someone whom you can share a rude joke with, and cackle away together at it.

A true friendship that knows no bounds can take you further than you have ever experienced. That friendship has no barriers and can make you fly far across the world. Such a bond is to be treasured, and the two friends united as siblings can be.

You all either have experienced it or wish to experience it. Yes, it is the crux of the matter.

Those who have this friendship are lucky, you think. Yes, such people are together in mind and spirit. These friends are close merely because they are supporting each other, being there for each other.

Those who think they don't? Think again. You do have it, but you don't realize it because you can't see us. You have us, and we do give you that friendship. Aren't we around when you need a shoulder to rest your weary head, providing you with comfort and gentle words? You may not see us, but we are there anyway. We support you and encourage you to take advancing steps into a new life or adventure. And in sickness, we are always there for you. We also enjoy a good joke, no matter how bad it can get. If it makes laughter, then it's a good joke.

You are never without a close friend when you have us around you. It's not that hard to realize and remember when you think about it.

Be well, my friends, I am always with you all.

Raphael"

***

7 MAY 2015

Daily Message from the Angels and Ascended Masters:

"Do you realize how fortunate you are? You have the air on your world to breath. You have the ground to walk on and the soul that is full of divine light. You are lucky, indeed.

Luck has nothing to do with money or personal material belongings: real success shows in your smiles, laughter, and synchronicity.

Opportunities that open for you are not just luck, but it's because we have heard your call and created the doorway for you to step through.

Yes, real luck is divine. And the events causing all your 'lucky' moments? Us! We are producing these events for you. Ever realized that the long-lost friend that just came into your mind just before they rang you up on the phone? Us!

A lost item that was missing for a while, suddenly appearing as if out of nowhere? Us!

We are your luck also. Long may the relationship last for both of us. We make things happen for you, and you bring us joy when you feel joy.

We're lucky to have each other.

Be well, dear ones.

Gabriel"

***

8 MAY 2015

Daily Message from the Angels and Ascended Masters:

"Wishes are the dreams of future potential. You wish this, and you want that, but because they are dreams of future potential, they shall remain just potentials.
To make them come true, you must stop manufacturing 'wishes' and make them become dreams. You must make them become hopes and targets.
When you do that, they change from 'potentials' to become future promises.
And that is a different story. Potentials mean they have a big chance of not going anywhere if you do nothing.
Promises can happen if you have made the right decisions and are going to take that first step. You have the direction and aim.
Potentials do not, for they are often left behind at the side of your path of life.

You all can change the potentials into promises; take the first steps, and do something about them.

It's all up to you, dear ones — only you. It is a fact of your own life and development. So be it, for you cannot grow if you cannot make an effort to improve.

Be well, dear one.

Raphael"

***

9 MAY 2015

Daily Message from the Angels and Ascended Masters:

Sweetheart, you have all the time in the Universe to make things happen. You do not need to hurry for anything. Your destination will remain the same.

Now I'm not talking about your career or any appointments, though you all need to slow down the fast-paced life you lead there. Instead, take the time to stroll in the park, chat with people and friends. Visit distant family and even make time to play with your children.

Life without stress is a life that is full of happiness. Even your pets and children will be happy also.

Are you losing a job? Don't stress about it, instead ask us to lead you to another, even if it is just creating your own business. If you have the skills, go for it.

Never worry about things that cannot be changed. For that is a waste of your time and energy, which is more useful on a more positive target.

If the problem is inevitable, then sit back and focus on something that you can do to help yourself. You can't deter the unavoidable, but you can make plans to soften its impact.

Yes, always think outside the box. More you do that, the quicker you can see opportunities and new directions.

Don't become too hide-bound on one subject. Spread your wings and fly to new heights. Expand your knowledge and experiences. The more you know and learn, the more information you can utilize.

Don't worry, be happy. And let us take care of the hairy moments in your life.

Be well dearest ones.

Ambriel"

(I should have known that talking about Ambriel will bring Ambriel to visit me. *sigh* LOL!)

***

10 MAY 2015

Daily Message from the Angels and Ascended Masters:

"Never mind the complaints of others. If you want to dance? Then dance. If you're going to sing? Sing with all your heart!
It brings you happiness and joy to do so, then that is all that matters. Don't let anyone try to ruin it for you. Just sing and dance away, for that is all that is important to you. Enjoy it!

If you find joy in art, go for it and enjoy every little bit of it.

It is the same if you like any art or hobby with a passion. Go for it and live it. You all know what I mean. After all, if it gives you great pleasure, then it is perfect for you, no matter what it is; whether it is skydiving or sculpting.

We do draw the line at harming others, that is not a pleasure but a problem. It is so because the nerves in the brain are not working right and causing a chemical imbalance. How easy it is to cure it depends on how bad the imbalance.

But enough of that. You are all invited to live your life to the fullest and take great pleasure in doing so. You can do this any time and place, at your convenience. Those who don't like it, you can leave those who do alone and let them have fun.
Your turn will come, dear ones. Your turn will come. And when it does, we will enjoy your singing and dancing too. We'll join in with you.

Your life is yours to enjoy, no matter what. It is what you were put here for, to enjoy the wonders of life: yours and Mother Nature's.

So why are you all sitting on your backsides right now? Hmm? Get out and have fun.

Be well

Haziel"

***

11 MAY 2015

Daily Message from the Angels and Ascended Masters:

"Aren't you all such beautiful people! You create machines, delicate instruments, create significant medical breakthroughs, and save lives. Yes, we are pleased with you in your advancements. But what does it all cost?

The cost is:

Mines are bored into the ground, and the precious minerals are brought up. And often enough, the conditions in the mines were terrible, and the workers not paid enough.

The environment suffers due to mismanagement or just plain neglect.

People treated as cheap labor until they fall ill, then they are thrown out. Yes, those sweatshops you all complain over.

Have any of you considered what the actual costs are in what you have?

You want food, then grow it or pick it from the wild. Your mother supplies enough for all. It's only greed that stops the freedom to share it around for all.

It is time for you to realize what happens in your world. For a diamond, other peoples lives become endangered. Why? A Diamond? A diamond may be rare, but it's just a stone. That's all it is, a mere pretty lump of rock.

There are more precious things in your world: children, flowers, and trees. All that walks, crawls, flies, and swims in your world. Mother Gaia is more precious than your money. Let her keep her pretty stones.

You are more precious than mere rock. Far more valuable in our eyes. More expensive than rubies, gold, and silver. They're nothing in comparison to you.

See your true worth within yourself. There is only one YOU, and there are more so-called precious stones and such out there, that there is you. It is natural; you are the rarest gem in the

Universe. You weren't mined out, or anything like that. You are the creation of the most beautiful thing in the universe: Love.

Forget about your precious stones as they are genuinely worthless in comparison to you. You are priceless.

Be well, dear ones, and I hope you realize that you are more critical than mere rock.

Gabriel"

***

12 MAY 2015

Daily Message from the Angels and Ascended Masters:

"As you were an innocent when you were born, you were the innocent until you grew to an adult. Then your innocence was smothered by others who told you to drop the child within you and work in what they called the "Real World."

It is wrong.

You are what defines your world. You created your world.

Bring back that innocence and the child within you. Let it come forward and run free. In doing so, your world will turn into a much happier place. It will be so full of wonder and magic. Bring back that childlike wonder of the world around it.

The child within you is beautiful and should be free to express itself. It is your real nature. Bring it forth, dear ones. Play with the Nature Spirits and explore the wonders of your world.

Let the Adult in you sleep as it should, and be the open-hearted and enlightened child that you were meant to be.

Is it too much? I don't think so.

You will find yourself much happier when you bring in this beauty and innocence into your life. Forget the hurts and the insults of the past for they belong there; in the past. It was over and done with, and you no longer need them. You control your world, so start taking that bit of power and let the child run loose with it.

Be well, dear ones. All will become obvious in time; no sooner and no later. Time to let go and let love.

Gabriel"

***

13 MAY 2015

Daily Message from the Angels and Ascended Masters:

Time for that particular moment in your life. Time to move onto to higher levels. Greener pastures and gentler experiences.

It is time for you to leave toxic situations and go to where your heart truly lies.
It is time for you to stop harming the world, and instead take care of it.
It is time for you to let your heart open to real love, and instead of hiding from it.
It is time for you to grow into your spiritual gifts instead of denying them.
It is time for you to be the beautiful person you are and don't close your eyes to it.
It is time for you to grow into your unique self and remove those who wish to drag you down.

Yes, it is time for you all to spread your wings and fly into the beautiful world you have now, share your inner light, and spread your incredible love to others.

You are the perfect example to show that love between two people makes more love. Love is all around you, within you and made you. You need to show the world that all is much better than what others thought. You must let them see how beautiful your inner light is. Now is your moment, and this is your task in life. Those who wish to bask in your glow, teach them how to show their light to others also.
To those who wish to destroy your light, don't let them. Walk away and leave these people behind.
If these negative people persist in following you, their soul is yearning for their light to show. These people don't seem to realize that they want to learn.

Don't force yourself to teach all of them, teach those that you have drawn. The others are to be guided by others.

In time they will open and show their light.

As for those that refuse to open, showing their negative side? Walk away, and then ask for our help in teaching these negative ones the more positive side. Now, this is a task that can be much harder. We are willing to take that one on.

Be well, dear Light-Workers. I await your calls.

Gabriel"

***

14 MAY 2015

Daily Message from the Angels and Ascended Masters:

"Don't just sit there, get out into the day, and dance to the sunbeams. Feel the grass under your feet and let the birdsong trill through your soul. You need to let Nature take over for the moment, and it will bring you peace and harmony. Mother Nature loves you, and when you make yourself be taken over by her, she grounds you, rests you and nurtures you.

Let Nature take over for a short while. Be part of Nature, just as Nature is part of you. You can't deny that, as you are all children of Nature.

Dance and sing to the rhythm of Nature's heartbeat. Let the feeling of the Earth's energy source through you, cleansing and stabilizing you. Yes, it is known as Grounding. Sure, you can do that just by standing in the grass and just meditating. But dancing in the grass with Nature is a more fun way, heightens your vibrations and even is refreshing.

Don't worry; Mother Nature enjoys the dance just as you do.

Will you dance with Mother Nature? You will find I may join in with you too.

Be well, dear ones.

Ariel"

***

15 MAY 2015

Daily Message from the Angels and Ascended Masters:

"Beloved ones, there comes a time when you need to stand up for your beliefs. You need to make everyone know that you are not a pushover. You must show your inner strength and integrity and be true to your very own self.

You want this war of yours to stop, then make it stop — no good sitting around complaining about it and doing nothing. Actions speak louder than words my friends.
You want to save the world from greedy businesses and oil companies? Take the first steps in doing so. You will have a lot of support from those who believe in the same as you.
You want the beaches to be clean; it all starts with your actions, not words.

Sitting around has not fixed anything. But by getting and doing something about your problems, you can move mountains. A question that gets answered now is no longer a problem. It is one step closer to your next goal.

Your world needs you to look after it. We need you to look after your world too. Also, don't forget to look after yourself. You are all interlinked in this world of yours, and as it is going through the dimensional shift, this world needs you more than ever.

Stop the wars, and you will find a few other problems will immediately vanish.

Also, learn to respect each other. Christian or Muslim, you are all members of the family of God. God does not care what your religion is. God only cares about you. Do not let those who are negative try to rule you. They will use fear to control you. Don't let them. Stand tall! Again, look after yourself.

The world is your holy ground. Your body is your temple. Worship the Divine with your heart and soul, be free to do so in whatever way you feel comfortable. God doesn't mind at all, just as long as it is your love, and that is important.

Look after your world, yourself, and your inner spirit. You are the future of your world and your people. Your descendants will look up to you in admiration.

Be well and be a rock in endurance.

Muriel"

***

16 MAY 2015

Daily Message from the Angels and Ascended Masters:

Message from AA Gabriel:

"Just when you thought life couldn't get any better, ah... won't you be surprised.

The transition your world is going through will bring about changes and new situations. Those changes that appear in lifestyles, mindsets, and reality. As for the unique circumstances? The old way that you lived in your world will be obsolete and no longer relevant to you. You don't need to follow the need for cash for one.

All changes are meant to be and are part of the transition. Already some of you have gone ahead of this change and already transitioned before the others. It is intended to be also, for these people are the helpers, the guides, and they are all Light-Workers.

Some Light-Workers haven't gone ahead and are with you at your current stage: this, too, is meant to be. They will make sure that no one is left behind and will provide a helping hand to those who need it. And even some of these Light-Workers may also be the last to change, for they are the ones clearing up any stragglers and removing any negative energies remaining from the old world. They will have Healing abilities, for that's what they will be doing with your world, once the transition is over.

All in all, it is meant to be and always will be. Never worry about such things, leave that to us.
In the meantime, how about some fun and laughter? Hmmm?

Be well, dear ones."

***

17 MAY 2015

Daily Message from the Angels and Ascended Masters.

A message from AA Ambriel:

"Be in peace, wherever you may go. For you walk in the steps of your path, and your heart makes the path smooth or hard. You choose the way your path goes.

Let peace be in your heart so that your path is smooth and easy. That is the way we all wish it to go. That is the path of least resistance, and you will reach your destination sooner.
The stumbling blocks placed in your way, by doubts and self-recrimination, are easily removed; just let go of your past and accept yourself as being perfect the way you are. You are the way you are now for your lesson in your current stage of life needs you to be just as you are now.

When you let the seeds of peace take root within you, you will discover new worlds, new people, and above all, the divine love. In harmony, you are at one with us, to be loved. Order is the way of all intelligent life in the Universe. Don't be the exception.

Accept the peace and harmony that comes from us to you, for it is the path love and enlightenment. We feel that peace within ourselves, and we don't want it to be any other way, for it is beautiful.

You will feel the beauty of peace and love. Others will see it too, for it will show in your eyes and you will even glow with it.

You are all children in the eyes of the Divine, and the Divine wishes you to have the love, harmony, and gentle peace that you all want. You need to accept all that we have to offer you.

In peace, I bade you a temporary farewell and will return later with more messages.

Sweet love and affection to you all."

***

18 MAY 2015

Daily Message from the Angels and Ascended Masters.

Message from Gabriel:

"When all are losing their heads over nothing, may you be the one to keep your cool and see the truth. For those who panic at the slightest change, are not seeing the bigger picture. They are too focused on their own material needs and don't want to lose what they perceive as their physical needs.

Your real physical needs are this:

Divine love
Food
Water
Laughter
Joy
Harmony
Health

That's all you need in this world of yours. Anything else is only secondary and easily replaced or fixed.

Jewelry, gold, and other material stuff? Not so much. They're only valuable to you because humanity has put a price on them. It's only crystals, metals and so on. You put a value on the valueless.

The real values are those which I have listed above, your real physical needs.

When the brown stuff hits the fan, calm down and look at what will be affected. Often enough, the actual necessities are unaffected, and only the less essential things are touched by the uproar.

If you can keep your head while others are losing theirs, you will win your way on the road of life. A calm mind is a mind that is thinking clearly, analyzing, and seeing the truth. A decent brain, indeed.

A bit of advice from me, question everything that appears in your path. You may meet me on it.

Be well sweethearts."

***

19 MAY 2015

Daily Message from the Angels and Ascended Masters.

A message from Raphael:

"Don't ever feel down and sad about yourself. You are perfect in every way, and there's no need for you to be unhappy. You have the divine light within you, and that is all part of the Divine's grace. You are made the way you are because it is perfect for the task you have.

If you feel sad and unhappy because of illness? Have you thought that it is your feelings there that are making the problem worse? A lot of times it is just tiredness that's making you feel run down and sad. When it is like that, have an early night or a nap. Sleep is healing, very healing. That's when we work best with you.
Note I said, 'With You'? That's right. When you sleep, we talk and agree which parts of you need healing the most. We hear your words.

Tiredness can be the cause of a lot of unhappiness. But it's doesn't cause all of it. Illness can drag you down if you let it. Don't let an illness rule you. Instead, live your life to the fullest and have fun. Plenty of rest helps. But keeping those energies high is healing. Also, it shows the world that you are healthy, powerful!

Sometimes stress from a job or other situation plays on your mind. Don't let it! Let us take care of that side of things, and you need to start relaxing. Tell us what you are having the problem with, permit us to work with you on that problem, and then let us loose on it. All you need to do then is relax, have some 'ME' time. We will sort things out and show you the solution.

And of course, there's the depression of mental illness. That is the hardest of all to beat, for it is forever lurking in the background. Let us take you by the hand and ease your black hole of depression. We will not leave you alone in this but will stand by you. Let us heal you and bring you more into the light. And above all, believe us when we say we love you. We won't forsake you, but instead, you will have our company and love. Ask us to help you when it gets too much. We will hear. We will act. We will even find someone who can help you if wanted. No matter how bad things will get, we are there for you and will never forget you. Ask, and we will hear. Call, and we will answer. Release, and we will take care of you.

All of you, never think you are alone. We see all and know all. And we know how bad you can fall. But if you ever need a helping hand, we are always around.

Everyone is loved by us all and our mutual parent: The Divine. We will never lose sight of you and know that you will need our help and strength. All you need to do is ask.

Beloved ones never let your inner divine light fade but hold it steady. We want the best for you and will help. Just don't let go of your inner light. Nurture it, embrace it, and love it. In doing so, the darkness and negativity that lurks around will find it harder to attack you.

Be strong, be bright, and above all, be loved!

I ask this of you all."

***

20 MAY 2015

Daily Message from the Angels and Ascended Masters.

Message from Baradiel (Barachiel):

"When in the world of your own heart, you will find love will reside there. You are the physical embodiment of love. Please don't hide your love away. Let it show.

Open your heart to the delights of your world, and another person's love. And you will find yourself blessed. For your world is a miracle among the stars, and you are a miracle upon this miracle.

Open your heart to the many wonders out there. See how beautiful your world is. Also, the stars above, aren't they wondrous too? Open your heart to them too.

When did you begin to think that you cannot let any more love into you? Think again! You have an infinite capacity for love, and you don't even have to struggle for it.

As you feel this love, you will grow. Even the Divine can feel love and gives it. Yes, you know what that means. Prepare to give love in return for what you have received. It is a two-way emotion. You receive love, give love back. Again, it is infinite.

There are times when you love someone, but it's not returned. In this case, cut your losses and move on. You can't force someone to love you. Love is free and must be freely given and received.

Such is the way it is in our world also. We don't force anyone to love us. Besides, the best love in the world is love that is between each other. It is free and fulfilling.

Open your hearts, all of you! Receive our love for you. Receive the Divine's love for you, and return that love to us. There will be some who will reject this, so be it. We will not force you to love us. But we will look after you despite that.

Be love, for you are love. Feel the love, for you are love. Be yourself because you are lovely. "

***

21 MAY 2015

Daily Message from the Angels and Ascended Masters.

A message from The Divine Presence themself:

"Blessed be the ones who give their last penny to someone in need.
Blessed be the ones who give others a bit of their time, despite a busy schedule.
Blessed be the ones who stand up against those who would try to oppress others.
Blessed be the ones who sing with joy when they have no subject.
Blessed be the ones who share their love with others when they expect nothing back.
Blessed be those who feed the ones who have no food.
Blessed be those who support those who have no hope.
Blessed be those who care for those who have nothing.
Blessed be those who gave to others yet receive nothing in return.
Blessed be those who sacrifice themselves so that others may live.
Blessed be those who are kind when surrounded by cruelty.
Blessed be those who heal when others are ill.
Blessed be those who smile at you when you feel alone.
Blessed be those whose hearts are full of love, for they feel our presence.
Blessed be you, for you are all those and more. You do all these things because you are all Light-Workers. It is your destiny, and a beautiful future too.

Be well, dear ones, be blessed in many ways and all directions."

***

22 MAY 2015

Daily Message from the Angels and Ascended Masters.

Message from Zadkiel:

"If things aren't going the way you planned, then adapt. The reason is that there is a lesson in the incident for you to learn. It may not be as you expected, but it is going the way we expect it.

There are many reasons why we made it so, and some of them are these:

It is taking you from your correct path.
You are heading into a disaster, and we don't want that.
It could make you very unhappy.
Stop and think about the consequences of what you are doing.
You are interfering with someone else's path.
It's not meant to be.
You are rushing things, take your time.

There are many more, but the list would be too long.

But all in all, there is always a reason. If there is a hiccup happening in your life, learn your lesson from there. Don't stress about it or make a scene. You will not get sympathy from other people as you have noticed.
Just sit back, contemplate on it for a short while then move on.

There is always a reason why things happen. Don't bother with the 'Why does it always happen to me?' phrase. That is the words of self-pity and ego. It has happened to you because you are the best person that can deal with it. Learn from it and know that you are the best person for the situation.

But no matter what happens, we will be watching, noting your reactions. For we are testing your strengths and flexibility.

All are meant to be.

Be well, dear ones, and don't judge my words too harshly. I say things as it is. I do not use soft flowery words which can lead to confusion, but instead, I use words that are direct and easily understood.

That is all I wish to say."

***

23 MAY 2015

Daily Message from the Angels and Ascended Masters.

Message from Gavreel (a new one to me):

"Why do people always doubt themselves when they are in a situation that could be beneficial to themselves. I hear the words 'I'm not good enough.' or 'I'll never get the chance.' or even 'I'm not lucky.' To these, I say RUBBISH.

If the situation is in front of you, it's because we put it there. We think you are good enough, and here's your chance. We think you are lucky.

Stop putting yourself down and instead think you are lucky, you are more than good enough, and that chances open just for you. It is true! The more you believe that; the more such events will happen. That is due to us enjoying your pleasure at such things. We want to help.

Stop the self-doubt and begin the self-love. Be confident and show it. When it comes to job interviews, show your confidence, and be positive. Goes a long way, dear ones.

Well? Why are you waiting? It's time to start believing in yourselves, be powerful, be confident, and mostly be yourself.

Thank you."

***

24 MAY 2015

Daily Message from the Angels and Ascended Masters.

A message from my Healing Angel Tiriel:

"When you feel off-color and ill, that's the moments you feel the whole weight of the world is on your shoulders. Once that starts, then you must look after yourself first. You are an essential thing in the world when it comes to your health.

Never abuse your health, but instead look after it. It is all you have got between joy and unhappiness.

Take care of your body, and in doing so, you are looking after your soul.

When illness hits you, take the time to be with yourself and spoil yourself. Depending on the nature of your disease, it is how much you need to look after yourself — the more severe, the more care required.

Those in the hospitals, because of the severity of their illness, need a lot of care. So much so that they find it difficult in doing all of it by themselves. It is the moment where healthy members can be an aid. They can help others by only caring for those who have difficulties.

Treasure your health. It is part of you and your growth. A healthy body and healthy mind are perfect, and despite all your little quirks and fussings, you are still perfect in our eyes. Don't worry about the little kinks and quibbles. They all make a part of your character, your uniqueness. It makes "YOU."

Look after yourselves first, before you look after others. After all, what good is your help if you happen to be sicker than the one you are helping? Then when you are well, start looking after each other.

Of course, there are the 'Drama Queens' who claim to be sicker than anyone else. They make us laugh with their antics. Man-flu ring any bells to anyone?

Be well, and no pun intended. Look after yourselves and then each other. And keep laughing."

***

25 MAY 2015

Daily Message from the Angels and Ascended Masters.

A message from AA Raphael:

"What do you want in your life? Do you want a good job? A partner? Or even a holiday?
Well, they are all within reach of you, no matter where you are. The perfect job is yours for the taking. The loving other-half of you is just around the corner and waiting to meet you. And that holiday? It's there for the taking.

You have all that just ready and waiting for you. And it's all yours. Some say the holiday is too expensive and can't afford it. Well, when you think about it, you need to give up a few unnecessary luxuries like smoking, drinking alcohol, etc. to afford it. It's the solution.

There are those with no jobs and can't find one. Solution: Make one for yourself. It can either be permanent or a stop-gap until you finally get the job you wanted.

And all these beautiful things can be obtained by you at any time. The only thing that will stop you is YOU!

Less of the 'I can't do that' and 'I'm too busy' comments. And more of the 'Why not! I can do that!' and 'I've got time for that!' Instead of focussing on the negative side, start listening to the positive side. You can do all this and more. Aren't you all perfect? Ego is the one that will hold you back, so drop the Ego and instead accept the fact that you can do anything you want. You are the catalyst of your fate.

To reach the good things in life, you must go for them. We won't bring them to you, as they are already there. It's you that must take the first action.

Enough, I've had my say and hoped that you heed my words.

Be well."

***

26 MAY 2015

Daily Message from the Angels and Ascended Masters.

A message from AA Gabriel:

"When you feel wronged and poorly done by, forgive those who did you wrong. Never hold onto a grudge for it is a negative emotion, and it can poison you from the inside with its negativity.

Instead smile, silently forgive these people, wave a hand goodbye, walk away and forget about them. Your soul will thank you, and it drives the other person crazy.

You must show them that their words do not affect you and that you are the stronger of the two because you have let the light within yourself rule. For a person to create insults or do wrong to others, they are the weaker person. For only in such weakness, the negativity grows.

To be the stronger, you have to be confident, love yourself for what you are, open-minded, and filled with light. That is your strength with us, and it is given to you by us. We will reinforce that light within you in such confrontations with negative people. Don't let them put you down, for you are far better than the person who slings terrible words at you.
Walk away from them as they serve no purpose in your life path, leave them behind. Besides, why should you have to put up with them! Just smile as you walk away, for you have won the argument in spades. You are the victor, and in forgiving and not retaliating, you made them look foolish in their actions.

And as I said, it drives them nuts.

Well, that is my brief message to you all, and now I must leave as my channel is laughing away."

(At the beginning of this message, I had sensed Gabriel laughing away, and then what he had to say came through. Now at the end, we were both laughing. Gabriel's sense of humor gets me every time.)

***

27 MAY 2015

Daily Message from the Angels and Ascended Masters.

A message from AA Chamuel:

"Let peace dwell in your heart; soothing and gentle is its presence. The more peace that grows within, the more order there is upon your world.

Solitude is not the answer, but love is. No matter how much you try to be alone, you never will be. We are everywhere, just like the atoms in your body. We lie within you, and we are also part of your life.

So gentle ones, we are part of you and feel what you feel. Aren't we, after all, belonging to the same ultimate parent? That is what makes you all so unique. That we are all so different, yet we are the same.
That knowledge can bring satisfaction and peace deep within your soul. We Are KIN. And like the closest kin, we love each other very much. Take comfort in that knowledge also. We do belong to each other and will remain so till the end of time.

The love we have for each other can cross boundaries and dimensions. That is how strong it is for us both.

And we are the peace that dwells within you, loving you and caring for you.

Be at peace, beloved ones. And we will share our friendship with you."

***

28 MAY 2015

Daily Message from the Angels and Ascended Masters.

A message from Abraxas (New one to me):

"When you feel the pace of life is fast and going nowhere, you are the one who chose that path. Remember that. For you to find more in your life than just the usual hum-drum, you must go out there and make it. The universe is vast, and there is much going on. You chose to lead a non-eventful life.

You are a speck in the Cosmos, yet you are mighty with the light of the divine within you. New things are created all around you, so you have the choice of being involved. You don't need to live a boring life when you can make it fun.

A child's daydream, for example. You can help to make some of those daydreams come true by simply listening and taking an interest.

A person lost in a new city, you can help them find their destination and while you are at it, make a possible new friend. Be a host for your city and suggest more places of interest, and even visit them with your new friend.

Someone who has run out of cash for a cup of coffee? Then you must step forward and pay for it, and in turn, ask them to pass the gift along. You will feel good, I can guarantee it. And the reward will bring others a bright spot into their also dull lives.

You see, you are the catalyst for greater things to come. You can make things happen. You can CREATE new beautiful events.
It's not only the Divine who can do it, so can you and we encourage it. Why do you think we put ideas and plans into your heads when you ask it of us? Because we too appreciate your beautiful creations.

We are pleased to be around you when you do this, and so be assured that when you create something out of the ordinary in a dull day, we nearly sing with joy because you have shown your creative side. Artists do it all the time, and we do appreciate their efforts and skills.

They did make something to spark what could have been an ordinary life and made it into a life of color and beauty.

And so can you.

Be well my dear ones, I await your creations, even if it is as humble as a single painted hard-boiled egg. For it is a creation of part of your spirit and mind. It is called inspiration. No matter what you make and create, no matter how small, it is still a beautiful and creative way to brighten up a dull moment.

Do it my friends, and in doing so, you will have plenty of fun."

***

29 MAY 2015

Daily Message from the Angels and Ascended Masters.

Message from Metatron:

"Things are happening my friends. Events are coming together in the creation of a new world, a new future, and a new life.

You who are the inheritors of your new world will soon be required to move up into this new world: A world of light and beauty, a world that is more advanced in spiritual matters.

Already your usual religions like Catholicism, Islam and other such faiths, are beginning to show signs of changing. They are lagging because they do not belong in this new world.

And why? The old religions are of the past and are all unwilling to change. Change is fluid and to survive pressures and time; people must adapt and move with the flow. The old religions are rock solid and unmovable. Therefore, they will get left behind. They belong to the ancient world.

You too will need to adapt to changes, and I believe you can do this easily.

After all, the stars in the sky move, so can you, and you are the stars of the planet Earth.

Light-Workers, heed my call. Time for you to prepare yourselves to help others to grow, change, and adapt. You are the beacons, the mentors, and the warriors.

Every day, more and more are looking and moving towards the divine light. It is the moment of change — time for the first steps to be prepared.

My Light-Workers, you are essential in helping others in this new world. Yes, the very planet you are standing on is beginning to change, and it is shifting into a new phase. Its energies are changing, and a few of you are already changing with it. Yes, grow you all must. It is the new age of ascension. And you will see and experience amazing events and sights.

The time is nearly upon you all. Already your world is in transition, and the people upon it will change with the world.

Be prepared and grow."

***

30 MAY 2015

Daily Message from the Angels and Ascended Masters.

A message from Matriel:

"Let us teach you. Let us help you learn the fundamentals of our Love and Spirituality.

When you have a spare moment and are feeling a bit lost, go into your garden and sit in the grass. Be near a tree and relax against it.

As you relax, visualize the energy of the Planet Earth going up through your root chakra and rise upwards via your spine.

Feel the energy go through each chakra one at a time, setting each one spinning as the Earth energy goes through those chakras.

Let the energy flow upwards through the Crown chakra and up into the sky.

Now feel the energy spread through your entire body, cell by cell until you feel like your whole being, physical and spiritual is tingling.

Feel it burn away all the negative energies you have absorbed from others throughout your day. Feel how cleansing it is.

After a few minutes, withdraw that energy back and return it to the Earth. As you are doing so, you visualize a beam of gold light coming from the Heavens and following the path of the Earth Energy in you.

Let that gold energy pour throughout your body, cell by cell. You may feel tingling, or you may feel your energy levels recharged.

As the last of the Earth energy leaves you, replace it with that gold light throughout your body.

Let the gold light go through your root chakra and into the Earth itself.

The Earth will not mind and will accept this gold light willingly, for it is healing to the Earth too.

Keep that up until you feel within you that you have had enough.

That is when you may come out of your light trance state. Yes, trance state, because you will end up in a light trance. Take note of this trance for it could the first step in your voyage to the metaphysical. A lot of Light-Workers were started just due to this trance.

Now you are roused out; you may move and do what you need to do in your life. You will feel refreshed and cleansed. But also, you will find a spark of the gold light will remain in you. That gold light is from the Divine's love. You have accepted the Divine in your own heart and soul. It will stay for as long as you wish it to be.

Let it be so."

***

31 MAY 2015

Daily Message from the Angels and Ascended Masters.

A message from Ambriel:

"There is one easy rule for all of you, no matter who or where you are in your life.

This rule is: As you love others, you will do the same for yourself. As you heal others, you are treating yourself too. As you let the light shine within them, you make the light in you shine brighter.

You see, it's not a one-way system. As you are helping others, you are helping your soul at the same time.

All of humanity is as one, and they are at one with you. All actions that you do to them will reflect in you. That is why we ask you to be careful about what you feel or say. This simple rule has another name: Karma.

All of humanity is one - you are helping others strengthen that link and contribute to your wellbeing. Abusing that link will also hurt you as much as the other person, if not more.

Be careful about how you treat others. Be mindful of your words and throughout your life, be aware of your actions towards others.

Let it all rest there, and therefore help you on your path towards understanding -this giveand take through the links is a significant clue towards the answers that many seek.

You are all one.

So be it."

***

JUNE 2015

1 JUNE 2015

Daily Message from the Angels and Ascended Masters.

A message from Melchizedek:

"Let us all walk in the glowing grace of the Divine. Hold our heads high and bask in the divine love. Never look back when you do this, for what is behind you is gone. It no longer matters to you.

What does matter is the path you are walking. It's the path towards the divine promise.
Don't stop on your path but take each step day by day at acomfortable pace. You will all arrive at your destination at the perfect time. You will never be late or too early.
Walk the path with dignity, gentleness, appreciation, and joy. For it is a beautiful path to walk. There will be moments that could distract you and try to take you away from the road. Don't let it.

If the other members of your family are willing to walk the path with you in support and love, then you must let them join you, for they will also be blessed.

As for those who won't walk with you? They will try to take you from your path. That's when you must not falter but stride forward. Possibly they may be negative people. It could be that they have a different way than yours. If theirs is the same, they will quite happily join you.

Now and then you meet someone on your path, who will not follow your way or is unwilling to do so, but still they join you. It is their soul calling them to join this path of enlightenment, growth, and Ascendancy. That is a call that is very difficult to resist.

Let them join you and show them how beautiful it can be. But remember, if these people then decide to break away onto a new path, you do not have the right to interfere. Never have and never will be.

It's their choice. As simple as that.

Walk your path of life with peace in your hearts and the light of love shining around you. It is all worth it in the end.

Now so be it."

***

2 JUNE 2015

Daily Message from the Angels and Ascended Masters.

A message from El Morya:

"Well, you have made the grade. You have succeeded where others have failed. What area did you gain your accomplishment? Well, it's called the Game of Life.

You have come so far without any big disaster or hiccup. You have fought and the darkness and climbed the steps towards enlightenment.

Remember when those people in your past who said that you are no good, won't come to anything and being called rubbish? You can laugh at them, for you are nothing like they say. To us, you are fantastic, powerful, intelligent, talented and of course, beautiful. Leave those put-downers behind, because all their comments stem from one thing: Jealousy.

They want to be like you, but due to their negativity, they can't. These people have become their own worst enemies, aren't they?

They too could have all the glory they want, but they got to get rid of the poor attitude. It's harmful, and these people are unknowingly creating a negative version of reality for themselves.

You can create yours, and make it become a significant part of your life. All you got to do is let the light shine brightly in your heart.

That's all it takes! That and a lot of laughter and love. So easy, so pure and so lovable.

If you want us to help you, whisper. We will hear your whisper from the heart.

We will hear.

So be it."

***

3 JUNE 2015

Daily Message from the Angels and Ascended Masters.

A message from Daniel:

"Beloved ones, don't worry about a thing. We've got this; we'll take care of the problems. You need to relax and have fun.

Are health issues getting you down? Well, don't let it get to you. Laugh, joke, and do what makes you happy. It's all healing in many ways.

The happier you are, the better the healing. Enjoy yourself.

Finances in trouble, leave that to us. Just tell us what you want to do and how. We'll take care of things from there. Be very, very specific, as we do tend to be quite literal.

Other people getting on your nerves? Walk away and don't look back. These people are not part of your path, and so must be left behind.

Job troubles? Again, ask for our help. Tell us what you want and remember; be specific. We'll take care of it from there.

Lonely? NEVER! We are with you. You are our little sibling. And we look after our family members. You are never alone while we are with you.

I could go on and on, but you know what the undercurrent message is throughout this entire note? It is the message of "Trust!" And that is what we want you to focus on about us. Trust us. Let us take care of the dirty work. In trusting us, you are also allowing us to open doors for you.

Be well.

***

4 JUNE 2015

Daily Message from the Angels and Ascended Masters.

A message from AA Gabriel:

"When life throws you lemons, collect your fruits of labor, and make lemonade.

You see, all the things that have happened in your life are done to teach you. The quicker you learn something, the quicker you move on. It is all part of your spiritual and mental growth.

Yes, even as something as small as finding a mouse in your pantry. It is teaching you. Be humane. Be gentle and use a humane catcher.

All in this world is a little lesson for your life in this world is one big lesson, and you live on the surface of your classroom. Your significant experience is composed of small lessons linked to each other. It is all growth for you.

Never neglect yourself or your studies, for they will help in the next lesson. As I said, the quicker you learn, the faster you move forward.
Those who don't learn from their lessons will have to repeat it until they do.

And who are your teachers? You are your teacher, student, and friend. Your whole world is a classroom, so explore it, keep it clean and learn well.

So be it."

***

5 JUNE 2015

Daily Message from the Angels and Ascended Masters.

A message from AA Ariel:

"While you remain in your beautiful world, please take the time to say thanks for the many gifts around you.

The ground you stand on, give thanks to Gaia for providing it for you. Gaia will always support you and look after you. Gaia has always been around you and will continue to be your loving mother. Give thanks and gratitude for Gaia nurturing you.

The air you breathe, also Gaia's love for you. Everything that you have in this world is with Gaia's blessing. The trees, plants, beasts, rocks, water, and food. I could go on. But these were given with Gaia's blessings and love. Your Mother loves you indeed. Thankfulness and gratitude go a long way.

If you feel uncomfortable verbalizing your thanks, there are other ways. Plant a tree with love for Gaia in your heart. Feed the birds, heal a sick animal, or even something as simple as telling a pot plant your gratitude. They are all Gaia's children, just like you.

In caring for another of Gaia's children, you are also showing your gratitude. Gaia isn't fussy, just as long you are happy and caring for your environment. That's thanks enough for her, come to think of it.

Speak your thanks:

'My dearest Gaia, we love you and thank you for all what you have given us. We thank you with our hearts and our souls. We thank you with an exchange of love energy, and we ask for your blessing upon us, as we give our love to you willingly.

I thank you with gratitude once more, my dear Earth Mother for looking after us during all these years we have been with you.

Blessed be.'

And so be it."

***

6 JUNE 2015

Daily Message from the Angels and Ascended Masters.

A Message from Raziel:

"You are all feeling the strain of your worlds transition. Its energies are changing, increasing, and undergoing transmutation. All I ask of you during this time is ride it out. You too are changing with it.

You feel exhausted, wanting to sleep all the time, digestive upsets, skin irritations, and even migraine intensity headaches.

We are all aware of what is going on and how it is affecting you.

We are trying to ease as much of the symptoms as possible, but it still will take a while before the effects ease off.

So be patient with yourself and others. For they too are going through the same thing.

Be kind to yourself also during this time. Spoil yourself just that little bit more. If you feel like having a spa? Go for it and enjoy the session.

See, you all need this little extra pampering. The more you relax, the less the symptoms will be. Don't worry about major incidents. They become major because you have become too fixated and stressed over the problem. It's not all that large. Just take one step at a time and don't rush. Rushing adds to the stress and makes things worse for you during the transition.

Yes! Transition! You, also, are undergoing the same change of energies and frequencies as your world. That is why I ask you to be patient and spoil yourself, even if it is a long lie-in on a wet and windy day.

Look after yourselves, my dear ones. We will help as much as we can.

Be well."

***

8 JUNE 2015

Daily Message from the Angels and Ascended Masters.

A Message from AA Gabriel:

"Beloved ones, have you thanked your Divine parent today? For every gift and miracle that comes to you has been sent to you because the Divine heard you and rewarded you for good deeds.

Give thanks to your Divine parent, my dear ones, for all the love in the entire Universe is free to you, and it will reward you.

We are your Divine parent's messengers, and we deliver these gifts and such. It is on the orders of the Divine. We obey those orders, and because the Divine is our parent too.
We are family in many, many ways. We are your older siblings who watch over you and take care of you. It's what older siblings should do. And the reason why we do this? Because we genuinely love you.

We thank our Divine parent for having you as our family. You make us laugh when you have your lighter moments. And we join in such moments, encouraging you.
You sadden us when you are down. During such moments, we watch over you, sending you our love. Even our parent watches with compassion.

We are a family! Never forget that, because we never will. Little brothers and sisters, we love you. No matter what color, inclinations, religion, or handicap; you are our family, and we love you entirely without prejudice. You are ours to love, and we are yours to love back.

We are family, and I say again, never forget that."

***

9 JUNE 2015

Daily Message from the Angels and Ascended Masters.

A message from AA Raphael:

"Let the knowledge show that you have succeeded where others have failed. You who have worked this hard to prepare yourself for the final stages of the transition have done well.

You have done so much for so many, yet with little thought for yourself.

Well, let's change that now. It's time for you all to look after yourselves. No longer step back and let others take what we gave to you.

If such a gift presents itself to you, thank the giver and keep the bonus. It is a time of receiving. Receive love from the Divine and us. Receive tips from friends and family. Receive compliments and receive love. The award is not necessarily physical, for the greatest gift of all is LOVE. And that is what the gift for you is. Don't let others steal the gift of love that is yours.

There are also times to give the same equivalent gift to others, but it is from your own heart. The gift you received shall remain there.

It is also a time of pampering, re-energizing, and detoxification. You must prepare yourselves for the next steps: healthy body, healthy mind, and youthful energy. Love is purifying, so that is good energy.

Get my meaning?

The final stages of transition can be a bit difficult if one is not prepared. Expect bad headaches. As the shift happens, you will change with it - hence the migraines you get. So please, prepare yourselves. Change is imminent, constant, and forever. You would have long been extinct if you couldn't cope with change. You can do it and will. Aren't you humans a very adaptable people? Yes, you can do it.

So be healthy, pamper yourselves, and prepare for the final events. The changes will mean an increase in already existing abilities, and dormant abilities could become active.

I will be there waiting and helping you during these times."

***

10 JUNE 2015

Daily Message from the Angels and Ascended Masters.

A message from Ashtar:

"Rejoice! Yes! Rejoice! Your world is one of many in the Universe, but you have this one all to yourselves. You don't need a spaceship, for it is that already. And the reason to rejoice?
You are on it, and the higher levels have noticed. We are looking after you, and you have many Light-Workers among you.

Yes, the higher levels have noticed and are showing great interest. They will visit more often, and already, some are starting to prepare to interact with you all.

I am Ashtar, and I have been waiting for this moment. Now is the time to prepare your mind and souls for the meeting. The time will soon be upon you for the first contact.

So be happy with your race. The Light-Workers know of this coming and await it. For our meeting will be of the light. We will make sure there will be no interruptions.

No worries about where you are all headed. No need to worry at all. All is working out as it should, and the higher levels are making final arrangements.

Watch the skies? Quite a lot of you are already watching the skies. And many of you know and feel this meeting as it approaches.

Yes, only a certain few will come with us on this first contact and preparations are being made.

And the rest of you, don't worry. All is well. We have been contacting you for a long time, and the higher levels will be too. Your people are safe, and we will make sure of that.

It will be a time of great interest. Already eyes have seen visitors to your skies.

I await the next steps."

***

11 JUNE 2015

Daily Message from the Angels and Ascended Masters.

A Message from Ambriel:

"When you walk about on your business, do you stop for a moment and think of how lucky you are? You are fortunate!

And what is it that is lucky? You have your mind; you have your body; you have the Divine watching over you. You have us directing you and making sure you learn your lessons. You have the beauty of nature outside your door.

Yes, even a humble little Sparrow has much to teach us about beauty. You are lucky to have Mother Gaia looking after you.

You are lucky in so many ways.
Keep on thinking that. Confirm it to yourselves often, and you will find that more and more things around you are getting better.

Whatever you do in your life, there are always parts that do, even the dullest job in the world, seem right. That is also something I need to talk to you.
You think your job is tedious. Well, you're the one who is making it so. You need to change your mindset and be determined to make the post more enjoyable. It is all up to you to make that change. Only you can make your job enjoyable, and that is by being creative and using your imagination. Changing the mindset is necessary for you to find joy.

Notice that my message is telling you to change the direction of your thoughts into the positive? That is what it is. If you want to change? It's all up to you. If you're going to require to have more luck and opportunity? Again, it is all up to you.
Every direction and step you take in your life is all up to you. We can lead you to the crossroads, but it is you that make the choices. It's all up to you.

It is called Free Will, and we honor that.

Enough."

***

12 JUNE 2015

Daily Message from the Angels and Ascended Masters.

A Message from AA Gabriel:

"I keep hearing a lot of 'I don't care' and 'whatever' from those who are running away from their reality. You can't say that to us because we can see right through your words into your soul.
So your 'don't care's' and 'whatever's' are meaningless to us. We see the truth and know that you do care but are scared to admit it.
Why are you so scared? Are you afraid that we may judge you? We will never do that to you, for words are just that: Words. What we care about is what is within you. The real YOU! We care.

Simple as that.

So please, remove the negativity in your life and let in the positive. You will find that your life will take a turn for the better. Little miracles will start to happen. I say little because the biggest miracle will overshadow them. And that big miracle is you.

A positive mind will bring in a decisive turn in your lifestyle. Positive will attract more positivity. We will make sure of that.

So, my miracle child, are you willing to drop the ego and the 'Cant's' in your life? Because there is nothing more restricting than the word 'Can't.' It emotionally and mentally cripples your growth into the light.

You can do anything you like if it hurts no one. You can dream. You can laugh, sing, talk, walk and even imagine. In your dreams, you can also fly.

You are lucky. Some people are limited physically and are unable to do some of these things. They do not need pity, but they do require you to cheer them up, make them laugh, and at their request, a helping hand. Be their friend.

Have I given you food for thought?

Be well"

***

13 JUNE 2015

Daily Message from the Angels and Ascended Masters.

A Message from AA Gabriel:

"Darling ones. When you rest at night, do you ground yourselves and call the golden light to flow through you? Do you let Divine love surround you and protect you?
If so, then you are ready to carry on with your journey into enlightenment.

For those who don't, please do this. It is essential as it removes all negative energies that others have forced onto you. You don't need other people's problems pushed onto you. You are under no obligation to carry their burden on top of yours. These other people are trying to fob off their issues onto you, in the hopes you will do all the dirty work for them.
It's not your life path to do other people's work for them; you do your tasks and lessons. Let others do theirs, and they're the ones who need to learn.

There are of course those who are in genuine trouble, and that's when you can help, it is not only your duty, but it's an honor.

It's those who don't want to help themselves but expect others to help them; they're the ones you need to avoid.

Help your precious self first and then help those in genuine need.

Grounding yourself and removing those negative energies will remove any parasitic negativity from you, enabling you to help genuine people.

Do you understand?

Be well."

***

14 JUNE 2015

Daily Message from the Angels and Ascended Masters.

A message from AA Michael:

"Beloved ones, you have reached the stage of decisions, the decisions that are involved in your future. Now make them carefully.

Do you wish to go further in enlightenment and into the light? To evolve and grow into the presence of the Divine? Do you want to become a Light-Worker with a heart of divine light? To be the beacon to those who are lost? If so, then invite us into your life. Let us be your spiritual family. Let us be your friends and comforters. We are all that and even be your teachers.

By letting us into your life, you are allowing us to change you at the spiritual level. We will make you shine even brighter with your love light.

It is your decision.

Those who wish to remain as they are? That's okay. That's your decision, and we will respect that. Our contact with you will be limited because you have set that limitation by not inviting us into your life. But that doesn't mean we will neglect you. We will still be watching over you, protecting and nurturing you. But we won't alter you at the spiritual level. For that to happen, you must choose to allow it. And we will never infringe on that choice.

But if you ever change your mind, it's never too late. The door to that choice will remain forever open to you, and you are freely invited to step through that door whenever you desire.

Dear ones, you will all forever be loved by us all, and we will never leave you behind. All are protected and beloved by the Divine One, and we are obedient to the Divine, and also, we love you all. That makes it all a beautiful duty.

A task that is pleasant to do is no longer a task, but an act of love.

Be well."

***

15 JUNE 2015

Daily Message from the Angels and Ascended Masters.

A Message from AA Gabriel:

"When you look in a mirror, what do you see? Do you see your typical image, or do you observe the miracle that is within you? Look into that mirror and see yourself, please.

Sure, you see your reflection, but also note that you are also seeing the image of your soul. Yes, your body is perfect for the lesson provided. What you see in that mirror is more than just YOU. See into your own eyes, and you can see the universe in them. See the link to the Divine in them too. Your eyes are the windows to the soul indeed.

Don't look at the surface but look deep behind that surface. Look with your own eyes and the eyes of your soul. And you will find that you are beautiful, far more beautiful than you realized before. The surface is just that: Surface. It hides the deeper real you that lies within. That real, you are the pride and joy of the Divine. For you were made that way. It is only your world that has made you put up a shell to protect your real inner self.

When in private and you are sure you won't be interrupted, let your real inner-self comethrough and out from this shell and be free for a while. Your authentic self will laugh, sing, dance, and even play silly games.

It is all so worth it. Such will ease quite a bit of stress from you.

Your real higher self has another name; The inner child.

Play my children, play, and be free. Even if it is for a little while."

***

16 JUNE 2015

Daily Message from the Angels and Ascended Masters.

A message from AA Metatron:

"Time enough for work, and there's sufficient time for play. There is also enough time for meditation and repose. There is always time for everything you do. The only restriction that is stopping you is yourself.

Remember, humanity is the one who invented time and is the one who can ignore it too.

Remember, there is always time enough in the world for everything. All you must do is ignore your concept of time. That's the only thing stopping you.

There is no such thing as Time where I am, so we aren't restricted in our ways by it. Only humanity can make the change, and the change begins with individuals like you.

You can let time go away and be replaced by the life you would like, and by your rules. The only 'Time' you'll need to worry about is when it gets dark. That's an excellent way to indicate that the moment to sleep will arrive.

Never let 'Time' get in the way of your enjoyable and fulfilling life. Just enjoy every moment of your life the way you would like it to be — free, fun, and joyful.

The choice is yours. Let the others worry about things that they wish to worry over. They too can let go of things, but when it will happen? That is their decision.

So work on your own decisions, never mind the rest. You have enough to do as it is.

It's your path, your life, your choice.

Be well, dear ones."

***

17 JUNE 2015

Daily Message from the Angels and Ascended Masters.

A message from AA Chamuel:

"Never let an opportunity to better yourself go by. These opportunities are there for you to take a chance over. And you'll never know, one will lead you to an even more significant moment. They are all placed around you, and you need to grab the chance.

What is stopping you all from bettering your self and circumstances? Alas, it's yourself. I hear the excuses all the time: 'I'm not worth it!' and 'I'll never get the chance' and other such platitudes. Listen up! YOU are worth it and more. If you fail, it is because of two things: Self-doubt and not your path.

If it feels 100% right for you, and you feel driven to the opportunity placed in front of you? Then it is because we gave it to you. So never miss the chance. Sure, there will be more opportunities for you, but none are the same.

Throw away your self-doubts and negativity and let yourself grab life with both hands. As I said, you are worth it, and we know it. It's not the other people putting you down that you need to listen to, it's us. We will never set you wrong. It is your chance.

Set your mind on the situation, plan every little step, and then go for it. We will help.
So be strong, get ready, and live your life as you wish it. And if there are people around you that are trying to hold you back and down. You know what to do.

Be well"

***

18 JUNE 2015

Daily Message from the Angels and Ascended Masters.

A Message from AA Ariel:

"Never forget that as your world turns in the vastness of space, you roll with it. You are dependent on Mother Earth, yet you don't look after her very well. You put chemicals in the fresh, clean water she gives you. You destroy the creatures that share it with you: For sport and with chemicals. These creatures are also the children of Mother Earth, just like you, but you fail to watch over them.

Thankfully there are those among you who are ever alert to the problems her other children have and look after Mother Earth as well. To these people I say, you are blessed and much loved by your Mother. To care for your Mother Earth and her other children is what humanity was initially supposed to do: To be Guardians of Earth.
And these people who do look after your world have earned that title, and to be respected.
To the others, learn from these Guardians. They have much to teach you, and you have much to learn. You are all meant to live in harmony, not in a destructive war.

It's time to take responsibility for your actions, my dear ones. It is time. And it is never too late to start taking care of your Mother Earth. And right now, is the perfect time to do so.
It is what I want you to do, and in looking after your world, you are making it safer, more beautiful, and a more fabulous treasure than jewels. Life is more precious than gold, gems, and oil.

Be well, dear ones."

***

19 JUNE 2015

Daily Message from the Angels and Ascended Masters.

A message from AA Gabriel:

"Come together, all of you. All my Light-Worker friends, and all of humanity. Come along and join us. Now is the time for your part of the divine light to shine forth and be a beacon to those who wish to follow. It is time for the opening of the mind's eye.

When you come forward and join, you will create a vast energy field to trigger off the sequence towards the Universal opening. Yes, you are all the catalyst towards transition.
And you all thought you would either be missed out or forgotten, nope!

Combine your energies please and prepare the way for the first changes in your world. The final phase is coming, and we want you all to be ready.

Now I don't ask you of this lightly, for I know it can be a strain if there is little preparation done. I also ask the more experienced ones to help those who are new. Show them grounding and focussing. Show them how to strengthen themselves in mind, body, and spirit.

You have your work cut out I know, but I wouldn't ask of this if I knew you couldn't do it.

Prepare yourselves, my beautiful friends. It's getting near the time of the next stage.

Be well, dear ones."

***

20 JUNE 2015

Daily Message from the Angels and Ascended Masters.

A message from AA Uriel:

"Share this with my love.

The Divine loves you all, no matter what your beliefs, religion, or color.
The Divine loves you all unconditionally, and without restriction.
The Divine does not encourage prejudice or hate, but only wants love to reign in your world.

As for those who hate their fellow man just because of their orientation? Shame on you. The Divine loves them equally.

And those who hate because of differing religion. Shame on you too, for the Divine, belongs to no religion. The Divine is the One and shows no preference for any creed or cult. You are all equal in the Divine's presence.

Those who hate because of different skin coloring? Shame on you too. The Divine only sees the purity of that person's soul, and all souls are of many colors and equally beautiful.

Before you begin to attack another person for perceived faults, look in the mirror. Remember, did not Jesus say, "Let who is without sin, cast the first stone"? Now, remember that before you let hate to take over and hurt your beautiful pure soul. Your soul did not deserve such a punishment. It deserves something you need to learn; love, joy, and gentleness.

Think about that before starting something you may regret. You may begin a beautiful moment instead.

Be well and be loved for what you are: A beautiful soul within a pure body. Be humble, be accepting, and above all, be loving."

***

21 JUNE 2015

Daily Message from the Angels and Ascended Masters.

A message from Sananda Jesus:

"Beloved ones, why don't you care for your selves more? You who have so much in this world to gain, often ignore the beauties around you and sit in front of a computer or a television.
The world out there has much to offer you. And it is far more interesting than a box of moving pictures caused by electricity. There are things much more critical. Run in the sunshine, feel the rain, listen to birdsong, stroke a tree, laugh with children, feel the grass under your feet and above all have fun.

There is much in this world that is on offer to you, so please, don't ignore it. The way those of the negative forces, they seek to ruin it all in the name of money.

Take back your power and live your life. Let nature and humanity live side by side and be responsible for caring and loving your world.

Enjoy your world in all its beautiful and incredible beauty, for if the negative forces have their way, it will soon disappear.

Get out in your world and take over looking after it. Become the Guardians we want you to be. Have fun in doing so and enjoy the gifts nature can give you. Earth spirits will help you in this, so you will not be powerless.

Let the light rule on your world, don't let the darkness ruin it for you.

Be well and hear my words, sweet ones."

***

22 JUNE 2015

Daily Message from the Angels and Ascended Masters.

A message from AA Michael:

"Beloved, never let others success get you down, for their path is theirs alone, not yours. Never grieve over perceived lost hopes, for they were never yours to hope for in the first place.
We have plans for you and you alone. Never forget that. Our projects involve different aspects as they were made only for you. And they will be put in force at the right moment, no sooner, no later.
As I said, we have plans for you that were made only for you.

Let the others walk their paths and let them walk it alone. Your path is in another direction, and you will walk it alone. You cannot take others with you, hence alone. But you will in a way and you will not be alone, for we will walk with you on this path - just like we also walk with others. To make sure that all goes as well as it should be.

Dear one, you have a lot more to learn, but not much longer to wait for your path to become open to you, for you to walk on. And you will find how different your way is from the others. That is why you should learn that what others have done, can't be done by you.
Never grieve over being directionless or lost. You never were. You are only just waiting for your path to start. You have already

taken the first steps toward this path, and now you are just waiting for the right moment.

As for the unhappiness in your life, it is only temporary. Be patient, and things will get better as soon as you make the first steps.

Never let others success pain you. Their success is not yours. And remember you are successful in other ways, and you have a bright future starting to come to fruition. It is all on your very own path. You will receive direction to the right people at the right time and when you are ready.

So be patient, learn, and get ready. Soon you will be busy enough.

That's all I need to say for now. Be patient, beloved, be patient."

***

23 JUNE 2015

Daily Message from the Angels and Ascended Masters.

A message from AA Gabriel:

"Your path can be rocky, or it can be smooth. And the only thing that causes it to be that way is you. If you keep on saying; 'I can't do that,' 'I daren't do...' or 'No one likes me,' then your path will indeed be rocky because you have subconsciously made it be. All your mental put-downs of your self have all manifested your problems, bringing a lack of confidence and no self-love. You are afraid of your own shadow, and so you deliver about your negativity into your life.

Well, stop that! Instead, start thinking along the lines of 'I can do it!' 'I love being me,' 'I am lucky!' and 'I am perfectly capable.' These thoughts can start to smooth your future path. All are positive affirmations, and only you can make these words work for you. They will strengthen your resolve and confidence if you work on repeating the words to yourself.

Keep on repeating them every time you look in the mirror, and one day you will notice that you are much stronger than you are, confident and more out-going. You will become your words, and your path will be smoother in life.

It is all down to you and what you believe. Believe in your self, for you are the most precious thing in the world to yourself. Believe it, it's true!

That is all I need to say, dear one."

***

JULY 2015

2 JULY 2015

Daily Message from the Angels and Ascended Masters.

A message from AA Ariel:

"When all seems lost and fruitless in your life when things seem to get on top of you when you feel you can't take any more.

Stop!

Breath!

Calm!

You can do this. You are strong.
You aren't lost but need a rest.
Nothing is fruitless; it just needs patience.
You are just exhausted, that's all. You need a holiday away from the cause. Just get away from it all.
Then after a while, you come back and tackle the problem again. And you will wonder why you were making such a big issue of such a petty little incident.

Always the way, my dear ones. You all tend to make mountains out of molehills when you are exhausted. Hence the rest. Is it that important for you all to ruin your health over something trivial?

You see, you are the important one in your life. Yes, you! And it's about time you all took notice of that. You are first and foremost when it comes to your health.

When you need to rest: DO IT! No messing about or such.

If other people are the cause of your worries? Again take a holiday with the same results afterward. The other person may regret specific actions. Take a holiday when you feel a strong urging telling you. It's your Soul telling you.

Rest, play, explore a forest, go on a tour of other people's gardens. It will rest you.

That is all dear one. Close my message."

***

3 JULY 2015

Daily Message from the Angels and Ascended Masters.

A message from AA Michael:

"Enough! That is right, enough!

Let no wars stop our love and blessings.
Let no hate try to block us away.
Let no negativity try to harm our assistance.

We do not want that and never will want that. We want you to be free, loving, and peaceful. But we see wars, poverty, and illness.

I know that many of you are trying to fix such things, and it is a hard job for you, as there are always battles with the negative side who want such bad things to carry on.

The poor are dependent on the goodwill of others, but there are those who parasite on the weakest.

They take more than they should.

I say Enough!

To those who suffer, I say this; be strong, never let yourself be crushed and don't let others try to knock you back. Step forward and sometimes take risks. You know your true worth, and if you need help? Ask us, and we will find a way to help you in one form or another.

To those who help the sufferers as much as they can. Well done! But it can be a hard battle when the negative forces are trying to take away what you have brought with you to help others. Be strong and don't back down. Others are dependent on your strengths and drive. You are helping more people than you ever realize. We will help you willingly.

To those who are the negative ones? Eyes are on you. We see what you have done and said. You have taken more than you needed and made others suffer. It is now time to return what was not yours to take.

We can help you with this, ask.
If you wish to follow the light? Ask.
If you wish forgiveness, ask.
If you wish to change, ask.

Same goes for all of you reading this. If we can help you, ask.

Enough of my message, sweetheart."

***

4 JULY 2015

Daily Message from the Angels and Ascended Masters.

A message from The Divine:

"You who have nothing, think again.

You have the world before you.
You have the birds flying in the sky, singing.
You have the trees in all their glory standing with you.
You have nature surrounding you with all majestic beauty shown.
You have more than you ever realized, and it always has been.
You have become too focused on material needs, to be aware of the beautiful spiritual needs that really should take priority.

I don't want you to lose that spiritual link between us. I never want that gone. For you and I are closer than you think, and if I lose you to material needs, it saddens me a bit.
Though I will never stop loving you and watching over you, the wait for you to come back to me is part of my patience. I don't despair, for I know you always come back to me as loving and open.

As a family, we are. As parent and child, it is and must be.

I wish you all to take care of your spiritual needs, for they are essential also. You are of the same essence as your siblings, my Angels. I made you with my will and light, and that is why I don't want you to forget your origins.

Never worry about churches or such, for I never wanted a brick building in my name. Instead, pray with your soul, for your soul is also my true church - my temple and my loving light.
That is why I wish you all to shine in my light, my love, and my presence. You must all become more than you think you are.

You are the same as my Angels, but with fewer restrictions than they have. They learn from me, and I learn from you. Am I not within you all, seeing all, feeling all, and doing all? Through our link, I learn of your wishes, your desires, and your hopes.

Let the links be strong, for through them I can work with you too. I can pass my words to you. Send my Angels to guide you through them.

Be faithful, honor yourself, and above all, let my light shine strong within you. And you will become so much more. My children, you are already mighty, but you allow others to lead you astray.

Be honest with yourself and follow your path. For others have no right to take your Free Will away from you. I didn't give it to you for others to take control.

Use it, learn from it, and grow.

Until we all finally meet again in the light of love, I shall watch over you. So be it.

My message is delivered, my child."

***

5 JULY 2015

Daily Message from the Angels and Ascended Masters.

A message from AA Michael:

"To those who are happy and filled with joy over a significant achievement in their lives or a new family member: Bless you! You feel what we all want you to feel often. You are at your peak in energies when you feel this emotion. You are closest to us then, feel it more often dear one, be joy, be happy. We love you like this so much more.

To those who are bored and think there's nothing to do. Rubbish! You have lots to do. You can walk in the park, offer to tidy up a disabled person's garden, do a chore that has been idle too long. Get in touch with nature even. There are meditations and even music.

Try this! Go to the nearest shopping center and smile at everyone. You will feel better, and you will make other people's lives much better while doing this. Again, your energies will start to rise as you finish each task, giving you a sense of completion. Nothing quite like that sense isn't there. Rather satisfying. And the job won't pop up again to nag you. We love to see that air of satisfaction, for it makes you happy. That's what we want.

Those who are depressed and are sinking? You are not alone and never will be. If you think you have nothing to live for, think again. You have lots to look after, care for, or even love: a pet, a young child, a garden, nature.
If you feel down like that, let Mother Earth hold you in her arms. Go to a peaceful spot near the water and lie against a tree. Invite us and Mother Earth to take care of you and heal you. Let us all help. We are here for you.

We can do a lot more than people realize, a whole lot more. We can do more than find a parking spot or find a lost ring. We can make your soul soar in the sky and explore the universe. Meditate, and invite us in. Let us take care of you.

Well, will you?

To those who read this, I hear your words in your heart and mind. Your voices are sweet to us, and so we listen to you all. We are here for all of you, and we don't care what religion you follow. We also don't care what your beliefs are, your sexual orientation, or what color you are. You are all equally beautiful in our eyes and The Divine's eyes. You are perfect.

Be well, dear ones; I am listening."

***

6 JULY 2015

Daily Message from the Angels and Ascended Masters.

A message from AA Gabriel:

"Sweet ones, let your hearts be open to our gifts. Let your minds expand like the blossoms of a flower.

'Why?' you ask.

Why is this? When you open yourselves to us, we start opening doors to opportunities to you. We bring unconditional love, and you become what others perceive as very 'lucky.' Luck has nothing to do with it. It's us all the way.

Don't forget to bring those who are willing also to receive our gifts. So that they too can receive our blessings in their many forms.

As for those who aren't willing, they might change their minds if they see how much of a beautiful and fortunate person you will become. They might want to try the same thing. If they are willing to be shown, then bring them to us.

No forcing, just choice. Free will.

Always keep an open mind with other people as well, as they too have their own stories to tell. They also have experienced life's pitfalls in many different ways. Listen to them, hear what they are trying to say to you, and then with the goodness of your heart, help them grow and become stronger.

Love can do that, so can compassion.

Never turn away a person in need, for it shows that you are rejecting your self. Remember, we do visit your world in many disguises, and the person you turn away could be one of us or one of our subjects.

But if your instincts give you a warning about the person, a psychic danger sign. Obey it. For it means that you could be in peril. That person is NOT in need at all.

Are you all willing?

That is all, my dear one, and your new keyboard is a bit awkward."

NB: I've just gotten a new keyboard - ergonomic one, and I'm not used to it yet. The typos are constant. I had to go back often to correct what is written down. Gabriel was extremely patient with me and making cheeky comments about it.

***

7 JULY 2015

Daily Message from the Angels and Ascended Masters.

A message from AA Zadkiel:

"You who are reading this, you have been called to hear my words. You are to prepare the way for the new generation of Light-Workers, for they are getting ready to step forward into their roles.

You are selected to give the new Light-Workers direction and experience. Then you can let the Light-Workers be free in your world, in our service. You need to teach them how to use their gifts in the best possible way, and we will help you with this also.

Dear ones, you are the pathfinders. And you too will be helped on your path also. It's not all about the new Light-Workers, but also about you. As you teach the new members, you are growing away from your student levels and heading into the higher levels yourself. All to your benefit, as you teach others, you are preparing yourself and becoming the mentor to the new ones.

Growth, harmony, love, joy, and above all, the divine light, are all part of this growth. You are growing well, all of you -even those who think they are left behind. To these people I say: Wrong! You were never left behind. You were waiting until we had set things in motion, preparing your path for your next steps. Step forward, dear ones, it's time.

My message is brief, as it needs no padding. It is as it is, and that is the most definite way to explain things.

Step forward all and prepare the paths of the new generation. Call on us if you need our help in any way. We will answer in one form or another.

Be well dearest."

***

8 JULY 2015

Daily Message from the Angels and Ascended Masters.

A message from AA Uriel:

"Listen to my words, everyone. All that you have seen and heard in your lives is all that you needed to see and hear. Nothing is accidental but educational.

Yes, there is free will, you will always have that. You can choose what direction your path will take you. As soon as you wish, we set things in motion to help you on that path. Each decision you make, we adapt and prepare.

Nothing is accidental but deliberate. So many opportunities and you can pick and choose.

We do restrict what information that your mind can use about our realm. Too much information can only serve to confuse you if you aren't ready for it. The human brain is versatile, but it is somewhat 3D in its thoughts. We are waiting for you to reach the higher levels before you teach you more. You'll be readier to learn then.

Patience is a virtue there.

You will learn all you need to learn to help you on your path of your choosing. But when it comes to passing on to our dimension, your knowledge there is released back to you, and you will remember everything; of us, previous lives, your roles, and long-awaited friends.

Nothing is ever lost in learning, just waiting for you to come home to us.

Those who have Ascended are privileged to have their memories of their many previous past lives restored to them. Their minds have grown beyond the norm. They have earned their returning memories.

This happens to all those who have Ascended, including you. Yes, you will in time Ascend. Some will be in this lifetime, or the next, and so on.

All are meant to be. You all will Ascend at the right moment when your mind, heart, and soul will unite into one. Your energies and knowledge will have grown beyond their current state. That's when it starts.

That is all I need to say for the moment. Think on my words."

***

9 JULY 2015

Daily Message from the Angels and Ascended Masters.

A message from AA Gabriel:

"When you believe that the road to Heaven is in selling stuff for profit, you will find out that it's not that way at all.
Also following the Bible word by word and acting on their words? It's still not that way.
When you do what appear to be good deeds, you are stroking your ego. Again, it's not that way.

The real way is when you help others with no expectation of a reward - when you assist someone, or your heart opens up to us.

You see, you are your church. It is your very own soul and nothing else. Buildings are just that: artificial constructs. Bricks, mortar, and cement. Not the real church.
The REAL church is you and in all. You can worship the Divine in any of them, even if you go into a field.
You are the church. You are the most critical being in your life.
Your church is open to you, and you will never be locked out or turned away. No matter what your beliefs, color, or designation, you ARE important. And your church is where The Divine will hear you the clearest. The Divine sees the truth in your words that come from your heart, not by others telling you what to say.

Isn't it more than enough?"

***

10 JULY 2015

Daily Message from the Angels and Ascended Masters.

A message from Angel Nathaniel:

"Sit back and relax.

Relax in the privacy of your own space, and where you won't be interrupted.

Now breathe in deeply and slowly exhale, letting all your stresses and aches out through that breath.

Keep breathing like that, and at the same time, visualize the golden light pour down from the sky and surround you. You will be by then in a light trance state.

Breathe in this gold light, breathe it in deeply, letting it go through your lungs, and enter your body.

Feel this light flow through every cell it meets as it spreads through you.

Keep breathing, and soon, the light reaches your fingertips. Feel the tingling energies as they start to make you glow with the golden light.

Your whole body is tingling with energy, as the gold light is clearing you of any negative energy that you may have accumulated through the day. Feel the sensation of pure love that the gold light gives you.

Keep breathing in the gold light.

As soon as you feel you have had enough, slowly release the gold light back to its origin. Give your thanks to the Divine for allowing you to experience it.

Now still breathing, slowly release yourself from your mild trance state back to your awakened state.

You will feel lighter, enervated and you may feel a sensation joyful love surrounding you.

Whatever you feel, remember that the Divine has blessed you with his beautiful golden light.
It is free for you to reach for any time. If you ever need to reaccess it, follow the steps I mentioned. You can do this as much as you like. It's free.

Be well dear ones, be well and be within the Divine's love."

***

11 JULY 2015

Daily Message from the Angels and Ascended Masters.

A message from AA Gabriel:

"There are among you that do so much for others. Some do little things, and some do a lot.
But think about this, what do you do for yourself? Hmmm?

Yes, think of it. What do you do to reward yourself, or to have a little luxury?

Well, my little hard workers, you must spoil yourself sometime. You worked hard, and you deserve something for your labors: a reward, a treat, or even a holiday.

Exactly, you do so much for others, isn't about time you did something for yourself? You do come first, you know.

It is for the sake of your mental, physical, and spiritual health that you must put yourself first often. After all, if you are happy and relaxed, so are the people under your care, for they sense it. If they see you happy, they relax and become pleased with you.

If they sense confidence and satisfaction, then they too will feel that way.It is easy to get along with happy people. Whoever you are helping, let them sense your now relaxed self. If you're happy, so do they.

To be happy, relaxed, confident, and such, treat yourself, look after your own needs first. That way, you can best look after otherrequirementsappropriately and with less stress.

That is all, dear ones."

***

12 JULY 2015

Daily Message from the Angels and Ascended Masters.

A Message from AA Michael:

"Whatever you do in this world, be happy.

Be happy that the sun shines.
Be happy that the moon glows.
Be happy for the stars above.
Be happy for the seas.
Be happy with the air.
Be happy for the birds.
Be happy with the plants.

Be happy for the animals.
Be happy for the children that sing and laugh.
Be happy for a friend on a celebration.
Be happy with your partner.
Be happy with your laughter.
Be happy about everything in your world.

Aren't they all made to make you all happy?

We want you to be happy. Simple as that. We like to hear you laugh and sing. It makes us happy too.

There is so much strife in this world, only because the negative forces are creating it. The negative energies have no resistance to laughter and joy. They can't stop it; they can't fight against it. It weakens them.

Be happy for all your worth, for negative forces have no real power over you. Only by playing with your mind they make you think they have control. It is an obstacle easily removed.

Just be strong, stand up straight and proud, and feel our love and joy flow through you. Strive to be happy.

And laugh!

That is all I need to say, don't you think?"

***

13 JULY 2015

Daily Message from the Angels and Ascended Masters.

A message from AA Chamuel:

"Why do you worry so much? Aren't there many beautiful things happening around you, providing miracles, joy, and laughter. Aren't you open to these?

Worry is nothing more than stressing over a situation that is well and truly out of your control. If you change it or make a difference, and it is inevitable. Why worry about it!

All worry every got you was high blood pressure, headaches, and health problems.

Stop worrying about nothing you can change, and instead relax and let things go. Ask us to handle the problem instead. We can do that quickly enough. You only have to ask us, and then you go and have fun.

What's the point of struggling over a problem we can deal with efficiently.

Even when you think we've done nothing, that is because we work subtly and in the background. You may not see a result, but you can be sure we have eased the situation far more than you know.

Health problems? Again, stop worrying. Worrying makes the whole thing worse. Live for the day instead. Live your life to the fullest and let us take care of the dirty work. We have skills and powers far more than you can imagine, so your problems are nothing to us.

The only time we won't deal with a problem is when it is to teach you a lesson, and you must learn from it, for you can't advance further until you do. It's all part of your growth then, so be patient and be healthy.

Monetary problems? Ask what your needs are and how much money is needed. Don't be greedy at others expense though.

Hm! As my channel is known to call us as humanity's 'Mother Hens.'

That is enough; my message is over."

***

14 JULY 2015

Daily Message from the Angels and Ascended Masters.

A Message from Sananda Jesus:

"Help those who ask for your help. They need for you. Do not expect a reward back, for your support must be unconditional, like our love for you.
Do not put a price on your assistance to them. For then, it makes the gift of your aid worthless.
Instead, help them, do it willingly, and when it's over, say your thanks with friendship and love in your heart. Tell the receiver to pass it on.

And then move on.

In turn, the other person will remember this and know that the words to pass the gift on, will do so with the same instructions for the third person, and so on.

The more that do this, the more chance peace and love will grow. Just passing on a little gift is handing over the love that gift gave.
No matter how big or small is the gift, it is still LOVE; this means that there are no limits.
I would like to see this spread further into the world. I have had my say to you all, so please, pass it on."

***

16 JULY 2015

A Lesson from Angel Tiriel:

There is a way of healing without having to be drained of energy.

I shall let Angel Tiriel do the lesson.

Healing Without Losing Energy.

"As you relax, visualize green energy coming through your feet
Now imagine blue energy pouring down through your head, and meeting in the middle of your own body.

Place your arms to the front of your body, palms up and slightly cupped to each other.

As the energy pools in the middle of the body, visualize now the energy is reaching through your arms and then coming through your upright palms. It should be that of a ball of green and blue energy.

Keep feeding that healing energy into that ball, which is resting in the palms of your hands.

When you sense that there is enough energy in that ball, stop feeding energy into it. And instead, visualize holding and sustaining the ball in the palm of your hands.

During this whole process, you are not meditating, nor are you in a trance. But you are controlling the energies from the sky and earth.

Now close the energy connection with the sky and earth by again visualizing the energies retracting and leaving you.

You should still be able to sense this ball of energy in your hands.

You can now approach the subject that needs to be healed and apply the energy ball in that area. Ask the Guardian Angels of your patient to take the energy and place it where it is needed most, or you can ask them to direct you. That is when you focus on healing the subject's illness the best you can.

If the subject is far away in another part of the world, ask your own Guardian Angel to deliver it.

You all have more than one Guardian Angel. One stays with you, and the other acts as a Gopher. It is the Gopher that will deliver the energy to the subjects Guardian Angels, who in turn will use the power on the subject.

This method of healing is a way of making sure you have enough healing energy to deliver, but at the same time, won't drain all your strength. You too will receive a boost at the same time as creating the ball of healing energy."

***

17 JULY 2015

Daily Message from the Angels and Ascended Masters.

AA Emmanuel wants a few words:

"Never believe that the end of the world has come just because someone has left you. It is never that. Instead, it is the beginning of a new world for you, and a better one at that.
It's just that the other person no longer serves their purpose in your life, and it is time to let go and move on. You can look forward to better things.

Accept what we have given you, and you will learn that indeed, it is much better.

Don't hold onto the past; you can't save it. It is like water in your hands; it flows through your fingers. Nothing can stop it. And why would you?

That is so."

NB: I hadn't intended to channel due to my Cold, but a particular angel wanted a brief word. I can never say no to them.

***

21 JULY 2015

Daily Message from the Angels and Ascended Masters.

A message from AA Emmanuel:

"When people condemn you and tell you to grow up, ignore them. For they are envious.
Don't grow up ever! Let your inner child loose and feel the joy of life and the many wonders of this world.

It doesn't matter if you already know the facts behind what was considered magical to you as a child. The Divine created everything, so it is still magical.

Chase after Unicorns and fly with the dragons. They may not be in your world, but they exist in ours. And they do occasionally get in touch with those who have a heart that is as open as a child's.
Run in the falling leaves, splash that puddle, and roll down the grassy summer hills. Even build a snowman. It's fun, and you all should have more fun in your lives. The more fun, the better you feel. It is healing, after all.

Why do we ask this of you, well, it's all due to the fact, when you achieve a childlike love and wonder of what is growing around you in nature, you are closer than ever to Mother Gaia and us?

And, we love to see you laugh and smile. Every moment of joy you have is a moment we share.

Aren't your children the dearest of all to us and the Divine? If you have the heart of a child, you become that more precious to us. We love you, unconditionally, and we all want you to be happy, enjoy yourselves, and develop further into the light.

Let your inner child loose again, dear ones. You will never regret it and find still that wonder and awe that made your childhood a fantastic adventure. Even if it is just jumping about a rock pool at the beach, and yes, we do laugh when you slip and land in a pool unhurt.

Be well, dear ones."

***

22 JULY 2015

Daily Message from the Angels and Ascended Masters.

A Message from The Divine:

"When will you all listen? Many have spoken words of love and peace, but few obey. They have talked about helping your world, with oceans and creatures, but no one hears. These children of the light also risk their own lives to save you all from damaging your future. And you won't listen.

Heed them, my children, heed them. They are trying to tell you that your world is not infinite, but a lonely planet among many others. It is also your home. Ruin your home, and you will harm only yourselves.

You aren't listening to those who are helping the world. But you should, for these peopleare on your planet for that very reason; to enlighten you.

Instead, you listen to the words of others who spout phrases of war, famine, and plague. They speak of the negative path and a lot of you blindly follow them.

It's a situation not what we wanted for you. These people are controlling you.

Instead, you must take the first steps in reclaiming your right to enjoy your world, to look after it. To live free and in peace. That is what we want. It is your world, your home, and your life! Reclaim your rights to all and look after your selves and your world. It is your only home, my child.

Look after your world well, and it will look after you.

Did I not put on your world enough food, medicines, and water for all? Yes, I did. But it is the ones who control you, that are managing these resources. That is also something I did not want.

Where are the children? Where are they now? Are they lost amid the pressures that the negative ones have put on you? You are the children, but in a lifestyle, I had no wish for you to live. I wanted you to be free, enjoying the sunshine, and playing in the forests. I wanted you to be happy and dancing.

But I see pressure put on everyone to be a sheep in the society of wolves.

You are the free birds, not the penned in sheep. Shed the fleece that was forced on you and be free. That is what I want for you. Free to explore, free to feel, free to be yourselves.

That is so, my children."

***

23 JULY 2015

Daily Message from the Angels and Ascended Masters.

A message from AA Michael:

"Let today be the start of the new YOU. Let go of what bad moments in your past and leave them behind where they belong; in the past.

Instead, start to look forward and planning your new future. Plan a holiday, a house, a car! Anything! It is all original and waiting for you to create and do something in it.

Don't let hurts and memories of the past destroy what beautiful things that are coming to you. If you dwell and cling to the past too long, it can absorb you. Not physically, but emotionally.
The past can stop you from reaching new heights, can also pull you back into dark moments. So never let the past rule you:you rule!

Are you willing to take the next steps into your bright future, with all its promises and wonders? Are you going to create new beginnings?
I hope so. For every tomorrow is the first day of your life. There are so many tomorrows, and each is new to you, awaiting yoursignature on it — a day of interacting with new people and further talks with friends.

The past has no power in the future, never has and never will have if you let go. It is by holding onto it, you give it that power, though it is temporary.

It is all brand-new, and many wonders are going to happen. I can see into the future, and if I look far enough ahead, I see such amazing events.

It's all ready and waiting for you.

Be well, be well."

***

24 JULY 2015

I have AA Michael here with me, and he's come to say this:

"I have heard so many of you asking as to why our messages are always about love, light, and all the good things that some of you consider 'fluffy.'
I tell you; we will always tell you all these such messages. We need you all to listen to us. We don't say all these things just for fun.

You see, the path to us involves lifting your energies, and forgetting what hurts that have been committed to you and by you in the past. You don't need that emotional and mental baggage. You need to be free from all that.
You also need to open your hearts more to let in more of the divine energies into you. We are helping you to forward to the light.

Yes, we are trying to get you to grow into the light, be purified and ascend.

The journey is yours to take, but we will guide you and arrange doors to open for you on your path. It is a learning path, and letting go of your past is one of the lessons. Once you have learned that, your spirit grows brighter.

In the end, your spirit will reach a level where it can not stay at its current stage, and that's when we will arrange for you to ascend.

So, we will keep on speaking soft words of love and divine light. We all want you to grow into the divine light. Letting the light shine through your eyes and becoming what you all are; the essence of divinity that lies dormant, but never dead. You will become one of the hands of the Divine.

You will be one with the Divine, just like we are.

That is why we always encourage, help, and love you. Our messages are to try and waken you to your potential gradually.

That is all I need to say, my friend."

(This is instead of my usual Daily Message)

***

25 JULY 2015

Daily Message from the Angels and Ascended Masters.

A message from AA Uriel:

"It is now time for the release of your past. We have spoken to you about this and that it has been necessary for you to all do this. Well, this is a way one can do this.

Go to a place that is secluded and where you are relaxed, and you can be sure of no interruptions.

Go into the meditative state, and envision white light coming down through your crown and into your entire body and coming out through into the ground.

Let that light pour through every cell of your body.

Now envision pink light joining the white light and pouring into you also.

Let that pink light also pour through every cell of your body.

Say this:

'I shall let go of what is no longer required.
Archangel Michael, please cut the cords of what is needed no more in my journey to the light.
Let the cords of what pains and hurts that have happened in my past be severed and left behind when I move forward.
Let those who have held me back, release me so that I can grow into the light.
Let the light of love and the Divine shine in and through me, cleansing my heart and soul from the damages the past has left on me.
I ask this in the name of the Divine and love.
I ask this with love and gratitude.

I thank you, Archangel Michael, with my heart and soul.'

Some may feel a sudden release, but then some may feel relaxed. There are other feelings, too, but each one of you will react differently.

Enjoy the feeling of the pink and white light pouring through you, and let the pink light pool in your heart, for it is filling you with healing love.

As soon as you feel you have had enough, then release yourself from the meditative trance.

And be free, my lovely ones. Fly!

That is all, dear one."

***

27 JULY 2015

Daily Message from the Angels and Ascended Masters.

A message from AA Chamuel:

"Trust, that's all we want.

Trust in your inner strength, for it is yours and only yours. It makes you reliable, independent, and dependable. It also makes you a force to be reckoned with when the going gets tough.

Trust in those closest to you, for these people will stand by you when there is a need for strength; supporting you when you fall and will remain to help you until you become into your power again. And after that, will still be around if ever you need these friends again.

Trust in your feelings. They will tell you when something is hazardous. Your intuition will let you know when trouble is brewing. Listen to it; it will never let you down.

Trust in us, for we all have your well-being as our focus. We will supply the Guardian Angels to surround you, watch over, and love you. You are the closest to them, and they trust you. They know you the best, despite all your quirks and prickles. They love you, as simple as that. And will never leave you.

Trust in The Divine, who knows how hard it can be for you at times. But will never lay on too much pressure so that you can no longer cope. The Divine knows your limits, and so do we.

If you ever need our support, trust in us to answer your call. We will always listen. You may not see us, and you may not understand what we do. But we are there. Our motives are not apparent because we work in the background. But when the incident has passed, you may realize how it could have gotten much worse.

That's where we have helped, by lessening a significant problem into a much lesser one.

Trust in yourself, your closest friends, your Guardian Angels, and above all: The Divine.

There is love in all those."

***

28 JULY 2015

Daily Message from the Angels and Ascended Masters.

A message from AA Ariel:

"Listen! There will come a time when we will call upon you. We will ask you to do a task, which could change your life and others. And in some case, a sacrifice of some sort, whether it is of a memory, a connection or that of a precious gift. The time is not yet now but will happen at the right time.

We ask this of you, for your strength, belief, love, and your inner Divine light, as we will require it and you.

Not everything is hidden, and a time will come when an incident will shake your world, and this incident is when we will ask you to step forward and be steadfast. Stand for the light and with us. We will need you, as it will involve you.

Will you step up and stand at our side in mutual support? Your world is starting to suffer, shortages around you. Your world needs you to start looking after her; your Mother Gaia.

Will you all stand together and fight to save your world? We will help you if you decide to.

Will you help your world, and the future of your descendants to enjoy what nature has? To fight against those who wish to destroy it? We will help you in looking after your beloved Gaia.

There is no bloodshed. Just you all taking back what is rightfully yours to enjoy, to love, to nurture.

Will you?"

***

29 JULY 2015

Daily Message from the Angels and Ascended Masters.

A message from AA Gabriel:

"Self-belief is a positive thing. It has long been neglected by yourself in the pursuit of others.
It has been left at the wayside when it comes to other people, who take advantage and abuse it.

You must remember to believe in yourself. You MUST!

When you believe in yourself, you will find yourself becoming more beautiful in mind and spirit. You will be stronger, and you will attract like people who will see your growing confidence and happiness very magnetic.

As you grow stronger in this belief, you will find those who wish you ill, will remove themselves from you. Why? It is because these negative people have no more control over you. These people are weak, and you are far worthier of better. And with confidence in your self, you will get to meet better people.

You must trust and believe in yourself. You are your individual and mighty self. Growing in spirit involves believing in yourself. It's all part and parcel towards the path of enlightenment. That's what makes it all worthwhile.

So please do this: love, listen, trust, and above all, believe in yourself.

I like to see people who do this, grow stronger. Their light grows immensely. Well worth it and so beautiful.

Please, believe in yourself, because we believe in you."

***

30 JULY 2015

Daily Message from the Angels and Ascended Masters.

A message from AA Raguel:

"Have you ever considered what could happen if you just took a step out of your routine?Instead of going through the routine daily grind, you just turned a different corner and walked a different route? Or, instead of doing the shopping and cleaning house, you decide to sit in the sunshine at the park?

Such little changes are far more than they seem. They indicate CHOICE.

Sure, you can carry on, as usual, same route, same day by day grind. Or you can make a conscious choice; to make your day fuller, more vibrant and take a different direction than usual.

Explore your town. Introduce yourself to a neighbor. Smile at everyone, visit the lonely ones in the hospitals, even if it is just going to your local park. All changes that can enrich your life and create the beginnings of many more adventures. From a visit to a park to maybe a holiday overseas.

One thing can lead to another. And your choices make the events start to grow and make your life an incredible fun-filled adventure. Now isn't that better than a dull day to day routine?

Even those days have their moments. You can create those special events yourself, just by choosing to do something different, no matter how small.

Out of acorns, great big Oaks grow.

Well, my little acorns? Are you going to grow into big Oaks?"

***

31 JULY 2015

Daily Message from the Angels and Ascended Masters.

A message from AA Chamuel:

"For you to wonder and to grow, you must first wonder about where you have been and are going to. As soon as you have related the right points in your past, then apply them to your current life.

Had a happy childhood? Then show it by being pleased with what you are. Your childhood makes you.

Had a memorable and loving moment in your past? Then remember that beautiful moment.

Don't dwell on the hurts and pains that had happened, for they are now past and gone and never to return. Let them go; you don't need them anymore. Instead, dwell on the happy moments. They are useful things to store and keep in memory, for they make your inner light glow with pleasure.

Yes, this is all about you.

To be happy is to let go of what is pulling you down. To release old hurts and insults and to forgive those who have hurt you. Forgiving helps you release those memories much better. And above all, forgive your very own self for the hurts and pains you have caused to others and your true self.
Then leave the memories behind in the rubbish where they belong.

We can help you with this if you have difficulty. Just ask Michael to sever the cords that hold you to negativity. Ask, and you shall receive.

Don't forget to thank him, though. It all helps and talking to us helps also.

Be well dearest ones."

***

AUGUST 2015

1 AUGUST 2015

Daily Message from the Angels and Ascended Masters.

A message from the Highest Source:

"Blessed ones, walk forth into my light and show me your love for your fellow man.
Embrace them and call them kin. Show me your worth by loving someone who needs love.
Show your love to those who have been harmed by those who are false.
Show those in need that you care and will listen.

Is that too much to ask?

Let my beasts walk with you without fear and instead with companionship.
Let my beloved children be free to be children. Let them play, laugh, and explore.
Let them be safe from those who would harm them.

My children let your love and your light shine freely and with no restrictions upon you. For you are my children and I will not tolerate anyone trying to smother your beautiful soul into subjugation.
Be free and without pressure. Be yourselves and fill your hearts with love and peace. You are everything I wish you to be, so be faithful only to me and to your selves.

You do not serve humanity, but you serve me. If someone tries to force you to be subservient to another human, leave. You were all made to be equal, not more or less.

It is what I wished for you. And it is called Truth.

Remember, all life in your world is equal to you and is not anything else. Even the humblest of beasts is thesame. Treat each other with respect, kindness, and patience. That is all I ask.

Be at peace within yourself, for I have reasons for asking this of you. I would not ask you to do something that could harm one of my many children, no matter what those extremists say. I do not follow their word because they do not follow mine.

I stated many times, 'Thou Shalt Not Kill' and yet they ignore me.

It is something I do not want.

Make peace and love your entire life, and you will find that peace and love will make your life very close to divine, this is what I want for you – to feel what I feel for you.

Be at peace, no matter how you envisage it. I shall await your presence with my loving heart when the time is right.

Enough, my child. Let the message end here."

***

3 AUGUST 2015

Daily Message from the Angels and Ascended Masters.

A message from the lovely AA Gabriel:

"Sweet ones, you have Light-Workers among you. Some are aware of yourselves, but some Light-Workers who don't even know they are such. Now it is time to wake up to that fact. You are reading this because you all need to be aware that is what you all are. Light-Workers.

You may think you have no ability and wonder how on earth could you be a Light-Worker?

Well, it's simple. You do have abilities, but you are either ignoring them or not aware of them. Some of you have been bursting at the seams with your energies, but seem oblivious of them.

Have you been feeling restless and full of vim lately? Hmm? The urge to go out and spread the love?

Light-Workers come in many shapes, forms and energies. Not one is the same as the other. You are all unique in many ways. Some have abilities that cross over each other, but they each have the person's unique 'signature' to it. It is a feeling or sensation — all unique but with one aim and cause: Enlightenment of the world.

Some of you may have to make big decisions about this. That's okay. If your heart tells you not to be a Light-Worker, that's okay also. If your heart tells you not to, then it is not your path to follow yet.

Look at your selves and see within. You do have the power.

Farewell, for now, my Light-Workers.

And Em, I still find your keyboard awkward."

NB: I still haven't gotten used to this new keyboard. LOL!

***

4 AUGUST 2015

Daily Message from the Angels and Ascended Masters.

A message from AA Zadkiel:

You know that moment when all seems to click into place when a plan goes right and something precious that was lost a while back just suddenly appears? Have you thought about why such things happened?

I tell you why.

It is because some days or even months ago, you asked us to intervene and help you in this situation. We got going and started to arrange things.
We set events into motion so that the conclusion will happen; you found long-lost items, a job interview that got you that perfect job, or even that big idea that solves everything.

It's all us working on your behalf.

Give credit to your Guardian Angels, for they have heard you and have informed us. And with working together, we have created your event.
Also, give credit to your self for setting Ego aside and asking us for help. We heard and listened to you.

Keep on telling us what your needs are, for we are listening. We rarely do things instantaneously, for we can see into your future and if it conflicts with your destiny or could do harm to you, we will not activate the events immediately. Instead, we do it gradually so that nothing can create conflict and we can adjust things here and there with plenty of leeways.

Just that simple. Nothing is too much for us. And yes, we can find parking spots or lost keys. But you could ask for more, like a new job, or a new place to live.

Just ask, nothing more, nothing less.

Let it be so. That is all I need to say."

***

5 AUGUST 2015

Daily Message from the Angels and Ascended Masters.

A message from AA Gabriel:

"Sweet ones, reach out to those whom you love and will love you back. I ask this because you are all deserving of love, and you need each other to return that love.

So why fight?

If a situation becomes intolerable, walk away from it.
If it's only temporary, then seek a space away from it until things settle.
If you can't walk away because negative people are stopping you, call upon us to help you, because no one has the right to force you.
If it is within the soul, call upon Michael and Chamuel. Michael to cut the cords of the cause, and Chamuel to give you love of self.

I can hear some of you saying: 'It is all very well saying that, but what if it doesn't go away?'

I say: 'What lesson are you learning right now?' Yes, it is a lesson.

That's the only time we delay our help. Once you have learned your lesson, then we step in.

Yes, all the events in your life are lessons, and all are part of your significant experience: LIFE. Learn, learn quickly, and make sure it stays in mind, then you can move on the quicker.

But don't forget to give and take love, that too is part of the lesson: As you learn to give willingly and freely; you must be prepared to receive willingly and voluntarily.
And don't forget to love yourself without ego. That helps much more than you realize. That too is a lesson, an important one also.

Enough! I have waffled on long enough.

Be well, dear ones. Be well."

***

6 AUGUST 2015

Daily Message from the Angels and Ascended Masters.

A message from AA Uriel:

"Will you follow the path of light when your time has come, when you are called to join the ranks of those who work in it?
Will you come forward and stand before the Divine and open your heart?
Will you accept the divine light that grows within you and merge with it?
Will you Love yourself as being an extension of the Divine? An actual living part of the divine light?

That is what we hope you will do, for all go through this and it is a fantastic experience and a pleasant one, for no harm will ever come to you.

Do you wish to do this when your time comes? For some have already gone through this several times and it is a beautiful sight. Your energies will be released and shaped into your pure form.

You are all colors of the rainbow, and brighter than the stars. When you are in your solid forms, your light is much dimmed but still there. That is why we are trying to bring you enlightenment. To let your rainbow light shine through again.

And when one of you reaches that stage where their light shines fully while in solid form?

How exquisite you are then. You will have Ascended.

Will you go through this pleasurable experience with us? Let us help you in reaching the goal of your current levels?

Will you accept our love and guidance in doing this?

We hope you will.

If so, call upon us, any of us, for we are all unified in this. We will help.

That is all I need to say, for actions speak louder than words."

***

7 AUGUST 2015

Daily Message from the Angels and Ascended Masters.

A message from AA Michael:

"When will you believe us when we tell you that you are beautiful in our and the Divine's eyes? We see you as magnificent as the stars, yet you are always putting yourself and others down.

Stop it!

Instead of insulting someone for an unfortunate comment they made, tell them that what they said wasn't helpful and you forgive them for it, for rash words made in the heat of the moment, are made without thought. Then tell them that they are beautiful inside.

Ask their Guardian Angels to ease the tensions, to forgive harsh words, and that the other person has learned a step in their path of life. Be beautiful inside and let them see it. And teach them.

If someone physically attacks you, forgive them in your mind and leave. You don't have to stay around, and you don't need that added stress. Young souls can be violent, and for the simple reason is that they haven't learned the first steps yet.
You were like that once, so forgive them, and again ask their Guardian Angels to show their child what bigger adventures lie with love, forgiveness, and compassion.

If someone psychologically puts you down, shake your head, and move away. Again, you don't need such people, so forgive them, they too are still learning. Thought and compassion are what they need to learn. In a few days, these people will likely regret what is said, for their Guardian Angels may have managed to teach them compassion.

Neglect is something else; it shows that the ego has taken over big time. Again, a young soul. They too will learn via Life.

Keep telling those who deride you, that you can see the beauty deep within their hidden depths. In time, they will believe it, and what an incredible change will come over them. Tell them that they can do things, and if they seem reluctant, keep telling them that they have the ability and you can see it active in them.

Encouragement works more miracles than any negativity can destroy.

And don't forget to do the same for your self. Instead of 'I'm not good enough,' try instead: 'I'll give it a go.' You will surprise yourself on your strength. Self-criticism is very destructive; you don't need that sort of negativity in your life, so, ditch the attitude.

But if someone comes to you and shows their feelings the same way you show yours; befriend them. We have brought them to you to be a companion. Learn from each other, and you will support each other. Don't be surprised if such a friendship becomes a friendship so deep that your souls will be unison. It means that you are both on the same path, and you are twin souls.

Such are treasured.

Ah, that's enough. Short messages like this mean a lot to some. And we shall leave it that way. Be well, dear ones."

***

8 AUGUST 2015

Daily Message from the Angels and Ascended Masters.

A message from AA Chamuel:

"Out of the fire and the ice, came the Spark. As time passed, the Spark began to take on independence.

As time went by, the divine light shone on this Spark and endowed it with sentience. The Spark began to think on its own.

And as more time passed, the Spark grew in size and power.

The Spark once more was visited by the divine light, who decided that the Spark should havea form. The Spark was molded and shaped with the help of energies and love.

The Spark became Life.

Soon the Spark was encased in living flesh, and it reveled in it. The Spark could move freely, see and feel where before it could only float.

The Spark began to realize that it was not alone, noticing other Sparks who were also blessed the same way.

The Spark looked around and heard a voice say: 'You are the Spark! The Spark of life. You shall grow and spread across your world with more Sparks. Grow and be free with your Spark of Life, and let it glow across your world.'

Indeed, the Spark did take heed and spread the Spark of Life across the world, taking many forms in its travels.

And the story carries on to this present day.

You, my dear children, carry the Spark of Life within you, and you have spread it across the world. It is now time for that Spark within you to shine forth and bring the blessings of the Divine down upon you. These blessings within you are free to all who bare their Spark to the Divine. The many creatures who walk, swim, fly, and crawl have already opened theirs. I'd say it's about time you also did.

The more Sparks that open, the stronger the miracle that will happen.

How do you bare that Spark within you? Just open your heart to the divine light and let it pour into you. There's nothing more or less than that.

We are waiting for you, dear ones; we are waiting."

***

9 AUGUST 2015

Daily Message from the Angels and Ascended Masters.

A message from AA Uriel:

"When the heart weakens before another person's comments and put-downs, you are undermining yourself.
When the heart weakens, so does your will.

This the power of negativity coming into force.

Never let your heart weaken, and never let your freewill crumble. Fill yourself with resolve and know that we love you, and so does our mutual father; this will help your resolve grow stronger. The drive from that will help you when your world seems to be collapsing around you. Be strong.

But it also can bring new things. Be strong in your heart, and only let in those who can help you strengthen it more. No one is an island, least of all you.

You may think you have no one, but you have us.
Do you want a mate? Tell us.
Do you want more love? Tell us.
Do you want more laughter? Tell us.
Do you want peace within your soul? Tell us.

You are never forgotten and never will be, for we are always around you all. Don't let your heart weaken by the thought of loneliness. You are not because we are here.

All weakness in emotions isn't helped by exhaustion either. Rest plenty and always arrange a time to relax in — any time, and no excuses to avoid it. You must rest.

Enough of my words. There is much more, but not just yet.

Be well"

***

10 AUGUST 2015

Daily Message from the Angels and Ascended Masters.

A message from AA Gabriel:

"There is a time for work and a time for rest. That work time is when you create events with your hands and mind. But you do need time for rest.

Rest is necessary to re-energize and of course, to ground yourself.

This rest is to build up lowered energy levels, not to waste on arguing, doing chores, and for creating more work. Rest is REST and let nothing change that. Work time is for other activities. Yes, housework is just that: Work!

Self-sacrificing your rest time is self-destructive. Your body needs rest as much as it needs oxygen. Both essential.

Resting will improve your mind, your health, and your sleep patterns. It gives you time to dream of what you want, to read a favorite book or follow a loved hobby.

Rest is for renewal and to improve your mental state.

Too much work and not enough rest will make your energy go lower, tired, increasing poor health, and hampers your thinking. You need to rest.

Set apart some time during your day to do whatever pleases you. Use this time as your rest time. Even if it just involves playing with a kitten or doing a crossword, it is your time to relax.

Working non-stop doesn't help you; I hope you realize that. It will hinder you. Making you tired, and of course, very grumpy. I have seen so many of you become over-tired and taking out your stress on innocent people.

Children do not deserve to be hurt. Your partners do not earn a verbal attack, just because you didn't rest enough.

Of course, if you aren't allowed to rest, because others keep pushing you to work, and won't lift a finger to help you. Hmm! I'd say that a few harsh words would be justified, wouldn't you say?

After all, you aren't their servant; all must help if a job needs fixing quickly.

Rest my dear ones, you all need your rest. And let no one ruin that for you. It's beneficial on so many levels and if a cat-nap is on your list for a rest, then don't let me stop you there. Go for it!

Enough, I'm stopping you all from resting.

Be well."

***

11 AUGUST 2015

Daily Message from the Angels and Ascended Masters.

A message from AA Metatron.

"Remember all that you have done in your past have made you what you are now. And what you do now in your life, will make your future.

Those choices you made and followed, all influenced you and your world. Your preferences are yours to make, and no one else's.

We respect those choices, and we only get involved if you ask for us to step in.

Do not blame others for your own mistakes. For you chose your path, and you decided to follow it. If you selected a life of crime, then again, it's your choice. Do not blame society or other people. They had nothing to do with it; they are innocent.

Look to yourself and note that no one forced you into that life, you chose it. You can also choose to walk out of that life and into a better one. Again, your choice.

No one is stopping you. Only you are stopping yourself.

What I said is an example; your choices make you. You make your choices. Take responsibility for your decisions, and stop blaming innocents for your mistakes.

I know my words appear harsh, but they are not meant to be. For that, I apologize, but I have seen so many innocents harmed by other's choices, and it saddens me.

Please think carefully about what decisions you make. For they will affect more than just you, they can affect hundreds in the long run. If you make the right choice, then those hundreds will benefit from your choice, and you will help the most. Make a bad choice? Ah, then many could suffer.

It is never too late to change your mind about your path. Ask us to guide you on the right track or decision, and we will do so. The doors of opportunity are always open. Take it.

I have said what I have needed to say, and all I ask is that you think about what decisions you make and how it affects your future.

Be well."

***

12 AUGUST 2015

Daily Message from the Angels and Ascended Masters.

A message from AA Uriel:

"Do not be afraid of change, my friends.

Change is good for it expands your knowledge, gives you room to grow and keep your mind alert. It is all part of the evolution of the body and soul. Change is essential.

There are those among you who are afraid of change; they don't want to let go and hold on to the past with a viciousness that does not warrant its existence.
You must accept change and let go of the past. The past is dead and gone, and you cannot bring it back with you to the present and future. It is all a memory now.
To stagnate and become immovable, will mean you will be left behind. Stranded and left alone by the same people who accepted change and moved on. They cannot reject change just because you don't want to move on. They know they had to move on; it is part of destiny. It's yours too.

Change is needed, and you must change with it. Being left behind is not right, and it stops you from achieving your full potential. Please, let go of what no longer serves you and step forward into the sunshine of change, not the darkness of stagnation.
You will enjoy it. Let the past remain a memory, for it serves you best as that: just a mere memory.

Oh, and don't be frightened to try new things. It could be fun, and we want you to enjoy what changes bring.

I shall, therefore, leave you to ponder my words, and I will move on.

Be well."

***

13 AUGUST 2015

Daily Message from the Angels and Ascended Masters.

A message from AA Michael:

"We see you struggle with your problems.
We see you cry when it gets too much.
We see your pain when all you have struggled for, gets taken away from you.

It is hard, very hard the path of life, and for some, it is too hard. It is for these people this message exists.

You do not suffer alone; you must not. There are people in this world who will help you if only you would open to them. I know Pride has a say in it, but Pride cannot feed you and put a roof over your head. Pride is fickle and can turn on you.

Swallow that Pride and tell someone about your biggest problem. That person may be able to help; if not, they may know someone who can. Ask us to step in to direct you to the right person. We will.

As for that Pride, it is of no use to you. Dignity can easily be shed and regained. It is, after all, a state of mind. It repairs easily.

You are not alone and never will be abandoned. We see and hear all, and you do have your Guardian Angels continually watching over you. Ask them for their help in coping with problems.

It is upsetting for us all when you are upset by your struggles. Please never be alone in this. Ask us to send you help, and we will either guide you or someone else to you.

Let your Guardian Angels take over, dear ones. Let them, please. That is all they want to do to help. Let them take the problem. If it is harder than they thought, they will ask us to step in.

Nothing can stop us when you call upon us. And be prepared to accept help; in one form or another. You don't have to fight alone, but you can have a friend to ease your burden.

Ask, and we will help.

We await your voice."

***

14 AUGUST 2015

Daily Message from the Angels and Ascended Masters.

A message from AA Raziel:

"Do you remember the days of your childhood? The innocence and the wonder of your world? How everything you saw was fascinating and magical? It still is!

Believe in your magical world. Just because you are all grown into adults, doesn't mean that the world is no longer magic. It still is there, but your society has decided to blind you to it.

Believe in the fairies; they are the guardians of the Earth. They are the nature spirits. Right now, they are struggling to keep the world balanced, but humanities invasion and destruction of the world means that these Nature Spirits are starting to lose. They want your help.

Believe in the Dragons; they do exist on a higher level. They watch over your world, waiting for the day they come back. That event is soon, but they will be as friends.

Believe in the Unicorns; they too live in our level. They visit and work with the Nature Spirits, healing where they can.

There are other magical beings around and waiting. They want you all to revert to the belief and wonder of the child within you. When that happens, you will see miracles once previously lost to you.

Magic is as magic does. Forever there and hiding. Giving life and feeding it, nurturing and loving. Neither good nor bad, but is. A part of the Divine will make this too. Let the magic come alive within you and feel the stars within you. They will live in your heart and mind, and the servants of Gaia will be your neighbors.

Let it be so."

***

15 AUGUST 2015

Daily Message from the Angels and Ascended Masters.

A message from AA Gabriel:

"When you are feeling down in the mouth and blue, remember us. We love you and will never stop loving you. Even when you have done wrong to others, we may frown, but we know your soul is pure. We will still love you, and we will teach you your lesson.

No matter what you do in your life and no matter what happens to you, it is all part of the big picture. You are learning to become a better person throughout each incarnation. Your learning makes your soul grow with knowledge and wisdom. That's what we want.

Maybe this will help you understand what I mean.

Your world? Consider it as a large school, and everybody is in a classroom of various levels. Your life consists of lessons. And each incarnation, you go up a level.
Those who don't learn and consistently misbehave, don't go up that level but kept down. Those who commit crimes against others also kept down. It includes those who harm others. Once they show a sign that they have learned their lesson, then they can take a step up. This step could either happen in their current incarnation or their next. It all depends on the circumstances.

To learn is to grow, to grow is to become enlightened. And the enlightened one's are only a step below Light-Workers, and it is only a tiny step between them. The only difference is that one is aware but doesn't do anything about it. And the Light-Worker is also aware but spreads and shares their abilities to bring others to light.

Light-Workers have a few steps before Ascension. Only a few steps and the more is learned and practiced, the closer the goal.

Practice what you preach. Do not say one thing and do another. It makes others lose confidence in you. Instead, be true to your word and beliefs, let no one sway you from them and above all, be loving to all living creatures. They too have their path, and you were once like them.

Be well, dear ones."

NB: Gabriel is still teasing me over my keyboard. :P

***

16 AUGUST 2015

Daily Message from the Angels and Ascended Masters.

A message from AA Ariel:

"Times are changing. You must change with them. You must look after your world better so that the survival of your race is assured. You must care for each other and see that the returned love is the reward that is more than enough.

Stop the bickering and fighting. If a situation becomes intolerable, then leave it behind. Let go! You do yourself no favors by staying back.

Treat the child with some respect, but remember the parent is before the child. Parents must take on that role full time and not expect others to do the parents job. It isn't their duty. It's the parents.

Teach children to respect others and politeness. Such go a long way in life, more than hate. Those who teach their children hate will find they have made more problems for themselves. Teach them to love instead, and watch the children grow into beings of love itself. Much preferable, and so beautiful.

Teach the world that war is not required. But words of peace and compassion work.

There are always those who are the fanatics, be wary of them, for they speak words of hate from a damaged mind. Their souls are beautiful and perfect, but it is the mind that has the souls enslaved to an incarnation of hate.
Those who spout words of hate and bigotry? Be patient with them and don't follow their words. They too have their issues caused by parents ramming their beliefs onto their children. That is going a bit too far, and it has again damaged their mind.

These are the results of not enough love and gentle guidance from parents. Instead, it is the result of other people's beliefs forced into the child's mind with the threat of or with physical pain.

Not good.

Be patient and take steps so that none may get hurt. Protect those you love. And those who are deranged? They need protecting too, from themselves.

You all need to take steps to change your lifestyle. Your world is starting to suffer because you take without giving back. You damage what's left so that no more can live in the area. You need to change NOW! And take responsibility for what you do in life.

It is all up to you. If you wish to be the Guardians of your world, be the Guardians.

Enough! That is all I need to say. Post this and let those who feel drawn to the message, become the messenger."

***

18 AUGUST 2015

Daily Message from the Angels and Ascended Masters.

A Message from Ascended Master Ashter:

"Welcome to my world. A world of light and color. A world of beauty and cosmos. You are living in it, and you see what I see in the sky above. The stars are beautiful, aren't they? They wait for you.

The trees are reaching for the skies, yet only you can take them there — no other race in your world. In time, your kind will reach those stars, and with them, they will take the seeds of the trees. We will welcome the mighty Oak.

You will spread on the face of these new worlds, and some will change in time to adapt.

But please, I ask this of you, look after your worlds and stay in communication. You can start with this one. Look after it, clean it up, and respect it.

What you do now in your world, is what you will be doing on other planets. Others are watching you and seeing how you treat your world. Your actions will determine the Other's effects.

Yes, prepare for the Others to visit.

Who are the Others? They are the race that had your world before you came. They moved out to the stars and now have spread there. And they have watched over you. They initially moved away to make room for you, and they will step in if necessary.

They are the Golden Ones, the ones from the long past and into the future. They are the bringer of gifts or changes, which one depends on you.

The Pleiades is one of the systems they inhabit.

Their next course of action is dependent on your course of action. Look after and heal your world, and friends from the stars will come to help and advance you. Destroy your world, and your kind is lost. Those from other worlds rightfully don't want you to destroy theirs.

Enough, enough! If I say any more about this, I shall only confuse you. I shall leave it that. Thank you for relaying my message.

Until the next time."

***

19 AUGUST 2015

Daily Message from the Angels and Ascended Masters.

A message from AA Gabriel:

"There are days where one has moments of sadness and depression. These moments can be taxing and even exhausting to the body. I ask you to be patient and rest a lot more during those times. Tiredness is a factor for many of these conditions, and just an extra hour of sleep will help you. Go to bed earlier. That's all you must do.

But there are those which are caused by outside circumstances that affect you — a loss of a beloved one, or a verbal fight with a friend.

In the loss due to death, be patient, and keep that person's memories alive in your head. Think of them when they were happy and smiling. Even though their physical form is gone, they are visiting you in spirit. Watching and loving you. They talk to you, but a lot of you don't hear them. But they are still with you. Talk out loud as if they were physically there like they used to be. They're still there, listening. In time, some of you may end up actually "hearing" their answers. Depression during those times is futile.

As for the verbal set back with friends or family? Swallow that silly pride and apologize. If the argument was too vicious and due to incompatibility, again apologize. You don't have to embrace them back into your life. The separation was due to diverging paths. Accept that, forgive them and move on. Don't dwell on the negative side, as it will rot. Move on and forget.

Depression that is due to chemical imbalances is another matter. There I ask everyone to be patient and supportive when someone has this problem. The sufferer can't help it, it is beyond their control, and they know it. They do try to stop it, but it is a continual struggle, so they don't need people's judgment, for they judge themselves. Instead, they need people's understanding. Some find temporary relief with their doctor's medication, but it is still a struggle in the long run.

Understand all that is going on within others, is also happening within you. Feelings hurt due to other's rash judgment.

Please understand and accept as such. No one is immune, but you all have different ways to cope.

Be well, and thank you."

***

20 AUGUST 2015

Daily Message from the Angels and Ascended Masters.

A little poem from one Angel who occasionally tells me them - Raphael:

"Rest in your heart and mind
Relax and meditate
And feel within your third eye find
That the stars will come to life
With words of peace
And not of strife.
Let your heart wander the waves
Of the oceans of the heart.
Let your soul exit the caves
That your ego lies hidden within.
Be at peace within your soul
And find the golden light in you.
Let the beauty of the Divine call
Upon you to its might.

Are you not beautiful inside?
You are that and more.
Ignore those who deride
Your belief and put you down.
They are young and yet to see
What love the Divine can give.
You are perfect and will ever be.
You are ours to love and keep.
So, walk with your head high
And leave the negative ones behind.
They're envious and will sigh
At the opportunity they missed.
To know you is to love you
That is a fact.
The soul within you is true
No doubt about that.

You are beautiful, all of you."

***

21 AUGUST 2015

Daily Message from the Angels and Ascended Masters.

A Message from Ascended Master Hathor:

"Many civilizations have risen and fallen. Many have grown too big for their own good and destroyed by the very people they harbored. Sometimes nature itself took a step in the destruction.

There are many ways for the world as you know it to change. Your civilization can also vary, either to the better or worse. That part is up to Humanity. Look after your world and each other freely with no intention of repayment, and your world will look after you. Look after your world with your heart, not with financial profit.

The heart makes you the better Guardian. Then your civilization will change to the better.

But if you insist on keeping on the path of profit, overusing natural resources, and plundering fossil fuels which destroy your air, then the worst will happen.

Note that I have said, 'WILL' because there are no 'ifs' or 'buts' in it. Self-destruction is not pretty, and that is what your leaders are doing. Why do you put up with it? It's your world, too; you are the ones that must live in it. Take back what is also yours, and don't let others take it away from you again.

Some risk their lives every day in trying to preserve your world. We honor them because they cared for this world with their heart and soul. They loved their world so much; they were the true Guardians.

You have the choice to select which path you need to follow: Self-destruction or self-improvement.

Choose and choose well. Your world depends on the right choice.

Enough. My message has been passed on. I am Hathor."

***

22 AUGUST 2015

Daily Message from the Angels and Ascended Masters.

A Message from AA Gabriel:

"I want you all to get out into the garden or to the nearest park, anywhere you can walk on grass with bare feet. That's right! I am going to get you to be in touch with Mother Earth. I want you all to commune with her.

Walk in the grass, bare feet, and all. I want you to push all the negativity that has built up in you throughout the day and force it out through our feet, and into the ground.

Visualize pushing dark masses of energy down through your body and into the ground below. Then at the same time, let white and pink energy flow into you from the top of your head.

Let that help you push out that dark energy.

As that dark energy leaves you, flush it out with that white and pink energy, let that white and pink energy surge through every cell of your body. Cleaning you at the atomic level and destroying any remnants of that negative energy. When you do this, you may find your fingertips tingling, or feeling slightly lightheaded. Don't worry about it, it's cleaning you up and at the same time recharging.

The white energy is mine to give. It is cleansing at the same time purifying. The pink light is Ariel's; it is love.

You may end up feeling rather lively and comforted. But you will feel pretty good.

When the white and pink energy has thoroughly cleansed you, close off the connection between you and the ground.

You are merely visualizing the link being withdrawn and shut down.

Then you can move away feeling good, and dare I say it? Spiritually squeaky clean?

Enjoy!

Farewell for now.

Gabriel"

NB: This time Gabriel didn't tease me about my keyboard, but he sure made me laugh with this message.

***

23 AUGUST 2015

Daily Message from the Angels and Ascended Masters.

A message from AA Uriel:

"May many blessings shower upon you all.
May the gold light of the Divine reach your heart.

All within you is perfect, and all you need to is for you to teach your soul.

Never hold back on the lesson, but open yourself up to learn new things, new adventures, and growing current ones. The more you learn about what is within you, the quicker you will understand. Never run from new experiences; it is all part of the big picture called enlightenment.

You are reading this message of mine shows that you are willing to learn. Just needs one small lesson to start a sequence of new ones. Start small, dear ones. And you will find within that short lesson; there is much to learn, for it will lead to more experiences.

The lesson could be as small as showing an animal some kindness or even looking after a garden. It's the little lessons with significant potentials indeed.

The more you learn, the quicker you grow. Simple as that.

Sure, there are times when you need to rest. Please do and often. Take your time over learning also. Rushing things does you no favors, and only adds to the stress. Relax and don't hurry, the lesson will go at your preferred pace.

It all brings me to say this, think back on today's events. What did you learn? You will find that already, your lesson had started before you woke up.

A lot of these lessons are rather pleasant, so don't worry. Those that are unpleasant, we won't bother you with until you are ready to take them on.

Again, no rush there.

Be well"

***

24 AUGUST 2015

Daily Message from the Angels and Ascended Masters.

A message from St Germain:

Dear ones, all of you are sweet to us. Give yourselves credit for all the good things you have done in your life. Some of you have brought forth new life. Congratulate yourselves on that. You have done well. Some have saved lives, again, congratulate yourself.

You all have done good things in your life, and it is about time you recognized that fact. It is a beautiful experience, and I want you all to know this. These are splendid deeds, for they arewith love and strength.
The combination of those two will make your soul that much stronger.

Because you have done well in your life, your energies will be higher when you acknowledge them and feel happy with the knowledge. It is all part of that all-encompassing power: LOVE.

Love yourselves for doing such good. Yes, do so. It's not egotism, but self-empowerment. Were you strong then? You can be the same again. And you can change worlds with that strength. So, what's stopping you?

Those feelings of self-doubt, procrastination, and fear? All negative. By making yourself feel good, that negativity goes out of the window.

Don't self-doubt, for you are perfect the way the Divine intended. We can see that perfection, and yes, you can ask questions at others. The worst you can get is a 'No.'
When others ask you questions, be positive in your answer. None of this 'I don't...' or 'I can't...' unless it is someone trying to make you do harmful things. Then speak up and out, stand your ground, and give strife back.

Procrastination? Are you putting things off for another day? Also known as laziness. Don't put off things. Instead, start doing them as soon as possible. That way, once it's gone, it's off your mind. You are free of it – finished.

Fear? Ah yes, that insidious emotion that can destroy civilizations. It is scary, isn't it! But you are stronger yet. The only time you should let fear help you is when you are in danger. Such fear can save your life. You heard the saying that fear could give you the power of 'Flight or fight.' So unnecessary anxiety is debilitating. Don't let it rule you, never let it, because you are stronger! You order it! If you feel it coming on without no reason for it, then distract yourself with more pleasant thoughts or a beloved past-time. I recommend watching a kitten play. You will end up laughing there.

Ah! Perhaps a baby goat! Thank you, Emrayel. Yes, that is also distracting and amusing.

Enough, now all of you, stand up and be proud of yourselves. You've done well. We are happy with you all, and more and more of you are turning to the light. Be happy and let the Divine take care of the annoying stuff.

We are proud of you too.

Be well"

***

25 AUGUST 2015

Daily Message from the Angels and Ascended Masters.

A message from AA Gabriel:

"Wherever you are, whatever you do, you are always in the presence of the Divine.
The Divine and we will always watch over you. We can see all and are aware of all. Nothing is hidden, no hurt ignored, no love missed, and no runaway lost.

We are watching you all, with love, expectancy, and patience. You may find that comforting. Some find it disturbing, but soon realize that we don't interfere with your lives unless it is to improve it.

That's right! We can improve your life.

A situation that is getting rather tense can be eased off by asking us to divert pressures into another direction or only by putting a dampener on.

You can't hide from us, and you have no reason to anyway. We are your closest friends, your spiritual family, and above all, your protectors. Now isn't that a beautiful thing?

Right!

Let us guide you, leading you to the right decision, by only letting you access the full information of the choices. A well-informed decision can help many ways in your path.

So much to say, I want to say a lot more, but I am restricted. Most of you aren't ready yet, so those who are, I shall speak to individuals. But I can say this; your world is changing. Changing faster than you realize, and it's about time you knew it. You must be ready to cope, grow, and mainly adapt.

That part should be natural for you; afterall, Humanity is very adaptable in many environments.

But change is happening right now! We will help as much as we can, as, after all, we can't interfere with your free will.

Hm! Someone somewhere mentioned that we don't have free will, and your will is what we look after. Partly right, your will is what we look after, and we do it out of love. But we too have free will. We chose to look after you. And we made this choice out of respect for the Divine and you. We can pull back to have a moment to ourselves, but others will watch over you during that time. Never conflicting.

Now, did you enjoy my little snippet on what it's like on our dimension? A bit of knowledge goes a long way. Enough! I've rambled long enough.

Be well, dear ones."

NB: I'm now suspicious. Gabriel is not teasing me at all today. He's up to something. He's just said: "I'm always up to something." and laughed.

***

26 AUGUST 2015

Daily Message from the Angels and Ascended Masters.

A message from AA Michael:

"Where ever you are in this beautiful world of yours, look around you and be thankful. The Divine has given you trees, flowers, birds, water, animals, grass, the mountains, the air, bees, and of course, you.
All around you is a gift to you. A gift of nature and you are the holders of that gift.

Child, it is time for you to enjoy your gift.

Your world is so beautiful with all its large amount of variety. So much more important and enjoyablethan all your computers and phones. Your electrical devices are only temporary and have limited use. But nature in all her wonder is nearly infinite. So much to see and learn from such charm and beauty.

Nature is more than your world, for it abounds in other planets too. She is the mother of planets, and nurturer of all living creatures, no matter what they are. They are all her children, including the plants.

And you!

Enjoy her wondrous gifts, for they are miraculous in their way, including you.

Yes, I am mentioning you a lot in my message, because you are part of nature, just as much as the lowly rocks to the mighty planets. You are all her children as much as the Divine's children. Life is part of the Divine's own will and is a beloved sibling to us. Enjoy your world, its many wonders, and your interaction with them should be that of peace, harmony, and understanding. Through the gentle care and loving of Nature and her many children, you will grow. You will grow in love, spirituality, and strength of spirit.

Ahhh yes, if only you could see what we can see in you. Such beauty, perfection, and you are all the children of Nature.

I have said enough and no need to say anymore, for you will understand what I am getting at.

I shall remain your friend in need. Farewell for now."

***

27 AUGUST 2015

Daily Message from the Angels and Ascended Masters.

A rare message and lesson from AA Raziel:

"When you wish for a reasonable conclusion, you are attempting to materialize an event to happen. The more you concentrate on this, the more likely it is to happen. It is called manifesting.

How manifesting works?

When you put your sights on something you want in your life, you must either create a picture board and place it in plain full view, or write what you need on a piece of paper and read it often out loud.

Concentrate on your subject of want.

Then tell us what you want. Ask us to create the sequence of events to bring the item/subject of desire to you. Describe the series of events in detail every step by step, which will bring the desired result to you.

It will not be instantaneous, but slow to happen, and that's because we must arrange things that don't interfere with your life path and others life path. So steady and careful means a better chance for us to plan things.

Now keep thinking of what you often want throughout the day. Keep it in your daydreams and heart. Never let the dream fall to the wayside and be forgotten.

Sure, there are moments when you must put such thoughts to the side to concentrate on something else; expect that. When done, return to the original idea of what you want.

You must keep the dream and the wish alive so that it will become active. Be patient also.

If there is a set time, you got to get the item of desire, due to urgency or such. Tell us OFTEN.

We can perform miracles, you know.

We will hear and see your wish. And we will act. (Even if it is to shut you up)

Keep the dream alive, my children. For the vision of the present will be the future reality. All ideas have that potential.

Be well."

NB: I like the humor, Raz. I love it.

***

28 AUGUST 2015

Daily Message from the Angels and Ascended Masters.

A message from AA Raphael:

"This time, I am going to make you look within you and interpret what you feel deep down.

I want you to all have a moment where it is quiet. It will only take a short while so that I won't be holding onto you for hours, just a few minutes.

Right! I want you to push your ego to one side and instead, reach out with your mind and go deep within to your soul. As you do this, see if you can feel your Soul's feelings.

Gently sense what is going on there. Your Soul is aware of what you are doing, and if asked, may help you.

Try it.

Some try using meditation for this; some reach in with their minds. You are all different, so use what method is most comfortable for you. Ask your Soul to help you if you wish.

Send your Soul some love through the mind. Your soul, as I said, is aware.

What do you feel deep in you?
What sensations do you feel?

Now I am asking you to do this because I think it is about time some of you started to try and communicate with your Higher Self. Your Soul is exactly that, your Higher Self.

When you get that link established, communication will be more accessible, and you will discover how amazing you are. Your Higher Self will help you in many aspects of your life, providing advice, guidance, humor, and even love. It wants only the best for you.

I know what the results are, but I want you to know it for yourself. That is the best way.

I will speak again later, my dear ones.

Be well."

***

29 AUGUST 2015

Daily Message from the Angels and Ascended Masters.

A message from AA Chamuel:

"Rest, relax, and be at peace with your inner self. As your heart softens with love for your soul, let your soul show its appreciation for you. By resting, you are letting down barriers and allowing the Soul to heal the weary part of yourself. Your Soul will also talk with us, providing you with further information.

Resting is renewing, rejuvenating, and necessary.

As you sleep, that is when we step in, healing and loving. We talk to your Soul during that time. Rest is important. It's both "our" time: You and me.

Be calm and know that your Soul has only the highest intentions for you and will always be with you through thick and thin. Did you know we talk to you, using your Soul as a conduit?
When you feel us around you, your Soul is aware and letting you know.

Thank your Soul for being a part of our lives, you and me. And thank yourself for having a Soul that is as beautiful as you.

Hmm! Believe me; you are beautiful. Some may not believe in us, but we believe in you.

Be well, dear ones. Be well."

***

30 AUGUST 2015

Daily Message from the Angels and Ascended Masters.

A message from AA Anael:

"There is in your world an interesting spiritual element; it's called Love. It is spread widely around and found in easily accessible places. It has a strange pink color, and it glows non-stop.

When gently rubbed, it grows warm. But when scraped hard it hardens and goes cold.

This strange element looks like a crystal and is in the hearts of every living creature in the world. It is protected.

Now and then these living creatures do expose the crystal to the light, and if nurtured, will grow. But some will try to damage that crystal, so the children of nature must look after them carefully.
This Love is brittle when exposed. It can be harmed or damaged. The only way you can fix it is by giving Love to Love. The more Love it receives, the stronger it gets.

This fragile and beautiful crystal of energy is beautiful and to be treasured, and familiar in your world, but it is more precious than diamonds.

Its Element name: YOU.

Think about it, dear ones. Think about it."

***

31 AUGUST 2015

Daily Message from the Angels and Ascended Masters.

A message from AA Zadkiel:

"Sweet dreams and pleasant thoughts are what makes your world sing with joy. When you dream of something beautiful, your Soul and mind are glowing with pleasure. Your heart sings. And your world, its heart is your heart too, and it sings.

We wish you keep on dreaming beautiful things. Make your wishes as beautiful, and never stop the pleasant thoughts. The more you keep on with this, then expect wonders.

Don't worry about what is inevitable, as fretting only gives you health problems. Instead, dream big and beautiful.

That brings to my other message.

There are people in your world that are all colors and shapes. Love them all, please. The Divine made them that way, so they are perfect. Don't judge them, instead smile in greeting and friendship. Some of them are not what they seem and maybe more than you realize.
Remember that you may be entertaining an Angel in disguise.

Yes, we do come down to your world often, testing, seeing, and bringing forth a significant event in the growth of your world. And we do start such things without you knowing.

I'll let you go now, to think about what I have said.

Be well."

***

SEPTEMBER 2015

1 SEPTEMBER 2015

Daily Message from the Angels and Ascended Masters.

A little poem from our wordsmith AA Raphael:

"Sweet small child, don't be blue.
The Divine above is watching you.

With love so pure and strong,
It seeks your heart, to belong.

So, do not cry my little one,
Let the sadness be far and gone.

The Divine's love is true,
And it is aimed at you.

Do not worry or start to sob and cry
Your words come to us upon a butterfly.

There we hear your very heart,
And begin the process of miracles to start.

Beloved one, you are ours to love,
Don't be scared; you're precious to us above.

So, lay your worries and struggles down,
Start a smile and remove that sad frown.

Begin to laugh and let your heart fly,
And your voice will sing, and not cry.

We are your beloved friends, that's right.
You are ours, throughout the day and night.

Beloved, let us walk beside you in joy.
Guiding your path and bringing light, enjoy.

So, let go of those who hurt you in your Soul.
Let in our love, our guidance, and your goal.

Our love is within you, that is right,
For you are beautiful, a lovely sight.

Don't forget you make your light too,
And leave behind those feelings so blue.

Walk your path into our divine light
And let us lead you to future bright.

In harmony, we will sing you to sleep,
So your dreams are lucid and deep.

Relax, and leave the darkness behind,
And walk into the light, no longer blind.

Your heart is open, let it sing its song
To the Divine, pure and bright, belong.

Hear me, child, listen well to me,
You are growing into the light, and see

You are part of the light that's true
Us, the Divine and your soul are part of you.

Fare you well, we'll speak again
And never let others give you pain.

My little birds you all are at that.
Your dreams and hopes that you begat.

Live your dreams; make them real.
Make the promise become that more real."

NB: Raphael is sitting beside me, arm across my shoulder, and telling me I need to rest more.

***

2 SEPTEMBER 2015

Daily Message from the Angels and Ascended Masters.

A message from AA Michael:

"What can I say? You can make your dreams come true. It's all there. The reason I say this is because I still see people too frightened to move forward. They fear failure. And because of that fear, they fail.

Instead of manifesting failure, how about making the right moves to create your perfect solution. To do this, you will need to make the first move. Less of the: 'I don't know... ', and the 'But they won't...' Yes, recognize the words?
Instead, more of those: 'Why not! Let's do it!' and 'I'm going to make this work.' All positive affirmations and the only way you can get what you dream of is to ask us.

You see, you know you must dream hard, imagine events and such to manifest the desired result. But you forgot one primary and essential item: YOU. Yes, YOU! YOU must make the first move. If you sit around and do nothing but expect others to do it for you, then expect failure. We step in to help when you step up and start making things happen.

That's the way you and I roll. We help those who help themselves. Stand back and hide, will get you nowhere. You fail yourself. We can help you if you help yourself. That's the way it is. There is just you and us. And we can be a great team when we work together. Nothing will stop us then.

Will you help yourself by making the first move to making your dreams into reality?

Be well."

***

3 SEPTEMBER 2015

Daily Message from the Angels and Ascended Masters.

A brief message from AA Ambriel:

"In peace, let your heart rest safely.
In peace, relax and be yourself.
In peace, let enemies forgive each other and themselves.
In peace, be on good terms with your neighbors.
In peace, let no harsh words be said.
In peace, be true to any promise made.
In peace, you will let time flow like a gentle river.
In peace, the wars of ignorance will vanish.
In peace, you will find enlightenment.
In peace, walk free and untouched by harm.
In peace, let your soul sing to you.
In peace, let the only running you do will be for the joy of it.
In peace, let the blind see with their souls.
In peace, laugh with others and with happiness.

All these and more are possible in the name of peace. I say this:

Be at peace and let none disturb it. For it is right for you and everyone else."

***

4 SEPTEMBER 2015

Daily Message from the Angels and Ascended Masters.

A message from AA Raphael:

"It is that time again. Time for you to take stock of what you have learned and experienced.
To reflect and contemplate the wrongs done to each other.
Yes, time to forgive those who have done wrong to you. To let go and move on, forget these people as they are no longer part of your past. If you are still in the same situation - leave it. It no longer serves your purpose, and no one has the right to harm you.

If you have done wrong to others, forgive yourself for the mistakes. Send out to those people you have wronged, your love instead, and wish them well. Put an apology in love also.

Then move on. Go forward.

Once you have let go of all the wrongs in your life, you will feel free, lighter, and more alive. It is the part we wait for because that's when you start to grow into the light of the Divine — becoming purer.

When you have done all the releasing, start sending out your love to all, and never speak of wrongs again. Now is the time of renewal and learning. You are the Students of the light, and you are all in the Divine's classroom. We are your teachers, and you are here to learn.

Don't worry, the lessons are exciting and expect to have fun.

For those who have difficulty in letting go, you must call upon Archangel Michael to help you release. He can cut the cords that are holding you back, removing the ones that are holding on to you. But remember you have a part in this too, you too must walk away at the same time and don't look back. You are leaving behind those who have tried to hold onto you.
Negative energies are parasitic; you MUST leave them behind.

Enough! Enjoy the sensations."

***

5 SEPTEMBER 2015

Daily Message from the Angels and Ascended Masters.

A message from AA Emmanuel:

"Do you wish to know what it is like to have an Angel see into your heart, to live there, and to be part of you? Would you like that?

If so, first invite us into your life as friends and kin. Let us be part of your family and home. To be always welcomed.
In time you will find that things in your house will change. The negative moments will become less in time; the atmosphere of your home will become brighter and happier. We will even cleanse your house of any negative presences that may infringe. In the end, your home will become protected by our existence and the divine light.
We want you to be happy.

In time, you will invite us into your heart as well. That is when we put in some of our gracious Love there and put in the golden light. This gold light is the light of the Divine itself. Nothing is purer and more loving.

Expect your heart to open more with that, and you will find that not only we have taken residence in your heart, so will the Divine's love for you. When we are in your heart, we will protect you also from any negative forces. And you will become stronger, more advanced and grow further into the light.

It is a beautiful thing to behold. And there is nothing stronger yet more loving.

My child, who channels my words, has invited all of us into her life, and we love her so. Let us be part of your life and let us love you more.

Be well, dear ones."

***

6 SEPTEMBER 2015

Daily Message from the Angels and Ascended Masters.

A message from Sananda Jesus:

"When you walk in my footsteps, you are walking with me in your heart. I am with you in each step, holding you in friendship.

When you stumble, I will reach out and pick you up.
When you falter, I will wait with you.
When you run, I shall run with you.
When you jump, I shall catch you.

I am with you every single step of your life. Encouraging and loving you. I am always there for you.

No more hiding from me, for I can see you.

No more denying me, I will still save you.
No more running from me, for you will end up running to me.

I am your friend and savior. I am your ally when trouble seeks you out.

Do not run or hide; I will always seek you out from within your own heart and soul.
Why would you want to do that, though? I will never harm you or reject you. I am always with you with open arms.

"Who am I?" you say.

You know me by the name of Sananda Jesus. I am your friend and brother, and you are always welcome in my life.

Bless you, all my dear friends. Bless you."

***

7 SEPTEMBER 2015

Daily Message from the Angels and Ascended Masters.

A message from AA Michael:

"Darling ones, when will you stop staring at what's directly in front of you and being oblivious as to what wonders that are happening around you. Look up from your phones and computers and see the Divine's miracle of love in action. Birds and trees, the flowers, people are walking and talking. Yes, LIFE!

It is the pure proof of the divine miracle.

It is going on always around you, yet you are more interested in a piece of dead-weight electronics. You are restricting yourself; in fact, you are dumbing yourself down.

You were not intended to become a robot yourself. Put down that phone and turn off that computer. You need to get out in your vast and beautiful world and become part of that divine miracle.

Life is varied in many ways, from the lowliest bacteria to the massive Blue Whale. You are all linked to each other. You are all part of Life, and all are related to you and each other. Even the little sweet Daisy has some kinship with you. Are you all not descended from the one thing? The divine miracle of love.

You can start living again under the umbrella of divine love, and protected from the sudden storms that fate can throw at you.
Start by merely hugging or saying; 'I love you!' to your friend, sibling, parent or partner. It will all start from you, dear ones. That's all it takes to begin another miracle. You!

Ahhh, I have gone on enough. Get out there and LIVE the divine miracle. We'll be watching.

Be well."

***

9 SEPTEMBER 2015

Daily Message from the Angels and Ascended Masters.

A message from AA Cassiel:

"I wish you all to laugh with joy, happiness, and amusement.
I don't need to tell you about such high energy emotions are enlightening and empowering, you already know that and are quite aware of what such feelings can do.

It's just that you all need to remember this common saying: Laughter is the best medicine.

And it is.

As you laugh with happiness, your heart rate improves, your stress levels decrease, and your body starts kicking out those hormones and chemicals that reduce pain. Even your brain gets a good dose of stimulation of the right kind. Your lung capacity also gets better.

You start to heal.

Also, healing is your mental state. So, watch a comedy, share a good joke with friends or us, even laugh with young children. You won't ever regret it. It can even be bonding with these friends. For the sharing of laughter can also share love. A good thing isn't it? Yes!

Nothing wrong with being happy or laughing. Some people among you, who frown upon such, calling it frivolous and sinful. Psht! Nothing sinful at all. We Angels want you to be happy. The Divine gave you the ability to laugh and joke, and the Divine wants you to be joyful too. So those negative ones are missing out on the big picture.

You were born and made for laughter, joy, and fun. Yes, fun!. You can enjoy yourself freely. And yes, we too, enjoy a good funny joke. We do the same among ourselves. And we play harmless pranks on you and each other also. You see, you aren't unique in laughing; we all enjoy happy moments. You, we and the Divine. We want you to be joyful, and that's the facts.

Only those with a higher brain function can appreciate a joke. Don't expect a Sea Anemone or a Jellyfish to have one though. But your pets have that higher brain function, even a little squirrel has.

I've held you all up, dear ones. Enough. I do ramble sometimes. Have fun and laugh."

NB: Before this screed, I had been teasing Cassiel about hiding from me and avoiding giving out any messages. Next thing I know he had grabbed me by the shoulders and began reciting this message (and making cheeky comments at me between sentences).

***

10 SEPTEMBER 2015

Daily Message from the Angels and Ascended Masters.

A message from AA Gabriel:

"Take on what is new in your life, for we have placed them in your path for you to learn.

A trip overseas that you have often thought over? You have the means, but always putting it off. Why? Do it! Live it! And you'll never regret the new experiences, for they will enrich your mind.

There are many such examples of new paths or adventures -even new experiences. They are all placed in your way. Most of them are doorways to new paths. Some are lessons to help you grow forward.

Don't back off and say you can't do this, or you can't do that. We all know that those are fob off comments. Both of us know it -you and I. They do not wash with us.
Throw away such negativity and instead try something new. You may surprise yourself. If you don't like the experience, you don't have to stay there, and you can back off. But you can always say that you have tried it. Even if it is mountain climbing, camping, hang-gliding or such, you can then honestly admit you have been attempting it. It will give you a bit more respect for yourself, and you will by then realized that you were braver than you thought.
But then again, you may find such experiences fun. Good for you and feel free to enjoy yourself. We will help you with this

also. We don't expect you to over-reach yourself. Work within your capabilities, though; we don't want you to hurt yourself. So, don't go driving a 16-wheeler rig if you happen to be blind. Be sensible, please! ;)

Never give in to self-defeating regrets of lost opportunities. Instead, go for these opportunities. These 'regrets' are a form of negativity and can bring you down. If you have any, drop them and move on. Live for the now.

Well? Live it up!"

NB: Thanks for making me laugh, Gabriel.

***

23 SEPTEMBER 2015

A brief message from our friend AA Gabriel:

"Beloved ones, I am Gabriel. I need you to hear my word.

There are times when pressure and stress will get to you and affect your mindset. It is not good. I want you all to slow down and learn patience.

When things go wrong, look at what you are doing. You could be learning a lesson there. The teachings on tolerance - take heed of this lesson, for when things go wrong, it is because patience is part of your learning.

As you note this lesson, slow down and take your time. It is better to do a job that is perfect due to your patience than a rushed, messed up task. Always be patient as there are those around you who will test your patience. Just step back and let them learn for themselves that you are not someone to mess around.

Be calm, and you will find that through slowing down, your health will improve.

Of course, I am aware of emergencies. In those cases, you must call upon me to help you keep your mind clear, so that you may cope better. That is what I am there for, for you.

Now, I must let my channel go, for she is showing signs of tiring out.

Be well, dear ones, and keep up with the laughter."

***

26 SEPTEMBER 2015

A bit of wisdom from AA Emmanuel:

"When others take to judging you without knowing you, then be assured you are on the right path and doing the right thing. Those who aren't on their properway are jealous and will try to pull you back to their level.

Instead, pass by with your head held high and a smile on your face. You are going places, my child, and they are not. Besides, when you smile and move on, you have risen above the haters there and then."

***

28 SEPTEMBER 2015

A brief message from AA Michael:

"How about this for you to note. Instead of saying 'I wish I could do...' or 'I'd like to try this sometime': Do it!

Procrastination does not solve problems but can create them. Do them, and you can always say you have done this or that and feel satisfied because you have. You have experienced something that would usually be held at a distance by you.

Stop making excuses for yourself to others. You are not in this world to please others; you are here to live for yourself and learn — less of the delaying tactics and more action. You'll be surprised at what you can do, and you might even relish it.

All of you, get out there and LIVE your life to the fullest, it's more fun."

***

OCTOBER 2015

1 OCTOBER 2015

Daily Message from the Angels and Ascended Masters.

A message from AA Gabriel:

"I wish to you heavens Grace and Joy in your life. You all deserve to be free and filled with love for your family, friends, and yourself.

Let go what does not serve you, whether object or person. If they no longer help you, leave it for someone else to take on.
Ignore the barbs and hurtful words of jealous people. They wish what you have got but are not willing to get up and go for it themselves — their loss, not yours.

Stride forward with your head held high. You are more than you think you are. You think you are kind, friendly, pleasant and content. You are and more.
Some of you think less of yourselves too. Some of you think you are unworthy, forgotten, sad, and insecure. You ARE NOT! You ARE more.

We think each one of you is equal. You are all worth it and deserve every little bit of Divine LOVE. No matter what your position or role in your life is, no matter how small or big, you are all one in the Divine's eyes. You are all precious beyond jewels.

You are beautiful.

We do not care about monetary riches, high fashion, or other mundane, shallow subjects. We care about your soul, your love, your happiness, and above all, we care about YOU!

Yes, YOU in all your original form, spiritually and emotionally.

It's all about YOU. And that will never change, no matter what happens around you and others.

That is all that matters in reality: YOU!

So be happy and be assured in that we want you to be satisfied in the best possible way. It doesn't take much, you know.

Live your life the way you feel is best for you spiritually, and you will find riches heading your way. And don't be surprised if we 'meddle' with a miracle or two. We want the best for you all the time.

Enough, I need to let you all go and enjoy your life as the way you wish it. Have fun!

Be well, dear ones. Be well!"

***

2 OCTOBER 2015

Daily Message from the Angels and Ascended Masters.

A Message from AA Azrael:

"Hail to you from deep within my heart. I speak to you from far away, and my message to you all is this.

Do not fear what loves you the most. Too many times, I have seen you back away from those that wish you nothing but love. Some even deny our existence, saying we're a myth.

We are not!

We are real, and we often walk on your world among you. You don't see us because we wish you not to see us. But sometimes we allow ourselves to become visible. There are still those who avert eyes and hide.

No more!

It is about time you looked around you and see that we are in fact, surrounding you.
We wish you no harm, only friendship.

Those who call upon our Ultimate Parent to condemn other people who don't share the same views:

Shame on you!

Our Divine parent will never respond to those requests. And the reason why? You are ALL the Divine's children. You are ALL loved. No matter what or who you are. YOU ARE LOVED. Therefore, I say, never fear us. We are always there for you, but only in a protective, nurturing role. We won't fight your battles for you, but we will protect you from those who send harmful thoughts your way.

We want you all to accept us, the way we do to you. There's no need to run away because you can't hide from us.

I shall also say this; there will soon come a time when you will need us significantly. Things are changing on your world, and you are changing with it. Don't fight it, instead accept it. It will be easier for you if you go with the flow. It won't last forever, but there are significant changes to happen. No, not the end of the world. Just the beginning.
It will happen, and nothing you can do will stop it. Don't bother worrying about it. Just accept it.

Child, it is now time for release, and I shall leave you with this thought. Nothing can stop you, and no one wants to. You have our support and always will. We will help you when you need us. I love you, and so do my siblings. Just call on us, and we shall hear.

Farewell for now."

***

3 OCTOBER 2015

Daily Message from the Angels and Ascended Masters.

A Message from AA Michael:

"Dance as if you have all your love put into it.
Sing as if your heart was full of music.
Laugh as if the light of the Divine was coursing through you.
Love as if it was coming from an unlimited source because it all is.

All these good things are there within you, and only you can show them out to the world. So why don't you?

If you need help in expressing your real beautiful self, then call upon Archangel Jophiel, who is the Angel of Beauty. Because these feelings are delicate and upon releasing them, you free them into your world. What a lovely sight it is, seeing your inner divine Spark grow so large and with such colors!! So beautiful that it makes us sing with joy with you.
Jophiel can help you with this and more.

That is all I wish to impart to you all and listen to this final word from me: I love you!

Be well!"

***

4 OCTOBER 2015

Daily Message from the Angels and Ascended Masters.

A Message from AA Michael:

"Do you know what it's like to feel the golden light of the Divine course through you? I shall tell you how you can do this.

Go into your meditation spot, where you can't be disturbed.

Now inhale and exhale a few times deeply, and then visualize roots growing out of your feet and into the Earth below, going deeper and deeper.

Envision the golden light coming down from above you and connecting to your Crown Chakra. Carry on visualizing this and keep up with the breathing.

During this, envision the golden light pouring through your lungs as you breathe, and at the same time, it's going through your Crown Chakra.

See that golden light pouring through your entire body from your head to your arms and hands. Then 'see' the golden light pour down to your legs and down to your feet.
Let the golden light pour through your feet out into the Earth below through the roots you have grown there.

Now keep the golden light flowing through you from top to bottom and infiltrating every cell in your body. Yes, that's right. Every cell will react, and you will feel this light course through you.

Soak up as much as you want of this golden light until you feel you have had enough. That is the moment when you slowly retract the golden light from the Earth, through your body and draw it upwards. Then withdraw this light from your Crown Chakra.

Close your Crown Chakra, by envisioning it closing like a door. Yes, by allowing the light through your Crown Chakra you opened it.

Withdraw the roots you have formed with the Earth, absorbing them back within you. Then gently come back out of meditation.

Thank the Divine for showering you with the healing golden light of divine love. This light is free for all, and you can bask in it whenever you wish and as often too.

Tell me, how do you feel?

I know what your answer is, but these answers are for everyone to see that you are all different, and you all react differently. That way, no one gets any hang-ups.

That is all my dear ones."

***

5 OCTOBER 2015

Daily Message from the Angels and Ascended Masters.

A Message from AA Chamuel:

"How many times do we all have to say we love you? Hm?

We tell you all the time, and yet you don't seem to listen. You rush headlong into assumptions and situations. Despite all that chaos, we keep on telling you.

Maybe it's time you all took a moment to stop and listen to us for once. And listen with your heart, not your ears. You will hear our love for you and feel it too.

Take time out of your busy day to listen to your heart and soul. Take the time and be honest with yourself and be frank.

You are all a piece in the universal jigsaw puzzle. When alone, you don't make much of a noise, but together, you all stronger and fulfill your part in this universe.

Therefore, we keep telling you that we love you. We see that bigger picture and know that humanity is the strongest when it joins together. That is one of your greatest strengths. You have more to add to it, and I won't explain it because you all know what it is.

Love.
Courage.
Intuition.
Family.
Friendship.

All those and more.

That is all I need to say because by now, you have gotten my drift.

Be well, dear ones."

***

6 OCTOBER 2015

Daily Message from the Angels and Ascended Masters.

A Message from AA Raphael:

"In peace, may you rest and wait.
In peace, may your love be patient.
In peace, may your light glow softly.
In peace, may your mind sing its lullaby.
In peace, may your body heal within.
In peace, may your Soul grow forth.
In peace, may your dreams come true.
In peace, may your words soothe the fire.
In peace, may your hands caress the lost.
In peace, may your prayer be heard.
In peace, may your eyes rest on life.
In peace, may your truth dispel the lie.
In peace, may your knowledge help all.
In peace, may your work be a pleasure.
In peace, may your ears hear us.
In peace, may your actions bring relief.
In peace, may your path be smooth.
In peace, may your voice be clear.
In peace, may you experience true peace.

Be well in peace, my dear ones, for such peace is something we all want and need."

***

7 OCTOBER 2015

Daily Message from the Angels and Ascended Masters.

A Message from AA Raphael:

"I see a lot of discontent over what you don't have, and other material wants. It's not necessary. You have all you need to grow in your life. You do not need the latest fashion accessory. You do not require such ego-building fads. You need yourself.

Just because an item has the latest top brand name, doesn't mean that you need it. Instead, ignore it.

You have what you need in yourself.
You have your self-confidence, your mind, your strength, and spirit.
You have us.
You have the Divine.

You do not need the materialistic ego-stroking. The only people who benefit from that are the people who sell these items.

Look around you. You have your world, and it is beautiful. That is more important. Look in a mirror; you too are essential.

Fads come and go, and none are necessary. Food and ordinary clothing are. Labels are not required, but common sense is. Think about what I mean.

Be well"

***

9 OCTOBER 2015

Daily Message from the Angels and Ascended Masters.

A Message from AA Michael:

"Wishing brings forth the dreams of potentials. Choose which one to follow.
Loving brings forth the possibilities of new friends. Choose which one to allow to come close.
Laughing brings forth joys of life. Choose someone to share the joke.

Meditation brings forth harmonies. Choose which tune to live in you.

Living brings forth new adventures. Choose which one to create a fresh start.

Friendship brings forth closeness. Choose the correct friend.

All these involve choices, and your preferences make your path to your future.

You wish to sit back and do nothing, your choice.

Do you wish to get involved? Your choice.

That is one of the many things about you that we protect and nurture. Free Will. You have it, use it. In doing so, expect things to happen. Good or bad, it's still your choice. Choose carefully and wisely.

Be well, dear ones."

***

10 OCTOBER 2015

Daily Message from the Angels and Ascended Masters.

A Message from AA Ariel:

"There are times when you feel you can't take any more in life and feeling lonely. The darkness of the mood takes you further downhill.

We feel sorrow when such a mood takes you. For it means you have forgotten about one thing: YOU ARE NEVER ALONE.

Instead of going into the black hole of despair, let us pull you out. Ask us to sit with you. Talk to us as if we are your closest friends because we are.

Where others ditch you or run away from you, we will stand beside you.

When others don't listen, we will stop and hear your voice.
Where there is no one for you to turn to, we will be there.
When you fall, we will pick you up.

We are always with you through thick and thin.

Talk to us. Laugh and share jokes with us. Lean on us. We are loyal to you and always will be, from beginning to end.
And the reason why? It's because we love you, unconditionally!

Let us wrap our love around you."

***

11 OCTOBER 2015

Daily Message from the Angels and Ascended Masters.

A Message from AA Michael:

"Beautiful ones, I have seen you all do many beautiful things today. Some have found new love, and that I found to be such sweetness to the heart. Some have explored your place in nature and relished every moment of it. Those who discovered their new gifts of Spirit? My, how your faces lit up when you opened them up.

And there are the ones who despite heartbreak and sorrow, have smiled at an innocent child laughing. In doing so, their hearts have begun to heal.

You are such beautiful people, and what wonders you have created for yourselves. Yes, you all make my heart sing with joy when you open to new adventures. It's all part and parcel of humanity. The three "L's": Learn, Love, and Live.

I too learn from you all. I have discovered that humans are resilient and robust. I also love you all. And as for the "Live" part? I live for you all and savor all your experiences.

I love you all, dear ones. I love you all in all your many phases and moods.

I am yours to talk to, my beloved kin. I am yours.

Be well."

***

13 OCTOBER 2015

Daily Message from the Angels and Ascended Masters.

A Message from AA Azrael:

"Do you wish to grow into our divine parent's light?
Do you wish to develop what gifts you have?
Do you want your divine light to grow further into this world of yours?
Do you wish to nourish your world with your love?

You can.

You do this with a straightforward thing.

You need to invite us into your life in all areas. And let us guide you.
Listen to us with your heart, not with your ears.
Follow what direction we give you, for we will want you to have the best in life.
But most importantly; let us be at your side.

When you have a decision to make, use us as a sounding board, and we will guide you to make the best decision of your choosing.

We are your teachers, mentors, and part of your spiritual family. Inviting us into your life makes our family stronger because we will be part of each other.

That is all I need to say, for you know that our love for you all is never-ending and remains so.

Be well, dear ones."

***

14 OCTOBER 2015

Daily Message from the Angels and Ascended Masters.

A Message from AA Anael:

"Be patient in your lives, for things are happening around your world. It is a time of changes and new beginnings. So, patience is required. Some of the changes will involve you, and we need you to be aware of what is going on. It means no distractions. If you try to hide from what is about to happen? Expect headaches or feelings of nausea. These changes involve cleansing, upgrading, and growth. Your energy is going to change with it too.

At the end of the changes, you may feel like as if you're full of energy and bubbling with new thoughts.

The best way to process this energy is to let it happen, open yourselves to it, and that way; it is quickly done and over.

You are all going to have this change happening to you all. Yes, even your pets will feel this. Every living creature in your world is going to feel the results, and there are also changes happening on your planet, and you'll never expect it.

Civilizations come and go, but yours is going to change. It needs to change or become extinct. And changing your mindset about what a 3D society wants, to a world that is evolving out of the 3D state is the best start. Old ideas and lifestyles will change. New beginnings are inevitable.

Expect new ideas, inventions and the new people that are coming. They are from far away and will visit. Yes, you are going to grow beyond your Solar System.

Enough, this is all I needed to say. For it is all that there is to say. Be prepared, be rested, and be your true self.

Be well."

***

15 OCTOBER 2015

Daily Message from the Angels and Ascended Masters.

A Message from AA Ambriel:

"You are all aspects of the Divine, just like we are. You have all the emotions and knowledge we have too, but we only let you touch the edges of it. The feelings can be powerful and can wend their way around the planet, overpowering the wills of others. We cannot let you have full access to it. Free will for ALL is essential.

The knowledge is there too, but again we can only let you touch bits of it. If we were to release all the knowledge to you, your minds would not take it. Only your Spirit Mind can comprehend it, not your physical brain.

It is the same way when we help you or heal you. A little bit at a time or your body gets overwhelmed. That's when the cure is worse than the illness. Your body breaks down if healing is too quick.

Help is also slow and steady. If it happens all at once, it could derail the path of life for the entire world. All things happen at their own pace and time. No faster or slower. Just the right speed.

So please, we won't rush things just because you want instant results. That's one decision that is not yours to make. You must be patient.

The Divine is patient, so must you. The Divine has been patient with us all, and you must be patient with yourselves. You are, after all, part of the divine will, just like us. And so, we must work together at our own pace. And when whatever you are working on comes to fruition at the right time, doesn't it feel fantastic.

I shall leave you with that knowledge that you must practice patience if you wish perfection in whatever you do.

Be well."

***

17 OCTOBER 2015

Daily Message from the Angels and Ascended Masters.

A Message from AA Michael:

"Generous people, you give so much of your love and joy to us, and we wish to repay you in same. We give you our adoration, and we want you to have joy in your life too. We want your life full of love and happiness, so we are going to make sure that you receive all this.

We want you to stand up and open your hearts, mind, and soul to us. And how? Just tell us and show your love. That is all we need — your willingness to receive.

You give out love and receive it back from us threefold. That is the right side of Karma.

We are ever willing to help you grow and open to the many wonders of your universe. Your universe is much bigger than you think. Much, much bigger. Your 3D part is only a tiny fraction of it.

Oh, how much we want to show you the magnificence of the Universe in whole. The power and its glory, and the one who created this Universe aremore significant than the Universe itself: The Divine. For the entire Universe is within the Divine. So are you, just like part of the Divine is within you.

I await the time with anticipation when we can all meet, and we can show you the sights of miracles. But we are patient, and your race has still got a little bit more growing to do, but not much.

I shall now say farewell for now and let you consider my words.

Be well, dear ones."

***

18 OCTOBER 2015

Daily Message from the Angels and Ascended Masters.

A Message from El Morya:

"Will you walk in my light?
Will you walk in my footsteps?
Will you heal what I would have healed?
Will you talk with my words?
Will you love what I have loved?

Will you?

I ask you to do this for it is for your benefit that you do so. These are the steps of my life and the divine will.

I wish you to take forth the hands of those who have struggled and help them stand up in the light.

I need you to step away from what is harming you and move into the divine love.

I wish you to be there to receive the light of divine grace.

No matter where you are or what you are, you are all beautiful in the eyes of our divine parent. We are the Divine's children, and it is about time you knew it. You are not riff-raff, useless, stupid, or ugly. You are not worthless or weak. You are all equal in the Divine's eyes, and those eyes are full of love for you.

As with any parent, the Divine sees you as beautiful, perfect, durable, and intelligent. Now you must believe it so because you are all that the Divine says you are, and more. So please, do not put yourself down or others. Instead, listen, accept differences, acknowledge, and step into the light. Nothing simpler. Tolerance goes a long way, but never lose yourself to other people browbeating you. Be yourself, for there is nothing more perfect than that.

I shall now leave my channel so that you may dwell on my words.

Farewell for now."

***

19 OCTOBER 2015

Daily Message from the Angels and Ascended Masters.

A Message from AA Metatron:

"I am here to explain what is going on with your world. Yes, I hear some of you say, "Finally!"

All your wars, conflicts, earthquakes, and even other disasters are all linked together by one cause: Your world is starting to evolve, to change.

Your old societies and standards are no longer able to cope and adapt, as the changes are too significant. It is now time for your cities, and people to change with it.

It is a scary time for those who don't know the reason, and the only way they can cope is by fear. And scared people act without idea or thought. That's why times are changing, and those who can change must help those who are frightened by the whole process. That is when new leaders will develop; modern humans can produce.

It is a time of change, and the old materialism of your ancient world is to be changed. A new world of Spiritualism isn't an evil place. It's peaceful, enriching and beautiful.

Time to change, and I don't mean clothing.

See you all on the light side of life."

***

20 OCTOBER 2015

Daily Message from the Angels and Ascended Masters.

A Message from AA Sandalphon:

"You who are waiting for what you deem to be the resurrection, think again. No such thing. What you are waiting for is the fruition of all your questions about life and death, and the world beyond. That is the real meaning of "Resurrection."
That the dead will not rise again, but, it is the long-extinct knowledge of your ancestors will be brought back to life.
The writer who wrote that was a simple man and had no concept of the world you live in now. His world was primitive, and that was all he knew.

You should not take all that is written in the Bible as literal, for they were again written by a simple people who wrote what they had heard from generations past, and then added their prejudices and views. And in times after that, each succession of rulers and religious leaders have had that same Bible rewritten to suit their own beliefs, and in turn, enhance their power over others.

Instead, accept the Bible as a journal of what has happened, but always have the thought in mind that not all is as it seems as it has changed by successive rulers. Yes, things have gotten lost in the translation, you could say. The actual knowledge is known by us and deep within your soul. It will guide you just like we do.

Trust in your true self and trust in your soul. It wants you to succeed and learn. It wants you to be happy. It is of the light, and therefore subject to the divine will. Yes, it knows the truth and will help you discern truth from what is in front of you.

You are the truth.
You are the will.
You are part of the One.

You are belonging.

The Akashic Records are never wrong, and you do have access to them. Some already know how to access these records, and some are yet to learn. But you will have access when the time is right.

Enough, be true to your self and seek within the truth. You know what is right and wrong, it is instilled in you. If you still have problems there, ask your Higher Self or us. We will help.

I shall leave you now so that you may search for the truth within.

Look in the mirror and look into your own eyes."

***

21 OCTOBER 2015

Daily Message from the Angels and Ascended Masters.

A message from Ascended Master Hilarion:

"When you think you know all of what is going on in your world, you prove to yourself you have learned nothing. Knowledge is more than what is in books and movies. Your very own actions and life are part of your learning process. And you still have a future hidden from you. So, you can't have learned everything.

To learn everything is to know the future in all its entirety, and the human mind is not yet ready for that. For the future encompasses the Universe and more.

You have learned very little. Be thankful for that, for it means that though you haven't determined much, there is still mystery and surprises. And there's a whole Universe out there to explore. You could say life would be rather dull if you knew everything, Hm? Only the Divine knows all, and only the Divine can do that.

Accept the fact that you all don't know everything, but instead, you all know a part of the knowledge of your world and a bit beyond. Join those parts together like a jigsaw puzzle, and you will find that your world has many more fascinating and beautiful mysteries you have yet to discover.

It's the discovery of new objects and ideas that bring a spark to everyone. You people are after all, incredibly curious and that's a good thing. To seek out knowledge is to grow with experience.

Now we don't mind the curiosity of your fellows, just if it doesn't interfere with other people's personal lives. Once you start poking around there, you will find yourself becoming rather unpopular with your fellows. So, a bit of restraint there goes a long, long way.

Learn and digest. Absorb and use.

Be well."

***

22 OCTOBER 2015

Daily Message from the Angels and Ascended Masters.

A Message from AA Uriel:

"I wish to have a little word with you all. Someone mentioned that Angels do not have souls. Well, we are beings that are beyond the Soul level. A higher vibrational level.
We have our equivalent. Yours is your Soul. Ours is the Grace that the Divine used to make us be.

What you have is a Soul made from the divine light. It's a form of Grace.

Ours is made that way too, but it's of higher energy. As we keep telling you, we are kin. We are no different from you, just different vibrating frequencies.

We too feel emotions, but without certain flaws that could hamper them. We do not feel hatred, andit is not needed either. We don't have it. We can love, but ours has no strings attached and free for all. We are without judgment and flaws. We are parts of the Divine. Your Soul is the same.

Remember what I said? We Are KIN. We have the same ultimate parent. We are your family.

And as for your Guardian Angels? They are your Life Partners. Do you realize what that means? It means they are there for you, any time you want them. You can speak to them whenever you want. They are there.
Also, when a Guardian Angel watches over two separate Souls, it is because these Souls forever joined to each other is far beyond the knowledge of your world. Far, far deeper.

There is an explanation, but you are not ready for it yet. If I told it to you now, it would confuse you. But some of you are starting to get that inkling. It is far more profound than Twin Souls or Twin Flames as you call them.

Enough. Let it be for now."

***

23 OCTOBER 2015

Daily Message from the Angels and Ascended Masters.

A Message from AA Raphael:

"This is a message to all of you.

Ears open!

Now, I have noticed a lot of people sitting around in front of a computer and doing little else. Your bodies were not made to sit around and be still; you were made to run, walk, and explore your world and to enjoy yourself.

Back away from your computers and cell phones, and instead walk in the garden, look around town and move around. Take exercise by doing a few aerobics or a jog on the spot; you need to move.

You need to move and keep moving. Make it fun. It is all part of your health and to improve it. A body that is doing nothing belongs to someone who is missing out a significant portion of life. And that portion involves you getting out and revel in the wonders that the Divine made for you in your world.

Of course, some cannot do all this for very different reasons and would love to do move about but unable to do so. We understand and instead ask you to instead, fly with your mind and explore the world within it. Use your imagination to expand your world and realize that your dreams are part of another world altogether.

Exercise! Exercise! Exercise! Off your bums and move your feet.

A person who gets out and becomes aware of their world, becomes fitter physically, emotionally, and mentally.

I have a reason to ask this of you all; it will come more apparent to yourselves as time goes by, and without any help from me. It will be your knowledge that you have learned for yourself. Ask me to give you the motivation if you find yourself lagging a bit. Hmm? I shall wait."

(After this I noticed Raphael grinning at me and a glint of mischief in his eye. Yes, I tend to plonk my rear in front of a computer and do nothing else. *grumbles*)

***

24 OCTOBER 2015

Daily Message from the Angels and Ascended Masters.

A Message from AA Michael:

"I like to say this. There is a time when you must be alone, so that you may communicate with your Soul and the Divine with clarity. For this is the time to join with all and let them participate within you in the name of love and healing. It is necessary for those who live a hectic life. So just being alone is a rare moment for them. But you must make the time, and it doesn't have to take long. Fifteen minutes is nothing.

You must do this to communicate with your inner self and for your mental stability. All are dependent on you keeping focused. Don't worry about tasks that are waiting. They're not as important as you are. This moment of rest is needed, so take it.

Relax and partake of the benefits of what meditation and reflection can give you.

There are times for joy, fun, and happiness, and you also need your rest. All contribute to your good mental and physical health.

I shall leave for now, and please practice balance and stability in your life in rest and activity."

***

25 OCTOBER 2015

Daily Message from the Angels and Ascended Masters.

A Message from AA Orion:

"Acknowledge the divine Spark within yourself. Give it the voice it needs and say out loud: 'I AM!' Those two little words mean the Universe shifts as the Divine one accepts your divine light into its realm of love.

It is not given willingly to all, for the only way one can get there, is by saying those two little words as is, with no added words. 'I AM.'

Those two words are potent. So powerful, that it can create changes within you. Changes right to the very core. They are the words of empowerment and strength.

As you say those two words, BELIEVE in them. 'I AM' is a sign of pure sentience and definition. Those words will make you steadfast and repeat them at times when you are under pressure from others. Believe in them.

Those two words are the words of strength, power, believe, and intelligence. Please trust in them, the Divine, and yourself. Considering those words, will, in turn, make you understand more in yourself, your spirit, and your confidence.

Words of power, I say.

I shall say these words with you: I AM. And indeed, I know I am.

Be blessed."

NB: this is the first time Orion has used me as a channel. I've met Orion before during meditation, but not for channeling. He has got the potent energy which nearly rocked me — good thing AA Michael had been holding onto my shoulders at the time, softening the powers.

***

26 OCTOBER 2015

Daily Message from the Angels and Ascended Masters.

A Message from Ascended Master Sananda Jesus:

"Will you understand when I ask you to let go of what is hurting you now? Do you realize what I am asking you to do?

I am asking you to remove what is no longer serving you. It means objects and people. Those who no longer help you or are now distancing themselves from you, are now heading on a separate path from yours. They are moving on. You are being asked to move on also onto your new path.

These other people have done their job in bringing you so far on your new path, at which they are unconsciously handing you to us so that we can help you further. Our help involves new people in your life who can help you. Even a modern lifestyle can be part of it.

It is all part of what I meant when I asked you to let go and move on. It has many names. Some of those names are Growth, Ascendancy, and Fate. All the same.

I ask you this with all my love, and I wouldn't want you to feel pressured to do this. Hence, I asked. Whether you heed the request is up to you, for I will never force you.

Be in the light."

***

27 OCTOBER 2015

Daily Message from the Angels and Ascended Masters.

A Message from AA Gabriel:

"Beloved ones, remember who you are in the Great Scheme of things. Remember your place in the Universe and don't even try to worm your way out of it. You have a responsibility to be where you are and stay there. Know your position.
And what is it that I sound so stern about, hm? Don't worry.

Who you are in the grandscheme of things is that of Light-Workers, and future Ascended Ones.

Your place in the Universe is that of a child of the Divine. And you can't worm your way out that as all were born to be the Divine's children.

Your responsibility is to love, love, and more love to yourselves, each other, the Divine parent and your world.

Your position is to be in the arms of the Divine as the Divine embraces you with love.

Now, doesn't that sound more like it. Hmmm? Thought I would catch a few out with that. ;)

Be well, dear ones."

***

28 OCTOBER 2015

Daily Message from the Angels and Ascended Masters.

A Message from The Divine:

"When you walk into my light, you are bathing in its constant rays of love.
You are walking with me in your heart.
You are walking with my other children, your Angelic brethren.

Never alone, and ever-loving, you will shine under my light.

How do I know this? I have seen it so many times myself that I have lost count. But then again, who is counting?

I have seen races and cities come and go, each one part of their path of destiny. Some roads were dead ends, but these races had selected that path, not realizing it had no progress in it. And that lack of progress was their demise. Other people had grown forward and stronger, and they exploited the lack of pace in that other branches of humanity that were left behind.

Sad, but it was necessary, they couldn't evolve. Those races who managed to accept the change and adapt, evolved, and they have grown brighter within. That is necessary and yet beautiful. You are all so adaptable when you put your minds to it.

As for the cities? If they can't change or adapt, they too get lost in the sands of time, making way for more changes in the future.

As it is with all things in this Universe, change is a constant, it is always around you and is part of your life in such a big way, and you can't exist without it. Yes, it is part of you. And change is what I want, to help you grow and learn. Ever-changing is your

world; you are too. And I am triggering those changes, as any good parent would do, to enrich your life and make you stronger.
Strength comes in many forms, don't forget that either.

That is what makes you so unique; you are growing and learning. Your world is changing with you, and you are evolving with your world. You both cannot stay still, accept that. And enjoy the ride.

Be well, my little ones. Be well."

***

29 OCTOBER 2015

Daily Message from the Angels and Ascended Masters.

A Message from Angel Ahdziel:

"Well, things have come to a point. You have many choices ahead of you, but the one we most recommend is the one to save your world. Yes, your world.

Stop the wars and violence. Instead, concentrate on bringing your world back to what it was. Your climate is changing because you are decimating the world for materials, and you are overcrowding it. So many trees have died, so many forests doomed, and your air quality is getting weaker.
Pollution does play a part in it, but the trees are the ones that are helping you to breathe. You cut them down.

You buy many things for yourself, all worldly goods. Not one will help your world, instead of thinking of material goods like gold, diamonds, and other unnecessary trash. Think of what you can do to make your world beautiful again.

More trees are an example. Let the forests grow again and bring back creatures from the brink of extinction. Once gone, they remain gone. There's no going back then.

Leave the diamonds, oil, and gold in the ground where it belongs. They are only stones, sludge, and metal. Your world has more valuable items than those — for example, its wildlife, plants, insects, coral reefs. Oh, I could go on. But it all comes down to this. Look after your world, or you will lose it.

Extinction for ALL is a possibility.

We are working on trying to stop that, but we do need you to pull your finger out and contribute to the well-being of your world. No just sitting around and expecting others to do the work for you. Life doesn't work that way.

No, we don't want you all to leave us. We want you to live with us because we live with you. Please don't ruin the only world you have.

We ask this of you.

Be well."

NB: Ahdziel is a new one to me. Michael had wrapped his arms around me and told me to brace myself. I did, and Ahdziel came through in a rush. His energy is powerful, making me rock in my seat. He was a tad annoyed with everyone. I also got the impression that he could be one of the Destroying Angels. As he finished his message, he began to relax more and became rather chatty.

***

30 OCTOBER 2015

Daily Message from the Angels and Ascended Masters.

A Message from AA Gabriel:

"Every decision you make is accompanied by changes. You see, before you were born, your soul agreed with us, their Guardian Angels and Spirit Guides to living in a set form of existence. It could be in a poverty setting or affluent. But they do agree for certain events to happen to them so that they can learn from the situation. Don't grumble at what straws you have drawn for yourself, your choice.
Your Soul has agreed to leave many choices open for later decisions by your physical self -your Ego.

That is when a lot of your lessons start.

Those choices remain open until you come across one on your path of Life and Destiny. And when you meet one, you can recognize it by the different directions each one will take you. That is when you choose what you want in life. Some prefer an event that seems reasonable at first but could be, in turn, a long path of hardship and sorrow.
Others choose a path that seems to be a bit risky and find to their surprise that it is quicker and more enlightening than they thought.

All choices are paths, and all roads are the result of your selections. You have many options and many ways. They are all placed there so that you can choose your lessons in life, as was agreed before you were born.

All we can do is respect your choices, and if necessary, give a helping hand if you find yourself lost. In that case, ask us to guide you, and we will. Sometimes we will even take it upon ourselves to remove obstacles that could stop you before it becomes apparent.

You don't need to ask us for that; it's all part of your path. And a lot to do with Love.

I considered I would give you a brief explanation as to how you choose your paths and choices.

Be well, sweethearts."

***

31 OCTOBER 2015

Daily Message from the Angels and Ascended Masters.

A Message from AA Gabriel:

"Have you ever felt the sensations of a hand gently stroking your head, and there is no one there? Well, it could be one of two things: Your Spirit Guides or us.

If you have been talking about spirits, guides, and other spiritual matters, then your guides will do this. It simply means they want to bring your attention to them. They wish to talk to you.

As simple as that.

But if you have been speaking of Angels, then you can be sure it is us. We're not trying to talk to you as your soul already hears us. We are showing love.

Again, simple as that.

Don't go flapping your arms or rubbing your head frantically, with your imagination going wild at the thought of insects or spiders in your hair. It's only us playing with your hair or stroking it.

Now if the sensation starts to feel like there's hands pressing on your head, and there's the sensation of pressure. Again, don't worry. We are downloading information into you to prepare you for your next step. It's all part of the learning process. Though in some cases, this process will give some of the receivers an intense migraine headache.

It gives us pleasure to provide you with our love this way. It's just a little something to remind you that we are with you. That's all. Now, does that short explanation help you with that sensation? Hmmm?

Be well."

***

NOVEMBER 2015

1 NOVEMBER 2015

Daily Message from the Angels and Ascended Masters.

A Message from AA Cassiel:

"While all is in chaos around you, and others may try to rouse your ire. Remain distant from it all and never let it enter your heart. Stand back and let it pass you by and never let it be part of your life.

Instead, walk on by with peace and tranquillity in your heart and let all the negativity wash away by the light.

You are that source of light, and you will let that negativity fall to the ground and be left behind.

You are a better person when you refuse to let it try to control you. That is when you become the stronger one, and the weak won't be able to work its lies on you.

Yes, negativity is the weak, and only people who allow others to control them have no resistance to it. That is why I ask you to be steadfast in the light and BE the light. Then negativity will never have any power over you, no matter what form it takes.

That is all I wish to say. Nothing else, it's enough for what I had wanted to pass on.

Be well."

***

2 NOVEMBER 2015

Daily Message from the Angels and Ascended Masters.

A Message from AA Chamuel:

"Why don't you:

Sing out loud and with pleasure.
Dance to the radio when you want.
Laugh at a good joke just because you enjoyed it.
Read an excellent, gripping book that will make your imagination take flight.
Enjoy the company of best friends that brighten your day.
Play with a child at each opportunity.
Learn a hobby and make it a pleasure.
Dream your dreams so that you can make them real.

All this and more I ask of you and enjoy every bit of it.

Why do I ask?

Why not!

Life is for living, making your life full of all the pleasant things. And you deserve them all.
These are all around you and are available around the clock. These are all free, take as much as you want any time.

Be well, dear ones."

NB: During this message, I felt drowsy, so I shook my head. Chamuel then flicked back: "Don't shake your head; something may fall out of it!" The cheek!!!

***

3 NOVEMBER 2015

Daily Message from the Angels and Ascended Masters.

A Message from AA Michael:

"I dare you!

I dare you to hug a stranger.
I dare you to share a joke.
I dare you to love yourself.
I dare you to embrace the light.
I dare you to sing to your heart's delight.

I dare you, dear ones.

I dare you to have fun.
I dare you to walk with nature.

Yes, I dare you.

The reason why? To get you out of your rut and to make you think outside the box.

I want you to explore beyond your limits and see what you have been missing. Things that were in front of your very nose the entire time.

I want you to be free, alive, and healthy. I want you to be yourselves. No longer hidden by others, not restrained by the prejudices of society, and open to love.

Be free my little birds. You are more precious than you realize. We know the secret of human origins, but you are all not ready yet. Be free in the knowledge that you are more than just human. We are a family.

Be well, dear ones, be well."

***

4 NOVEMBER 2015

Daily Message from the Angels and Ascended Masters.

A Message from AA Raphael:

"Just when you think you know it all? Ah, think again. You only see the surface of what is going on around your world. And even less of what goes on in your Universe.
There are worlds that at this moment beyond your reach. Dimensions that are forever sealed from your physical self, only allowing your spirit form to visit.
There is much out there that is far beyond your current level of education.

I can say this, for you to learn all this knowledge will take at least billions of your years, and only the Divine One has that knowledge. You are not at that level yet!

Learn what you have available, and of what's around you. It all helps, no matter how small it may seem to you. Yes, no matter how small. You may think it is trivial and not worth knowing, well guess again, it is worth it. A little knowledge can go a long way.
Learn what you can and make it fun to learn. Enjoyment and pleasure make the lesson easier to absorb. Boredom is the opposite.

Make your lessons enjoyable to yourself and others. You can't go wrong there. It will be better for you in the end, for an open mind is a mind that will advance the furthest.

Be well and learn with laughter.

Raphael"

***

5 NOVEMBER 2015

Daily Message from the Angels and Ascended Masters.

A somewhat confusing message from Ascended Master Melchizedek:

"When you walk the path of light, you are walking in thesight of the Divine.
The Divine sees you and will give you the strength and courage to carry on with your journey. You will receive the love and understanding that comes at each stage of your path,and you will never walk alone. Some will walk with you. The Angels and their friends, the Ascended Ones will walk with you.

The Divine has made sure you are always watched over and never left alone and lost. You do not deserve that fate, and no one else either deserves it. All will be watched over, loved, and nurtured.
You are the ones that are alone in your world, but others are coming. Alone no longer, and soon, all will be one.

Let the ghost rise above and cover your world; let the Divine show your world what is beyond your own. The Holy Ghost is one with you all. Let it fly and embrace your world with protection and love.

You will be all one. Alone, never! We are one, you are one, and forever we are all under the One. We are for each other, we are your friends and family, we are your beloved, and you are ours. Yes, never alone.

Be well dearest ones; I have had to say what I have said, for it was necessary. Words of light can be confusing to those not ready for it but will make sense to those who know of what is coming.

Soon all is revealed.

It is the prophecy.

I am Melchizedek"

***

6 NOVEMBER 2015

Daily Message from the Angels and Ascended Masters.

A Message from AA Gabriel:

"Hold on to your dreams. For they are all yours to cherish, visualize and work to make right. All yours, my dear ones. All yours.

You can do wonders with those dreams, and if you want it to be real, all you got to do is step up, step out, and work your way to it. Yes, work it. Some dream big, but don't do anything about it. They expect all handed to them for nothing. Well, it doesn't work that way. We help those who help themselves. We work with those who will work with us.

It's a two-way thing, and it always has been. Do nothing and get nothing. Do something, expect something back. Simple as that. Actions do speak louder than words, and aren't words just noises? Activities are motivation, intent, and conclusion.

Works much faster I would say.

Well, what's stopping you, Hmm? Yes, you are stopping yourself when you do nothing. So, don't blame others or the Divine. Blame yourself. Take responsibility and make things work for yourself. Take control of your own life and destiny and do something. Act!

Enough, I think my gist has come across.

Be well dearest ones."

***

7 NOVEMBER 2015

Daily Message from the Angels and Ascended Masters.

A Message from AA Haniel:

"Let's do something different. Let us see what you can do.
Would you like to shine above the world, to shower all with love and joy?
Would you like to be one with your world, caring and giving back to it?
Would you like to fly among the stars?

You can! Oh, yes, you can!

To shine above the world? All you need to do is give your heart and love to the Divine and accept the Divine in your soul. To provide and receive love in unlimited amounts brings joy to your world and to the source itself: the Divine.
When you do that, your very soul shines so brilliantly that it overpowers the light from the stars.

To be one with your world, all you got to do is love it, look after it and give back what you have borrowed. You take a tree for wood, then replace it with a seedling, to help your world sustain itself. Keep your area clean and encourage nature to visit. Once the creatures of nature realize that they are safe, you will be amazed at what life can bring to you. A beautiful flower coming out of nowhere is one example.

As for flying among the stars? Oh, yes, that is easy. You can do that just by meditating and bringing your energies higher to meet us. During that state, you will fly, and we will help you there. Just ask.

It's simple when you think about it. Even those deep within a city apartment can help in some way. Do pot plants come to mind, anyone? Nature is within you all and around you. From the humblest plant to the magnificent Condors in the sky. All around you.

And in you too.

Be well, dear ones. Be well."

***

8 NOVEMBER 2015

Daily Message from the Angels and Ascended Masters.

A Message from AA Gabriel:

"Remember the phrase 'Oh! What a tangled web we weave, when first we practice to deceive.'

Well, I see you often giving out little lies, some in the case of vanity and some in the case of hiding.

When it is in the name of vanity, you are making things worse for yourselves. In time you have created that web around you and caught in it. The spider is the lie itself; it has you trapped. It will be hard to break free of that web until you face the truth, accept it, and live it. Apologize to those who you have caught with you. Each one you apologize to will break a strand of that web, weakening it, freeing you.

Soon the strands will get fewer and break more easily. When that happens, accept the truth of what you are, and how beautiful that real person is. Accept yourself for that real perfect loving you. Let go of what is left of the web of lies and become the light of truth instead. There is nothing better than that.

You see, we can see the truth, no matter how much you try to hide it. The lies and excuses mean absolutely nothing to us, and we even consider them a waste of energy. So plainly stop it.

But some tell a lie to ease the pain of another. We see them in the hospitals, and we understand. That is when a fib that can calm someone is preferable to a truth that could make a person harm other people or themselves. We know very well the reasons. Don't worry about whether we would condemn you or not. The answer is: We will not. The Divine understands this too, for you say this lie in the name of compassion and love.
We understand and accept your reasons as right. We will share your love there.

Let us be your ever-loving, non-judgmental, funny, friends, and family. What do you say, hmmm?

Be well sweethearts."

***

9 NOVEMBER 2015

Daily Message from the Angels and Ascended Masters.

A Message from AA Raphael:

"Let us talk about healing. Whether it is healing your heart, your soul, your emotions, or your thoughts. We shall speak of all that at once, for there is only one way to treat all your troubles there purely. In other words: Love one another.

Open your hearts to the Divine and let their golden light shine on you. And then call upon me.
I shall heal all your spiritual and emotional wounds because that is what I can do. And I would love to do it for you.

****

To open your heart, find a spot where you won't be disturbed. Just relax completely.

Visualize your soul extending roots through your feet and into the ground.

And now envision that golden light being showered on you and being breathed in by you.

Feel the golden light course through your veins and into every cell of your body. Feel your Aura become infused with the golden light and you will become part of that light.
Let it run through you for a short while and then call upon me: Raphael.

Now ask that I help you heal which part of you that needs the healing, whether it be your heart, soul, feelings, or thoughts.

Visualize my green light of healing pour down on you and in you, mixing with the gold. Mixing in you, and healing.
Let it run in your body for another short while and then release both energies through the roots you created through your feet and into the ground.
You will know when you have absorbed enough.

Now slowly waken out of your relaxed state and take a few moments to relish the effects, before you start anew on your daily life.

Yes, Gaia will receive these energies too. Gaia will take any negative energies that have been washed away and cleanse them. Gaia will also do the same with any healing power and use it to heal herself. Nothing wasted, and all are loved.

Be well sweet ones."

***

10 NOVEMBER 2015

Daily Message from the Angels and Ascended Masters.

A Message from AA Chamuel:

"What is the most precious thing in your life?

Precious gems?
Words?
Money?
Family?

Or something else?

It is not gems, for they are mere stones. They have nothing else going for them. They are just one of Gaia's gifts to your world.

Words? Ah yes, that can be possible. For with words, one can say things of love, laughter, and even of the future. But still, one can always do all these without saying something. So, it isn't that.

Money? Well, the way some act you think it was. It's nothing also. Bits of metal and paper bring nothing but heartache when you are forced to pay for something that by rights is given freely by the Divine. It is not that.

Family? Indeed! Your family is precious, and it all belongs to you. We too are your family; you are invaluable to us also. So yes, that is high on the list. Cherish your family for what it is, a mixture of personalities all together and causing havoc when all meet under one roof. That's a family. Guess what! You love them.

There is always a few that create trouble that makes it hard for you to love them but be patient and don't put up with their antics. These family members will try to walk over you, so don't allow it.

As for the 'something' else?

Some are already starting to get the drift. That something else is you. YOU! Understand that. YOU are the most precious of all. You must look after yourself and after all, why not! There is only one of YOU, so make the most of it.

The Divine knows how precious you are and loves you all warts and all.

Start looking after the most precious thing in your world, yourself. And don't let others put you down. Walk on with head held high and loved with divine love.

Get my meaning?

Be well, dear ones."

***

11 NOVEMBER 2015

Daily Message from the Angels and Ascended Masters.

A Message from AA Gabriel:

"When you go out in your world of business, pleasure, and adventures, go out with a smile on your face.

Smile for that stranger who may be feeling a little down.
Smile for that child who sees the sun in your eyes.
Smile for the homeless so that they can see you didn't forget them.
Smile for the beauty of nature, so your world can smile back at you.
Smile for new people in your life today, for each one of them may need your smile.
Smile for the sunshine; it glows as bright as you.

Smile with the feeling of pure joy, as you venture out on your day. Let that smile sound in your voice also. For there are people out there who cannot see the smile but can hear it and will appreciate it.

No matter what happens, smile and the world smiles with you. Now if you laugh as well as smile, so much the better.

Enjoy yourself, have fun, create mayhem, in theright way I must say. Just be yourself, and have fun doing so. We want you to live life in the fullest and why not! You all deserve it. And no one merits anything less. Go out in your world of differences, changes, and happenings, and be one of those happenings.

Be well, my dear ones, and we will smile with you too."

NB: Just before I did this message, Gabriel came forward, wrapped his arms around my shoulders, and started singing: "Let Me In" (Osmonds song). I started giggling, which he joined in.

***

12 NOVEMBER 2015

Daily Message from the Angels and Ascended Masters.

A Message from AA Michael:

"Beloved ones, you must believe in what the Divine has given you. You have received gifts upon gifts from the Divine, yet some still don't see their way.

I have seen some of you saying you don't believe in the Divine, and that you believe in yourself and your reality. Oh, to understand so little. You are blind to the majestic wonders of the Universe because you cannot see beyond your sphere of ego.
Shed the ego, shed the blind sphere, and instead look around you.

The Divine gifted you this world, the plants, and trees on it. The beasts that fly, crawl, and swim on it. All yours to look after, nurture and love.

The Divine is around you, in you and is in everywhere you look. All is the Divine, and the Divine is all. To deny the existence of the Divine is to deny your existence. It doesn't make much sense. Instead, accept the fact that the Divine is in you, and you will soon notice that the Divine will open your heart for gifts. Don't be surprised at what shape these gifts may take as some be miracles.
Accept them, be grateful, send your love and above all, be happy in what gift you will receive. For it will be just the right item you need. All sent with love and tenderness, as our mutual parent does so love you all. We do too.

Enough, I am tiring my channel out. Be well, precious ones."

***

13 NOVEMBER 2015

Daily Message from the Angels and Ascended Masters.

A Message from AA Uriel:

"When you wish for something to happens, you should realize it is a type of prayer. You want for something beautiful to happen; then unconsciously you are praying to the Divine to make it happen. It is all prayer for there is no difference in wishes, prayers, and dreams. They are all received by the One Source. No matter what the object of desire is, the One sees and hears all. Even the darkest cravings.
Yes, some may have to look to yourselves at that, for it is true. Ego can only disguise your intentions to others, but not to the One.

We know you all have those moments. We know them all, and the majority don't act on them, thankfully. It is because you have self-respect and that is important. But those who succumb and follow those dark desires?
Do not condemn them or judge them. For those who succumb are the new Souls. Such souls are easily led and can be uncontrolled. Instead, just don't let them destroy your life while they are just trying to learn the first steps in your world.

When things seem wrong and show signs of affecting you? Back away, leave! These new Souls are the Infants of the Spiritual World, and all they have known is that of the animal side of their previous lives. They are Humans for the first time, and they are having a difficult time controlling themselves. Experience comes with each incarnation, so they still have a lot to learn.
Just don't get caught up in their world, as it is more violent in their eyes and mind. You get on with your world and don't get dragged down.

We are aware of these new Souls and know how violent they can get. We are always watching over them, making sure they do the task given to them. That is until they start to turn their heads the right way.

So again, I ask you to be non-judgmental and keep your distance.

Be well, dear ones."

***

13 NOVEMBER 2015

A Meditation session:

Uriel told me that someone wanted to speak to me.

I sunk into a deep meditative state and found Anubis waiting for me. As soon as I had reached the right state, he approached me and gently took my arm and told me that he wasn't going to keep me long.
He then led me to what appeared to be the front of a massive building, which had huge Pharaoh statues instead of pillars against the walls. Got the impression "Valley Of The Kings."

We went into this corridor that had hieroglyphics and pictures on the walls.

Anubis brought me into a cave which opened up into a room. It was well lit, had crystals on parts of the roof.
There were torches on the walls and fire in the center of this altar, which had crystals surrounding it. I was steered to a rock and sat me down. A white robe rested on my shoulders and a gold circlet placed on my head.

We began to talk about something which I can't remember, but the gist was that some changes are happening. Ah! Uriel is telling me what I had forgotten:

"That it is time for you to let go and let in. No matter what has happened within your life, there is a beginning in the past, the present, and the future. Some have come and gone from your life, and in the future, it will remain so. But you are to take the next step. Shed what is no longer functional and accept the change. The next step is upon you. Be prepared."

After a while, Anubis gently helped me off my seat and walked back with me down this long corridor again and brought me back to my body.

Right now, there's a sensation of fingers ruffling the left-hand side of my head.

***

15 NOVEMBER 2015

Daily Message from the Angels and Ascended Masters.

A Message from AA Gabriel:

"Never lose what self-respect you have. It is very much needed to help you in your world.
Some would cause pain and suffering to drag you down. They must not win. Hold your head high and say: "I will survive. I will go on. I will be glorious in my victory."
In saying this, you are strengthening yourself. If you can show your self to be your pillar of strength, then the others who will stand by you will become so also. And those who stand by them will become such. It spreads.

When the world stands up and says, 'No More!' and stands united and proud. Then you have won the battle against the negative forces.

Be sure about your abilities and beliefs. And let no one change them for you, as they don't have the right. You are your own master, and the only one who can give you orders is the Divine. And even then, you have free choice.

Show sympathy to those who need it, and they will stand with you.
Show compassion to the lost and lonely; they want you to find them.
Show kindness when others are having a rough time.
Show consideration when others are at the last of their strength.
Show strength when others are looking for a hero.
Show truth when lies have blinded others.
Show hope when others start to weaken.
Show the light within you to find the lost.

Never lose your strength and self-respect, for there are those in the world who will look towards you in hope.
Never be afraid to show such feelings, for there is nothing to be ashamed of in them. All I have named there are the real strengths of your Soul. And negativity cannot abide by these strengths, for it doesn't understand it. It will try to fight them, but it will weaken each time. And then finally it will go away to find a more accessible source.

You will win.

Enough, I have had plenty to say, haven't I. Be well, children. Be well in the heart."

***

16 NOVEMBER 2015

Daily Message from the Angels and Ascended Masters

A Message from AA Michael:

"Let me say this brief message to you all. I wish you all to hear what I am about to impart.

Let's give peace a chance. Put down your weapons. Yes, every single one of you. Put aside your differences and remember you are all the same. No better, no worse than each other.
Now shed all your religious dogma, no matter what it is. Then instead, love the Divine One as is.

That's all it takes. That's all we want.

Your dogmas are all human-made and therefore artificial. The Divine is for EVERYONE. No matter who or what you are. We all serve the Divine.
There are too many wars, and battles fought over what one single person thinks is the 'Right Way.' In truth, there is only one way, the way to the Divine is by your actions and soul. It is the path of Love and Joy.
But all too many of you are forgetting the one commandment that is for all: THOU SHALT NOT KILL!
No religion is good if it condones killing. For then, it is no longer a religion following the Divine; it then follows the darkness instead.
Let it be so for your survival. The path of violence is the path of destruction.

Enough. I have indeed said more than I intended, but I did decide that maybe more needed to be given.

Forgive me for tiring you, my channel.

Be well and be in peace."

***

17 NOVEMBER 2015

Daily Message from the Angels and Ascended Masters

A Message from Angel Anael:

"Why don't you all start a new hobby, explore your world, invent something, play, and dance some modern dance. In other words, be creative. You have all got the ability to create things in your world. Not surprising as after all, you do have the Divine's spark within you, and you are children of the Ultimate Creator.

Try a new angle on a hobby. If you are a sketch artist, try a new medium instead.
Those who sing classic songs, try a new genre.

Create! Create! Create! Don't stagnate. What you make with your new creation, could be the start of you expanding beyond your world. It is the same with meditation.
You do the same routines every time. Why not try something new? If you haven't done Reiki, why not try it. You limit yourself. Nothing is stopping you from exploring outside your box. Only you are.

If you think you can't dance? Except for injuries or disabilities, why not! Dance away, enjoy it.
Same with meditation. Touch the boundaries, ask us the help you in that area. If you are meant to go there, you will be allowed. We won't stretch you beyond your capabilities.

Don't get conned by your ego into backing off. Ignore what society says, for it too is ruled by ego. You are your own master, so if you want to dance in the street, do so. Have fun! If you're going to learn a new hobby, even if it is welding or engineering, do so and have fun.

The only thing that is stopping you is you, so excuses don't wash. Hint-hint?

Be blessed, my friends."

***

18 NOVEMBER 2015

Daily Message from the Angels and Ascended Masters

A Message from AA Chamuel:

"When in troubled times like this, you must set aside all that is not important and help those in dire need. These people need you, and you need them. So be prepared to give a distressed person a helping hand.
This help could come from either a gift from your heart or just being there when they want company. This help can take many forms, and you will know what is needed instinctively.

As events unfold around the world, innocents get harmed. And it is these innocents that need you. Earthquakes, bombings, and war, all take their toll around the world, even those who weren't there are affected. It is the moment where you come in. Those affected need you.

Healers unite! Your time and energies are required.
Light-Warriors unite! Your protection is needed.
Light-Beacons unite! Your shelter and compassion are wanted.

To all Light-Workers called upon at this time, it is now time for you ALL to start the process of healing and to help. None are exempt, for this is the purpose you are all trained. You will not be alone in this, for we will be with you, guiding you and giving you the right direction to work. We will help indeed!

Light-Workers hear your call and be ready. Do what you need to do and give aid where it is required. We will be there for you in turn.

Be well."

***

20 NOVEMBER 2015

Daily Message from the Angels and Ascended Masters

A Message from AA Zadkiel:

"Accept that there will always be things in this universe that you will never know at this moment. It is because you are not yet ready, and we don't want you harmed. The information is beyond your knowledge and your current frequency, so it only accessed by those who can reach that frequency.

The Akashic Records can be accessed any time by members or your kind, but there is still information hidden. As Humanity evolves, the nearer you will get to this information.
The information is what you call 'Sacred' and only accessed by the Divine, Angels and the Ascended Masters. This information is about your future, your world, and of the Universe. It tells of the beginnings, endings and the transitions of the Soul on the many levels to the highest level of all.

Just accept what is out there for you so far, as we will teach you. Never too much or too little, and just right. Don't try to cram as much information as you can, as you are unable to do so.

Don't ever claim to 'know everything,' you never will. Even we Angels don't know everything. We are omnipresent, but not omniscient. We rely on information gathered from others.

You see, you are not alone in not knowing everything. Only the Divine knows all and sees all.

Instead of overworking yourself in trying to learn nearly everything, try to play. That is learning also, the way of fun.

My apologies for my serious tone, for the occasion, merited it.

Be well, my friends."

***

21 NOVEMBER 2015

Daily Message from the Angels and Ascended Masters

A Message from AA Camael:

"Let us all join together, to unite as one and send your – no - OUR love across the world.

Fill that love with the weavings of peace and harmony. Let it flow around the world and surround everyone with peace and love.
Let us now add a strand of healing to the light material.
And now let the material absorb into each one of you.

Let it warm you inside and out.
Let it heal you.
Let it love you.

Let us all be one, hand in hand. And spread the most beautiful thing in your world: LOVE.

We want you to join us in that, and we can help you with spreading it. Invite us to share and help deliver that love.
We would are honored.

Be blessed, my dear ones."

***

22 NOVEMBER 2015

Daily Message from the Angels and Ascended Masters

A Message from AA Gabriel (as if you couldn't guess by the cheeky comments):

"We wish that all of you feel the perfect YOU that lies within you. This perfect YOU is your Soul.

Now feel that Soul deep within you and become what it is: Perfection.

That is what you are, perfection within. Now make that Soul of yours show through your physical self and make it real to you. Then you become perfection outside too.

Your Soul is kind, so be the same to others.
It is gentle, be gentle too.
It is wise, heed its wisdom.

Your Soul is so many things and more. It is the part of the Divine placed in you. The Divine can communicate to you through that. That is why it is so perfect.

You and we have all got that divine light within us. Yours is called the Soul. Ours is called Grace.
Same thing, different names, different frequencies. Just like you and us.

Now, have I confused you all enough? If so, GOOD! I have taken the first steps into making you think outside of your sphere of knowledge. The more you think outside the box, the more you learn and become more open to us.

You can't put us all in a box. I'd say it would get rather crowded, wouldn't you say?

Think away, my friends. I shall warn the others of the coming grinding noises and smoke that will result.

Be well."

***

24 NOVEMBER 2015

Daily Message from the Angels and Ascended Masters

A Message from AA Michael (whom I'm teasing right now):

"Have patience with yourself. You are only one person and can only do one thing at a time.
Do not try to do multiple things at once, for that is a prelude to either disaster or severe stress.
Just one thing at a time.

Take your time over each incident, mull over it, fix it and then let go. Move on into the next. Be relaxed over it. After all, a job well done is a job that has had someone being patient over it.
If others try to push you, ask them if they wish a perfect job or a botched job? Do they want what could be a big mess or a happy ending? All is the same in this game of Life.

I am asking you all this because a lot of stress is unnecessary. Don't rush things; instead, go at a relaxed pace.

I don't mean that you need to be so relaxed that you end up doing zip all, no excuses there.

Busy and stressed means health problems. Active and calm means a person at peace. Not doing anything means lazy.

Though I agree, there are times when it is good to have a lazy day, but only have it when you are finished. That way, you will feel happy about yourself, if not pride in yourself.

If you are exhausted, then that's another matter. You urgently need that rest, just for body and mind.

I must admit the only people who can manage to be doing several jobs at once because they have no choice in the matter; are Mothers. You must agree, they need eyes in the back of their heads. I bless the young mothers who work and look after children, for their lot is stressful yet at times - rewarding; the infant's first steps or their first word. Rewarding!

Be well, dear ones. Be well!"

***

26 NOVEMBER 2015

Daily Message from the Angels and Ascended Masters

A Message from Sananda Jesus:

"I hear your calls for help. I listen to each one.
I hear your calls of love. I listen to each one.
I hear your cries of laughter. I listen to each one.
I hear your songs of joy. I listen to each one.

I hear you, and I listen to each one of you.

I hear, I listen and learn what you require.

Some want my help; I give it.
Some want my love; I give it.
Some want my laughter; I give it.
Some want my song; I give it.

I give myself to your path of enlightenment, and I do this willingly. For it is through my aid, that your doors will open.

Will you accept my help also when you fall? Because I am there when you do, and I will help you up from the ground - this I will do for you, and I will do much more for you. I will bring solace when there is heartbreak. I bring comfort when you are lost. I bring laughter when depression starts to edge in. I bring myself when you cry for me.

I bring love.

That is all I need to say, for it says it all. Will you join me in this path of enlightenment, in bringing healing and love to this world? Bring your love to me, and I will combine it with mine.

That is all."

***

27 NOVEMBER 2015

Daily Message from the Angels and Ascended Masters

A Message from AA Gabriel:

"I wish to have a quick word with you all.

You all need to raise your energies as the next few days could be critical. Meditation, laughter, and good old love are what is required.

You see, there are conflicts in your world, and some of them may take a turn for the worse. I said, 'may.' It is dependent on decisions made at certain levels. We will help you in trying to ease this situation so that damage is minimal.

Yes, my darling Light-Workers, you are being requested to help heal your world. I believe that you all matter, and so does the Divine. You are all important to us, so please, do not lessen yourself by thinking you are not worthy. You are! And because that you are worthy, you are being asked to help heal your world.

Trust in yourself! Believe in yourself!

I have said enough as I think you all have the gist."

***

28 NOVEMBER 2015

Daily Message from the Angels and Ascended Masters

A Message from AA Uriel:

"When you are in need, we are ready for you. Call us. After all, that's what we are there for, always to be your support, teacher, and companion - still there for you.
When you request our help, expect the unexpected, for we work in ways that are strange to you, but typical for us. You may think that at times we do nothing, or too slow to respond.

Hmmm! Na!

We must travel back in time to trigger off a sequence of events and monitor them so that they do not damage another's life path to the point of no return. All is in balance in your Universe, and we wish to keep it that way. Anyway, this sequence of events will gradually filter back to you, and the response will come to you at the right time. Again, it is still monitored by us.

Some want to hear our responses and listen with their ears. Well, very few of you understand our answers that way. It's rare among you. So, we choose another way.

Your heart.

Feel our responses. Some feel a breeze, warmth, or a touch.

Some hear our voices in their heads. That's right! To listen to our voices does not mean you have schizophrenia.

Do you wonder how many have heard us and panicked, and ended up under a doctor? Too many and all due to lack of knowledge.

Sometimes we do take a physical form and do an instant rescue. That's when we MUST directly interfere, and it is all since we need to trigger off another sequence of events. Those events involve the subject's survival.

You see, we do take part in creating situations, changing them and my channel says we 'meddle' at times. If it is for the greater good, then we do interfere. Our reasons are for your well-being.

Be well, dear ones."

***

29 NOVEMBER 2015

Daily Message from the Angels and Ascended Masters

A Message from AA Nathaniel:

"When you journey on your path of life, never forget how critical events can be. What you may think as trivial, could be more important than you know.

The stranger who inadvertently cuts you off at an intersection may be sent by us to slow you down just a little bit, to avoid a crash.

The passer-by who picks up a bag or purse that you may have dropped could be one of us, gently directing you onto another path.

The running child in the background may be there to distract you from a misstep or a fall.

The bird that's flying low over you could be grabbing your attention that Nature wants to speak to you.

All of these little things are so important.

Listen to the voices within you. Listen to the rhythm of life that beats within your heart. Listen to the play of light across your soul.

All are of one beginning: The Divine. And all are cherished by us, because of that.

You too are part of the cycle of life and its interactions with humanity. You also will become to realize just who you are.

But in the meantime, to us, you are just beautiful and wonderful.

We love you and all your many quirky, strange ways.

Be well, and love your world, for it can love you back more so."

***

30 NOVEMBER 2015

The Angels have asked me that instead of their daily message, that I speak from within, from my Higher Self:

"Wishing within your soul is what is needed to get your dreams to come true. Believe in the fact you can make your dreams come true. You can make things possible, and you'll always have your departed loved ones ready to speak with you.

Dreams can be manifested by you, and just by continually thinking of them. All you need is to visualize what you need often. Now you must be detailed and go step by step to the result. That is how the timelines work.

You can make things possible simply because you all have the Creator's spark of life and creation. You are all part of the Creator, as well as the Creator, is part of you. You are all one, yet individuals. So, get creating, even if it is a simple thing like a small clay toy. It is still forming. Yes, even words can be creative. You are the Creators.

As for the departed loved ones? They are always with you; some are helping you right now. Taking the role of Guides or just simply because they love you. Never far away and can hear every word you say, including those words you wouldn't have said to them in the first place. Yes! THOSE words.
They will try to reply in many ways, and not all of them are by your ears — little signs such as coins or an ornament or photo that is well out of place. Maybethe odd knock on walls, or even that particular tune popping up on the radio at a specific time/date.

They are all there.

Now I must release my physical self. I thank you for listening to me. For it is by my family's call that I have spoken to you.

Farewell, my friends."

***

DECEMBER 2015

03 DECEMBER 2015

Daily Message from the Angels and Ascended Masters

A Message from Sananda Jesus:

"Will you follow me on my path? If so, will you do these for me?

Will you lay down your life for strangers?
Will you care for the homeless?
Will you heal those who are unable to ask?
Will you let your voice speak for the forgotten?
Will you do all these things?

I hear some will not and will step back from such a duty. Well, hear this, my friends.

I did all these for you, and I never stepped back from doing this.

Will you follow in my footsteps and do to others what you would like done to yourself? All in my name, and with no demand for compensation in return.
I did all this in the name of my father, and I did it with love in my heart.
Let me see you do the same in return.

And the reason why I did this for you because you were all worth it. You were the future, and you all had the promise of greater things to come.

I did it for the Love of my father, and the love of you all.

I ask again! Will you follow my path?"

***

4 DECEMBER 2015

Daily Message from the Angels and Ascended Masters

A Message from AA Raphael:

"Be patient with each other, for others are not like you. You see, you are all different in personalities, shapes, sizes, and it is all right down to the genetic level. Even identical twins have their little differences.

You are all individuals, and each of you is on your unique path of discovery.

It is a path of adventures, of learning and of loving. Each is individual as you are.

Do not put down others for their differences, instead encourage them. You don't know them as well as they know themselves. And only we know them better than that.

If you have an individual trait yourself, don't let others try to rub it out of you, or put you down. Stand tall, dear one. Stand strong! You are unique and beloved in your own right.

The Divine gave you that personally. It is because the Divine knows that you are more than capable of working with it.

If you have a hidden gift as an artist, let it show. And keep it secure in your heart.

If you have a deformity, make it a strength. You can help others to cope with theirs if you show them you can deal with yours efficiently.

Little or big steps, all of them are a lot better than standing still. Show the world you are mighty, the best thing in your own life and believe that you are beautiful in your perfect way.

Bless you, my sweet ones. Be well."

***

5 DECEMBER 2015

Daily Message from the Angels and Ascended Masters:

A Message from AA Chamuel:

"I shall be brief on this.

Have you ever looked in the mirror and thought: 'Looking Good!' Hm? Have you?
Well if you have, you are reconfirming your confidence and making it right. You see, when you say that to yourself often enough, you will end up believing it. When that happens, it will have the effect of making you look better each time. It also boosts the confidence, and your self-worth, making it right.
It is, after all, something we see in you all the time, and by complimenting yourself at frequent intervals, you will begin to see what we see. You will believe in yourself as this is what we like.

Belief in oneself is the belief that you are better than what others think. You are faithful and lovely. Up go the confidence and your vibrations. Up go the self-worth and own personal power of beauty.

Yes, we do see you all as beautiful, no matter what you look like because we see below the surface to the real you. And that is what we treasure. After all, physical beauty is only skin deep. True inner beauty goes to the very soul, and that is strong.

Believe in yourself and your beauty. You can do that; I know you can.

Be well."

***

7 DECEMBER 2015

Daily Message from the Angels and Ascended Masters:

A Message from AA Gabriel:

"There are those among you who do the most significant work for no reward whatsoever. They sacrifice their time, lifestyle, and even at times, their hearts to do this job. And it is a job that they do non-stop for a big part of their lives. These people have worked the hardest, never get paid, and most of them don't mind.
These are the ones that need you the most because you know them very well. And you know how much these people have sacrificed so that others can make their own lives.
Yes, they are the most beautiful of all -their gain in this is simple in its complexity.

And these people who sacrificed so much, who are they? Take note! These people are your mothers. They have brought you up from nothing at all into the beautiful person you are now. They did it not for money or reward. They did it out of love.

Yes: LOVE.

Reward your mother back and give her some of your love back — no greater reward there as it is so pure.

I realize that some never got to know their mother for various reasons. Some mothers were taken away in multiple ways. Then know this! Their soul will always remember you and will always love you, even though there may be conflict at times or loss.

Some of you are mothers also. I salute you and bless you. I love you! The Divine and your child do as well. What a perfect being of love you are. I thank you also.

Be well, dearest ones."

***

8 DECEMBER 2015

Daily Message from the Angels and Ascended Masters:

A Message from AA Uriel:

"I shall be brief. When you are exhausted, your mind slips into the lower levels of energy. You feel overcome with depression, and this is because your guards and protections have failed.
This moment is when you must rest. Take some time-out, you could say. I agree that there are some of you who are too busy to relax, but still, you must take the time to rest.
Your mind and body need it. Your psych and energy need it. Even the Divine rested after a big session of creating. Also, we chill when we can.

Don't push yourself, or disasters and errors will accumulate and then cascade en-masse. Rest is the best. After resting, you will find that you have a clearer mind and more energy.

Rest my children, rest."

***

9 DECEMBER 2015

Daily Message from the Angels and Ascended Masters:

A Message from AA Raguel:

"Remember the good deeds of your past and savor them as beautiful memories of a moment in time when you were perfect in body and soul to experience such a thing. Relive that moment in your mind and know you were loved. That is what good memories created for initially. The memories of laughter, perseverance, awakening, and growth. A baby's first cry at birth, the first steps, the laughter, and above all, the love.

All are part of the right side of life.

Forget the bad memories and let them go for they no longer serve their purpose for you. They have passed and can do nothing for you but ruin your life. Remove them from your life — it's time to, instead, concentrate on the great things.

Good memories are there for you, and you can make them happen also. Make them. Receive joy in making them too.

You are a Creator within your world, and you have the gift to create happy, joyful moments. The power is yours, and you must use it. Don't ruin that ability to make things worse for yourself and others. That is not what the original purpose of that gift we gave to you.

Besides, good memories raise your energy levels, and that is all for the greater good.

Enough! I give you time to reflect on this. You will need good memories to help you on your life's path anyway. It makes the way so much easier for you.

Be well."

***

10 DECEMBER 2015

Daily Message from the Angels and Ascended Masters:

A Message from The Divine One:

"I wish you all the wonders of the universe would stop and admire you, for you are the greatest wonder of them all.
I wish that the golden light would shower its love upon you all.
I wish that the stars would glow brighter with their love for you.
And finally, I wish that you all knew that you are all precious in my eyes and that you are all one.

No human-made religion can ever surpass the light that glows within you, for I am the only source of that light. Your petty little congregations that have twisted my words to suit themselves are false. They are of no consequence and have no right to tell you how to live your life and take what is yours to keep: your inner light.
I gave you that light so that you may see beyond the darkness if it should ever surround you.
I gave you that light so that others with their lights glowing, can seek you out and join you.

Oh, my children, how beautiful you are, and I relish the time when we can talk closer together.

I didn't create you out of a whim or just a fad. No, I created you with the intention of you reaching the stars and beyond. You are all destined to meet your final form: Divinity. Your souls are already on that path, and each incarnation they do takes them that step closer.

Yes, I wish my children to grow to become as One. But to do so, you must throw away what is holding you back from your growth. That one thing is called chaos. Chaos is war, dissent, negativity, ignorance, hatred. I could go on. But it needs to be removed and replaced by tolerance, peace, positivity, laughter, love.

You understand when I tell you to 'grow up' as I want you to become more than you currently are.

Enough! I have had my say, and it's time I let my words go out. It is for you, my children. Yes, you are no more and no less than that; my children! Yes, even the Angels themselves are my children too. They are your siblings.

Be blessed dear children; I love you all."

***

11 DECEMBER 2015

Daily Message from the Angels and Ascended Masters:

A Message from AA Raziel:

"When you think you know all you can about your world and the Universe around you? Think again. The universe is vast and contains a vast array of life, all of which are created by the Divine.

They live and populate their worlds and grow onto other planets. Some are more advanced than yours, and others further back. They are at all different phases of life so that constant messages to and from us always abound.

You see, we too look after these worlds. We watch over them, communicating, and even interacting. You are not the only ones we deal with in the Cosmos.

The universe is indeed vast, and thankfully, we can be everywhere at once. Dimensions are like that, y'know.

Yes, you are not alone. These other lifeforms are the children of the Divine also, just like you. You have many more brothers and sisters than you thought. Some of them are aware of your people's existence and are just ready for the right moment to visit. But take note, they are less likely to while your world is in such turmoil. It will put them off a bit.

There will be some who will step in and try to settle things down, and you won't even know they are among you, because they look like you.

Your kind has descended from these; this race seeded your world. You are the same, but your world has differences which have altered your type in little ways. Ways so tiny, you won't notice unless you look for them.

You see, you are all part of the universal family, and at this stage in your world's life, you are at the toddler level — all tantrums and dramas.

We wait for the moment when you all begin to settle down and be less violent, and then beautiful things will happen.

Be well, dear ones. I shall speak another time."

***

12 DECEMBER 2015

Daily Message from the Angels and Ascended Masters:

A message from AA Michael:

"Do you remember the time when all seemed beautiful, magical, and was an adventure?
A time when you were little and everything seemed big and challenging?
Yes, your childhood was a time of mystery, magic, and fun. Your world was a place to explore, to imagine strange and yet fascinating things when fairies and gnomes hid among the flowers and trees.

Yes, this was the time of purity and light.

That is the way all children should live their childhood. ALL children! But some never had that chance, and their childhood is that of pain. Those are the ones who need the help the most.
We do what we can to put people in their path who can help them, but it is up to the people themselves to create that helping hand. Free will makes people make many mistakes.

Just a simple, caring gesture can mean so much to these hurt children. Even if that gesture is that of a helping hand, sending of love, or a rescue from a bad situation. It all matters, and so do you.
If you know of such a situation, it is because we wanted you to be aware of it.
If you have experienced such a childhood, then we want you to help others in the same situation.

You all matter, no matter how little you think of yourself. You matter in many ways.

Be well and think about my words."

***

13 DECEMBER 2015

Daily Message from the Angels and Ascended Masters:

A Message from AA Azrael:

"Be at peace with others, and let the Divine reside in your hearts -however, you perceive the Divine to be. Once there, the Divine can make changes to your life. Things that you may not recognize as a blessing, but later in life, you will see it is so.
In your heart, the Divine can clear all obstacles and other negative hindrances. No more will peoples opinions of you matter, for only the Divine's view of you is the purest truth. To the Divine, you are beautiful, perfect, and so fascinating. That pleases the Divine.

Be accepting of the divine lightplaced within you, and let it shine forth from you like a lantern. You will soon find like persons who will walk with you in thislight and bathe you in theirs too, lighting your path in life.

I know my message is brief, for what I had to say didn't need fluff and frills. It just needed to be told as is.

Be well beautiful ones, be well."

***

14 DECEMBER 2015

Daily Message from the Angels and Ascended Masters:

A Message from AA Ariel:

When you feel an unexpected surge of love or joy, and there appears to be no apparent reason for it. Then think of the more invisible reasons: US.

It is how we talk with you, with your feelings. That surge of love is us telling you that we love you and that we are pleased with you. That surge of joy is us telling you we are happy with an essential choice you have made.

Sometimes we send out other feelings to get our point across.

Sadness mixed with a sense of urgency is when we want to tell you to help another creature in need.

Laughter: We want you to have some fun.

Calm: We want you to rest and be at peace within.

There are so many ways we can speak to you with feelings, with your emotions, and through them, understand our messages. With a bit of training, you could even sense what will happen in the future with them, or what has happened in the past. You sometimes call it Clair-sentience. We call it communicating.

It is one of the many ways you can speak with us. Do not try to hear us with your ears, for that is a rare ability. Listen to your heart, and you will find it more accessible.

Be well, sweet ones."

***

15 DECEMBER 2015

Daily Message from the Angels and Ascended Masters

A Message from Angel Matriel:

"Wish upon a star they say. Wish upon the star you are. You areof star stuff, and you are the star itself.

There are multitudes of stars, and each one has a home in someone's heart. Some you can't see because they are so far away, but you can feel it within you. You created that star when the Divine infused you with divine light. And that star became you. Is it any wonder why your kind is so beloved of all races?

You are a growing race, still young, and yet a lot to learn. But you are all on the edge of the next stage of your race's evolution. The next phase? Yes, the next stage is powerful, and it is part of your enlightenment process. Quite a few of you are already past that first step and well away on the next stage. They have crossed the barrier of space and time. They have ascended. And a few of you are straddling that barrier.

And then again, there are the very young souls, who are further behind. They have yet to learn their lessons, but they will reach that barrier and cross it when they are ready. None will fail.

You are the children of the stars, and you are born to reach them. Do not bother with artificial means at this stage, because in time, your kind will reach other worlds by a more energetic method, and it will be miraculous. And the only thing you will use to get there will be your mind.

Your evolution eventually will bring you to a level where your mind will be so overpowering that there will be no need for a solid form. You will be pure thought. Yes, you will have become one with the Universe, and you will be like stars. My Angel brethren will walk with you and work at your side. You are welcome, and what an ecstatic one it will be.

We all look forward towards this time, and it is getting closer with each revolution of your world.

Be in peace and grow, my children."

***

17 DECEMBER 2015

Daily Message from the Angels and Ascended Masters

A Message from AA Metatron:

"Well done those who have helped someone in need, no matter how small or humble the act is. You have made your Angels proud of you. You have done something selfless, and there is nothing better. You have shown unconditional love just by one simple act. It is excellent! A fantastic moment, indeed.

You see, this is what we hope your race will make into a fact of life for all. You all help each other when help is required. No money is asked for, no recompense except a simple word of thanks. It is what we want.
This sharing of love is how we Angels work with you too. We do selfless acts for you, helping you to manage events, arrange occasions and work tasks, and without any payment. All we want is your acknowledgment, your thanks, and love because that is what we will give to you.

Be thankful you have friends.
Be thankful you are the friend.
Be thankful you are wanted.
Be thankful you are beautiful.

To be thankful costs nothing, but it pays back with gratitude. We are grateful that we work alongside you. Despite your many little quirks and tantrums. We are happy with that.

Enough! Indeed, I have said enough and am thankful for my channel.

Be well, my children, and thank you."

***

18 DECEMBER 2015

Daily Message from the Angels and Ascended Masters.

A Message from AA Jeremiel:

"With all the pain, the troubles and strife that are on your world, I still see something beautiful in the middle of it. I see the human soul. I see how bright it shines and how it is ever ready to give and receive love.

No matter how much it hurts in the world around you, there is always beauty within you. It could be as simple as giving a mouth of food to a hungry creature, or as complicated as rescuing someone in dire need of help.

They all have one thing in common: You!

Each kind act you do enhances your inner light. Helps it grow, and once started, don't stop. It just gets better. Help others as you would have them help you. But remember, don't take crap from them either.

Nurture that flower within the midst of darkness and let it bloom. It shines with its light, and it shows through your heart and eyes. My child, please realize that you are that flower. You are the light within, and you are the beauty amidst the chaos. All have that connection that made you.

Revel in that combination and use it to further your growth and help others on theirs, just like the Ascended Ones did for others.

All part and parcel of humanity is this growth. Some find it awkward, but not for long.

Be well, sweetheart."

***

19 DECEMBER 2015

Daily Message from the Angels and Ascended Masters.

A Message from AA Gabriel:

"My thoughts on your world as I look upon it, are best described as contemplation mixed with a good dose of awe. You have created many wonders, and yet you have destroyed them too. You have created medicines, art, music, books and such, yet your world is suffering from the loss of its trees, animals, and the changing weather.
Asituation that's not right! While you remain on your only home, you are obligated to look after it. Keep it clean and clean up after your messes. We are not house-maids to do that, for it is your responsibility, and it is about time you did take responsibility for your actions.
You all know what to do and how to correct things, so why don't you?

My message is brief and to the point, because flowery words don't seem to make an impression. So, I chose bluntness.

Will you hear me?
Will you act?
Will you create a better world?

You can create a better world. You all have the Creator's light within you, and you are the children of the creator. Just remember this, the plants and other animals are also children of the creator as well.

By using your higher level of intelligence, you can look after your world better. That is part of your task here in this world.

I ask again, will you hear me?

Be well children."

***

20 DECEMBER 2015

Daily Message from the Angels and Ascended Masters.

A Message from AA Sandalphon:

"There is a time in this world for everything. There is time to laugh, time to love, and time to cry.
So much so, that time has become an integral part of your life. Do you not realize just how powerful you are? You invented Time! You created Time.
It is not essential to life for you or us. We don't have the concept of time as we live beyond it and are not affected. We can go back into the past, present, and your future whenever we wish. There is no barrier to us.

You have created your barriers!

You have decided that you can't go back to the past, so, therefore, you restrict yourselves.
You have decided that you can't go to the future, again you are restricting yourself.

And the cause? That 'TIME' creation of yours. Don't you find it somewhat restricting, because it does! It stops you from exploring your inner world and the outer universe. It prevents you from exploring other worlds.

Time does not matter and never has.

Once you have gotten over that time barrier, your world will open. No longer will the pressure of deadlines bother you. Instead, freedom will enfold you. Free to do what you want and at the pace you want it. Yes, even we do that. We have our moments where we back off and do our own thing. Relaxing isn't it.

I shall leave you contemplating what time means to you and us.

Be well, divine children."

***

22 DECEMBER 2015

Daily Message from the Angels and Ascended Masters.

A light-hearted message from AA Michael:

"There is the time and place for love, laughter, and compassion. And the time is as ever, the past, present and the future.
You must always have these moments within your life, and they must often be. A happy soul is a soul that shines brightest. The brightest soul is a soul that will grow and ascend the fastest.

Hmmm! As you can see, we are always asking you to take the higher road when conflict occurs. Yes, walk away from what negativity that is around and never bring it home. Leave it, and instead bring more joy into your life.

Someone gives you strife? Walk away.
An argument is occurring, and they're trying to bring you in it? Back off and leave there and then. You don't need that sort of thing in your life.

Someone is lying to you in the hopes of twisting your opinion to their favor. Ahh! Walk off! Again, you don't need another person's crap.

Yes! I know your slang.

The brighter you shine with your light, you will attract more like-minded people on the same path as you. You will end up helping each other, and the love bond will be secure. The 'best' friends, you could say.

We will bring these people to you, and together you will all shine the brighter. Each other's light is reflecting and merging. A strong friendship will form. And if some of these people are soulmates, their inner-light will be as bright as a supernova.

Always bring the light into your life. Bring on the laughter and joy. Bring on the love and compassion, and shine on!

Be well, my friends."

NB: Right now, Michael is groaning at the pun that I put at the beginning of the message: 'Light'-hearted

***

Interesting. I did a brief meditation, and Michael was with me. He told me to go deeper and send energy to the Earth.

At his request, I focused my energy, and the image of the Oceans came to mind, and I sent the power to there.

After 5 minutes, Michael told me to concentrate on going through the dimensions. So I did, seemingly traveling through a tube of various lights, deeper and deeper and with Michael at my side, guiding me so I wouldn't get lost.

Michael had taken a winged form, and I told him that I was aware that Angels don't have wings. He laughed and said that it was to make sure that I was following the right path. He would always appear to me in that form to catch my attention for something.

As I approached my destination, the bright light at the end of this tunnel was getting bigger and stronger. And soon I came through the end of the tunnel, and I found myself on a desert island, white sand, gently rolling seas, dead tree-covered volcano and some smaller islands further out.
All seemed so gentle, peaceful, and beautiful.

Michael then told me to 'Come back to Earth,' and I came back to my body.

Michael then told me that the island was for my use, as the little cottage no longer served its purpose as I had not been going there for quite a while. The island was to act as a focal point in meditation, and I can go there any time. He then added that the Gaia spirit had created the island for my use at this level.

Oh! I've just asked Michael if I have gone up a level. He said, 'Yes, and what did you think your migraine was.'
Since my migraine went away around 4pm, I assume my energies are settling.

***

23 DECEMBER 2015

Daily Message from the Angels and Ascended Masters.

A Message from AA Uriel (who is in a humorous mood):

"Did you know what your real origins are? We do, and we aren't allowed to tell you, because it is merely something you will need to find out for yourself.

This self-discovery of your origins is part of your path. A lot don't know it as they aren't advanced enough to figure it out. But those who are will find themselves knowing, and it will be instant that knowledge. The answer is all around you and in front of you. There are so many clues abounding your world to your origins, and yet very few realize it.

It is deliberate. For the time when you realize what your origins are, you will see the answers everywhere. And things will start clicking into place in your mind.

As I said, this is for advanced minds. Some of you are very close to that stage, very close. The knowledge is, in fact, a step up.

I shall tell you this; it will take a bit of thinking outside the box. Stepping out of your comfort zone of thought is required. And you will either be stunned, amazed or just chagrined as to why you hadn't noticed before. My channel had a bit of a shaky moment when she found out. So, we had to settle her down.

I am telling you all this as it is near to the time to a lot of you to open and step forward. It is close, and destiny has plans for you. Let's give Destiny another name, let's call it the Divine – The One Who Meddles The Most In People's Lives. I hear you laughing.

Be well, my friends; I wonder who will be the first to face-palm at the realization of what the answer is. I hear more laughter.

Always yours."

***

24 DECEMBER 2015

Daily Message from the Angels and Ascended Masters.

A Message from AA Gabriel:

"Are you so caught up in the trap of your own making? The trap of so-called healthy life. A pitfall of nine-to-five hours, work, and no play? Booooring!

Who is at fault here? You are. You allowed it to happen. Instead of living the life of drudgery, turn it into a life of fun and laughter.

Boring job? Well, liven it up! Even if it is just wearing a silly hat, or even singing to your favorite tune, your job is what you make it. Your life is what you make it. It all revolves around YOU!

Never mind what others tell you to do. If what they say suits them, then let them choose that path for themselves. You make your path in life, and you can make it as fun as you like.

Yes, even what you call naughty jokes can make a difference. Harmless pranks are good if it creates laughter. Hmmm! You get my drift.

Now, as I said before, you make your path, your own life, and your own choices. So, choose to make your world fun, live it to the fullest, and follow your heart. Live your life as you wish it to be, and LIVE! I have seen some of you do that, and the joy that is in their hearts is fantastic to see. Even when it gets tricky, that joy remains undimmed. They are living th life they love.

It is worth it, and when you live your life the way your heart leads you to, it is beautiful.

Yes! I know! I can hear the killjoys whinging away. Hmmm! To those, I say this: You live your life the way you want to, but don't influence other people's free choices. For it is not your place or right.

You can decide for yourselves; you're old enough and ugly enough.

Be well, and thank you."

***

25 DECEMBER 2015

Daily Message from the Angels and Ascended Masters.

A Message from AA Chamuel:

"I have a simple request for you all.

How about you and I go out in this world of yours and spread the light and love of the Divine? Hm? Well, this is how we go about it:

Just envision you are creating a ball of soft pink light between your hands.
Fill it with love, purity, and joy.
While it is in your hands, watch it grow as you fill it.
You will know when there is enough. You get the sensation of fullness and your hand's will tingle.
You then hold that ball of pink energy high above your head and call upon your Guardian Angels to collect this energy and spread it to where it is needed the most.

Now some will feel a sensation of hands and movement around them during this time; others will feel the energy surrounding them.
But as you finish asking your Guardian Angels, open your arms outwards in a gesture of release. Then take a step back and thank your Guardian Angels for their help.

And there you are. You have sent out the energy of love, healing, and other positive powers.

Guess what! You didn't even have to meditate to do so. You just needed to focus on filling that ball of light.

You can do this whenever it is needed, but not too often as you need some of this energy just for yourself. Yes, not everything needs meditation, only intent.

I shall leave you now, my children. Duty calls."

***

27 DECEMBER 2015

Daily Message from the Angels and Ascended Masters.

A Message from AA Gabriel:

"There are moments where you need to wind down, de-stress, and let go of the day's worries. Choose a walk in the park, or mess about in a garden. Either one will help you ground, settle your nerves, and sort your thinking out.

It's incredible how fascinating nature can be when there is a need. A simple sight of an actual living tree lowers tensions, for the tree has big shoulders and can take on the world. A simple flower is pleasing to the eye, also helps.

Always enjoy those moments, for they will help you ground.

That's what we are suggesting.

Give your self some time-out. Take a breather and chill. Your mind and body will thank you for it. And when you have relaxed long enough, you will find yourself thinking much clearer.

Take note though, don't bring the problems with you to the park or garden. Leave them where they belong, with the cause. That way when you return refreshed, clear in the head and they seem more comfortable to work.

Time-out is necessary, but not in the Naughty Corner.

Be well, my children."

***

29 DECEMBER 2015

Daily Message from the Angels and Ascended Masters.

A Message from AA Cassiel:

"When you see a fault in others, and you judge them by that fault. What does it say about you?
Weren't you taught to accept others as they are? It's in the Bible: 'Judge not lest you be also judged.'

When you see this fault in others, and you harangue that person because of that fault, you are judging your self. You are all mirrors of each other. What you accuse others of is what your problem is. When you attack others for something they can't help, you are again hiding your own.

I want you all to accept and unite. I want you all to be aware of how beautiful each other is in your unique way. After all, if you were all the same, wouldn't life be boring?

No judging others, instead accept and love them. The more of you that do this, the less conflict.

Already Light-Workers around the world are making steps in this direction. They are helping us to bring peace to your world. And we are helping them by directing them to the right place and giving energy. It is a lengthy task and a hard one. But the rewards are immense.
So less of the conflict, and more of the loving. It is all part of spiritual growth.

And we need more Light-Workers. The more open your heart is to us, the more willing we are to work with you. Will you join us?

Be well and be at peace and harmony within."

***

30 DECEMBER 2015

Daily Message from the Angels and Ascended Masters.

A Message from AA Raguel:

"So much is going on in your entertainment of late. Your current popstars, actors, and such. Very few of you realize that you are as equally talented.
Those who are aware of their abilities are afraid to show them, and all because of the self-belief that they are 'not good enough.' This belief is caused by outside negative influences which feed negative energy to the Ego and leaving the person with low self-esteem. It is unfortunate.

These same people are just as good in their unique way. They should never let anyone put them down or undermine their confidence. Instead, they should stand up and hold their head high. Show off their gifts and tell the knockers to leave forever. No one should have to put up with such negative influences. No one!

Positivity brings out a lot more results than negativity. Or as my channel says; you get more results with honey than with vinegar.
That says it all. Positive words are sweet, natural, and kind for you. Negative words are like acid that sour your thoughts.

Instead of saying, 'I think it's ugly' Say 'It's interesting!' or instead of saying: 'You're useless!' say, 'You can do it because I believe in you.'

Words of encouragement will make better people. And if those words become mixed with love? Well, you will make a superstar.

Also note, if you don't have a particular talent that you wish you had, you are probably skilled in another. You are all born with an ability, but some need to see it for what it is. Don't chase after something you don't have the skills for, instead choose the ability we gave you. It could be art, music, writing, or just that fantastic Personality Plus!

It's all to do with mindset and positive words in the right parts. And it's all to do with you.

Be well, my friends."

***

31 DECEMBER 2015

Daily Message from the Angels and Ascended Masters.

A Message from AA Anael:

"Beloved ones!

You must set your priorities.

We know it's a good thing to help others, look after them, and even give the energy to do readings. But are you looking after yourselves also? You, instead, put others ahead of you.

In a way, it's theright way, and we do approve of it but only so far. What we want to tell you is this: YOU must come first often.

If you give too much of yourself away, it will drain you. And you are not much help to anyone or yourself if you don't look after yourself first.

We request that you do take care of your health first and foremost. After all, what's the point of giving, if you have nothing left to give? All you do is get sick. You must look after your health and mind. Rest often and don't let others take-take-take, without giving back energy. Those people are energy vampires. Avoid at all cost. They are somewhat parasitic.

Now, remember what I have said, you must look after yourself first, to be able to look after others. It means timeouts, more sleep, better food, more leisure activities, and more moments of relaxation. Meditation is good there.

So, will my Light-Worker friends follow through with this? My words are for you, and I have been watching some of you drain yourselves. That I do not approve, therefore, I'm acting as your nurse in this. Look after yourself first and foremost!

Be well, dear ones."

End of 2015

www.ingramcontent.com/pod-product-compliance
Lightning Source LLC
Chambersburg PA
CBHW030259080526
44584CB00012B/377